1860	1870	1880	1890	1900

am Wordsworth 1770-1850

Thomas DeQuincey 1785-1859

Thomas Carlyle 1795-1881

Thomas Babington Macaulay 1800-1859

John Henry Newman 1801-1890

Elizabeth Barrett Browning 1806-1861

John Stuart Mill 1806-1873

Alfred Tennyson 1809-1892

Charles Darwin 1809-1882

William Makepeace Thackeray 1811-1863

Robert Browning 1812-1889

Charles Dickens 1812-1870

Anthony Trollope 1815-1882

Charlotte Brontë 1816-1855
-1848

950

-1924

1859-1936

udyard Kipling 1865-1936

m Butler Yeats 1865-1939

H. G. Wells 1866-1946

Arnold Bennett 1867-1931

James Joyce 1882-1941

Virginia Woolf 1882-1941

D. H. Lawrence 1885-1930

Ezra Pound 1885-1972

T. S. Eliot 1888-1965

VICTORIAN PEOPLE AND IDEAS

BY RICHARD D. ALTICK

PREFACE TO CRITICAL READING
THE COWDEN CLARKES
THE SCHOLAR ADVENTURERS
THE ENGLISH COMMON READER
THE ART OF LITERARY RESEARCH
LIVES AND LETTERS
BROWNING'S ROMAN MURDER STORY (*with James F. Loucks II*)
TO BE IN ENGLAND
VICTORIAN STUDIES IN SCARLET
VICTORIAN PEOPLE AND IDEAS

Editions

THOMAS CARLYLE: PAST AND PRESENT
ROBERT BROWNING: THE RING AND THE BOOK

A COMPANION FOR THE

MODERN READER OF VICTORIAN LITERATURE

Victorian

People *and* Ideas

RICHARD D. ALTICK

W · W · NORTON & COMPANY · INC ·

NEW YORK

FIRST EDITION

Library of Congress Cataloging in Publication Data
Altick, Richard Daniel, 1915–
    Victorian people and ideas.
    Bibliography: p.
    1. English—Civilization—19th century.   2. English literature—19th century—History and criticism.
I. Title.
DA533.A55 1973   914.2'03'81   72–10138
ISBN 0–393–04260–X
ISBN 0–393–09376–X (pbk.)

1 2 3 4 5 6 7 8 9 0

To John B. Gabel
discipulus · praeses · amicus

Illustrations follow page 145

CONTENTS

PREFACE

THIS BOOK IS rather like one of those "Music Minus One" records of a concerto, in which the orchestral accompaniment is present but the solo instrument lacking. The different voices of Victorian social and intellectual history here provide the background, that is to say, the thematic material which in a fully realized concerto is developed by the solo instrument. The unheard soloist—the real center of interest—is, of course, Victorian literature itself. The analogy is not quite perfect: literary history does figure more or less prominently in the opening chapter. But thereafter literature is present only in the form of frequent passing allusions, suggestions from the orchestra which, we are to understand, are taken up and elaborated by the soloist.

The chapters that follow are designed, then, to supply the accompaniment by which Victorian literature can be made more intelligible and pertinent to a reader in the last quarter of the twentieth century. The accurate understanding of any era's literature depends to a greater or less extent on a grasp of its historical context, but the danger of misreading and of anachronistic criticism increases when one deals with literature so intimately connected with contemporary life as was that of the Victorians.

Given—to use Matthew Arnold's excellent, self-illustrating word—the multitudinousness of Victorian society and culture, this book may claim at least the perhaps equivocal merit of audacity. It mercilessly simplifies topics which every well-informed student of the period recognizes to be extremely complicated; it makes broad statements which are, in reality, subject to all manner of qualifications. No effort has been made to prefix to every categorical use of "Victorian" a cautious but tiresome "many," "most," or "some." The reader is invited to take them for granted wherever they seem to apply. Nor has it been thought necessary to call attention to the numerous paradoxes and inconsistencies with which so rich, restless, and complex a culture as the Victorians' necessarily abounded. Most readers will find them apparent enough. Nor, finally, is this meant to be a comprehensive survey of Victorian life and ideas. It omits a number of topics which would figure prominently in any conventional historical account of the period but which have relatively few echoes in literature, among them party politics, foreign affairs, and the persistently worrisome Irish question.

The absence of explicit references to modern analogues of the Victorians' problems and crises is deliberate. To point them out in their entirety would be an endless task as well as a gratuitous one. Every reader will soon realize that, far from living in a world so remote from ours that they have nothing worthwhile to say to us, the Victorians belonged to a society that in many crucial respects is remarkably (frighteningly?) like our own. The silence of the following chapters on those resemblances is designed to reserve for the reader that most inexhaustible of the rewards offered by literature, the shock of recognition.

The book lays no claim to originality. If any fresh insights have crept in, they have done so unbidden and undetected. Provocative ideas will be found in sufficient abundance in the literature itself. The short book list at the end calls attention to some volumes of particular value to the reader wishing to flesh out his knowledge of subjects which necessarily appear here only in bare outline. But it does not pretend to be a complete roster of the many sources from which I have learned much and pilfered not a little.

So elaborate a set of disclaimers doubtless should be followed by a positive note. Although I have taken pains to insure that the book cannot serve as an ignoble substitute for the experience of reading Victorian literature itself, I have sought equally hard to provide in it the information which can make that experience more enjoyable and profitable. The full index enables it to be used as a reference guide, so that the reader can have immediate access to the historical vocabulary he needs to understand the true accents in which the Victorians spoke. In this not unimportant respect, the volume may prove to possess the sterling Victorian virtue of utility.

I OWE THANKS TO Professors M. H. Abrams, George H. Ford, and Peter Stansky, who read the whole manuscript and saved me from a number of factual errors and false emphases. My colleague, Professor James R. Kincaid, commented upon it, almost page by page, with an amiable severity exceeded only by the candor with which I report to him on his own productions; I cannot hope to repay him for the innumerable corrections and adjustments he suggested and I gratefully adopted. Dr. John Fenstermaker, the research assistant generously provided me by the Department of English at the Ohio State University, has once again applied his boundless energies and resourcefulness to the betterment of my pages. This inadequate acknowledgment must serve not only for his work on the present book but for his (to me) indispensable participation in several earlier projects. I have greatly benefited from the advice of my editor, John Benedict. Finally, I must thank the members of several successive classes in English 846 at Ohio State, who listened with much good will, and I hope not without profit, as I tried out on them the materials and approaches eventually incorporated in the fol-

lowing chapters. Now that the substance of those lectures is
in print, we will have considerably more time to talk about
Victorian literature itself—which is why I wrote the book in
the first place.

R. D. A.

VICTORIAN PEOPLE AND IDEAS

I

THE LONGEST REIGN

(1837–1901)

1. Romantic Heritage and Regency Twilight

OF THE THRONGS OF men and women who lined the crepe-hung London streets on February 2, 1901, to watch Queen Victoria's cortege pass on its way to Windsor Castle, only a few could remember a day when another monarch had occupied the British throne. The great majority had been subjects only of the Queen. They were, in the purest historical sense, "Victorians."

In John Galsworthy's *The Forsyte Saga*, the chapter describing the event is called "Passing of an Age." It was, indeed, an age; but its more than sixty-three years had been unified only by the presence of a single monarch, whose reign had been the longest in the nation's history. There was not one Victorian period but several. The "spirit of the age," as we interpret it from the records it left, was strikingly different in the middle of Victoria's reign from what it had been in the earlier years and was to be in the last. Seen in a century's perspective, the age merges at either end into epochs of very different tone, from which, retrospectively in the one instance, by anticipation in the other, those earliest and latest years acquired their distinctive coloration.

The eighteen-year-old Victoria became queen in June,

1837, and this obviously is a convenient date for the beginning of the epoch that bears her name. But historians often reach back to 1832, the year of the First Reform Bill, a major landmark in British political history. Which date is chosen matters little, because the 1830's were, in any case, a decade of transition. In literary history these years are sometimes called the interregnum, a fallow interval following the exhaustion of the romantic age's energies and awaiting the fresh invigoration that would soon come as new, identifiably "Victorian" voices were heard. To most readers, the early Victorian period is most readily placed in history and described as the immediate sequel to the age of romanticism, some of whose attributes it absorbed while rejecting or reacting against others.

The aging Wordsworth was still residing in the Lake District and composing poetry, though he had outlived his genius. His fame was gradually spreading to the larger public; after a slow start, he was on his way to becoming a classic, and his place would be confirmed by religious trends in the thirties and forties, when the unmistakable Anglicanism of his new poetry recommended it to members of the Church and his religion of nature appealed to readers of all shades of belief. Of the major romantic poets, Wordsworth had the greatest influence on Victorian writers. John Stuart Mill, John Ruskin, Matthew Arnold, and George Eliot—a variegated company—all came under the spell of his nature poetry.

His friend Coleridge died in 1834. Coleridge's own poetic inspiration had failed many years earlier, but he had compensated in a way by delivering interminable, nebulous lectures on metaphysics to pilgrims visiting him at the suburban London home of the physician who cared for him. He had a fair amount of repute among discerning readers of poetry and this would grow in time, but his main legacy to the Victorians was a body of religious and social ideas to which we will have several occasions to refer later on.

Of the younger romantic generation, Byron, whose celebrity during his lifetime had outshone that of all the others put together, remained in the public eye for a decade after his death in 1824 because of his surviving friends' acrimonious squabbling over issues connected with the writing of his biography. The popularity of his poems was assisted for some years by the heroic circumstances of his death (he died of malaria in Greece while preparing to assist in the Greek war of independence against the Turks), but in the 1830's a reaction set in, typified by Thomas Carlyle's shift from admiration to disapproval. There were several reasons for the Byronic decline in the Victorian period. His revolutionary fervor discomfited a national spirit dominated by middle-class insistence upon cautious, slow reform if reform was conceded to be necessary at all. His preoccupation with what Matthew Arnold was later to call "the pageant of his bleeding heart," his penchant for uninhibited confessionalism, and his extravagant rhetoric did not appeal to the more sober literary taste which had turned in the direction of Wordsworth and, among the percipient, toward Alfred Tennyson after his *Poems* of 1842. Byron's personality and career were alien to a moral climate in which rectitude, chastity, and seriousness had replaced easygoing sexual attitudes and gay cynicism. And, as often happens in literary history, the shoals of imitations and other dubious testimonies to Byron's fame killed, for the time being, the appetite for the genuine article. Boarding-school girls continued surreptitiously to pore over Byron's more luscious verse when they were supposedly asleep, but despite—or, perhaps, because of—this kind of loyal following, his critical reputation would reach its nadir in the 1850's.

Shelley was widely regarded with aversion because of his radical political views and his vaunted atheism. Only a few critics, writing in his lifetime and in the decade and more after his death in 1822, were able to dissociate his poetry, as art, from the "pernicious" doctrines it expressed. "Yon man Shelley," Carlyle told a friend, "was just a scoundrel, and ought to have been hanged." In the same vein,

the Reverend Charles Kingsley, who was no more acute a
literary critic than Carlyle but who, like Carlyle, faithfully reflected many Victorian prejudices, spoke disapprov-
ingly of "the lewdness of the gentle and sensitive vegetarian."
As late as the eighties Shelley's daughter-in-law was devoting most of her time to whitewashing his public image. But
among the discerning who were able to differentiate personal ill-repute from poetic genius, Shelley's fame steadily
increased. In carving "Byron is dead" on a rock when the
news reached remote Lincolnshire, the fifteen-year-old Tennyson was merely echoing a national grief, felt perhaps with
particular keenness among poetry-loving adolescents; but
in rapturously apostrophizing Shelley as "Sun-treader" in
his first poem (*Pauline,* 1833) the twenty-one-year-old Robert Browning enrolled himself in what was to prove the
vanguard of Victorian taste.

There was one group, however, to whom both Byron
and Shelley remained idols. These were the radical workingmen, whose enthusiasm was ideological rather than aesthetic
in origin. Byron's attacks on the political establishment in
Don Juan, A Vision of Judgement, and elsewhere, and
Shelley's *Queen Mab,* available only in underground
editions because of government prosecutions, were (if the
term is permissible in such a context) veritable Holy Writ
among the discontented workers, and their sentiments helped
inflame popular radicalism between the 1820's and the
1840's.

Keats, youngest of the great romantics, had been the
first to die (1821). Excepting only that of Blake, the eldest,
who died in 1827 and was remembered only by the few who
had known him as a harmless eccentric and seer of visions,
Keats's fame was the most limited. At the beginning of the
Victorian era he was a poet admired only by small coteries
like the Cambridge undergraduate "Apostles," to which Tennyson belonged. The corrosive reviews his volumes had received in leading critical journals, to say nothing of the legend
that he had been such a weakling as to be "kill'd off by one

critique," as Byron put it in *Don Juan,* had had their effect. His devoted friends, however, made a cause of his memory, propagandizing for his poetry and to a limited extent succeeding in keeping his name, if not the poems themselves, before the public. A more general fame would have to await the publication of his first biography, by Richard Monckton Milnes (1848: Carlyle dismissed it, most unfairly, as "an attempt to make us eat dead dog by exquisite currying and cooking") and the simultaneous discovery of him by Dante Gabriel Rossetti and his Pre-Raphaelite Brotherhood.

Of the other figures in early nineteenth-century English literature who are remembered today, Sir Walter Scott had died in 1832, the victim of his determination seven years earlier, when his own fortune was caught in his publishers' financial crash, to grind out novels until he could pay off his creditors in full. The Waverley novels would continue to sell in enormous quantities and, more than any other body of literature, would prove the inspiration behind the early Victorian idealization of the age of chivalry and Benjamin Disraeli's "Young England" program (see below, p. 23) for a socially responsible aristocracy wearing Tory colors. Scott had a number of imitators, but none approached his own skill, and the future of the novel in Victorian times lay instead with writers who dealt more or less realistically with characters and affairs of the present day. Jane Austen had died, a spinster member of a respected county family, in 1817; her memorial tablet in Winchester Cathedral does not mention that she wrote novels. Death had come to the critic and essayist William Hazlitt, a weary, life-battered man, in 1830; Charles Lamb, whose Elian essays had already won him a good deal of fame and whose companionable memory the Victorians were destined to suffuse with sentimental gush, followed him two years later. The two other leading romantic essayists, Leigh Hunt and Thomas De Quincey, lived well into the Victorian age. Both were to die in 1859, after long, checkered, and, especially in De Quincey's case, biographically obscure careers as miscellaneous journalists.

Thus mortality had interposed a barrier between the romantic era and the Victorian. (It is fascinating to speculate what sort of men Keats and Shelley would have been like if they had survived to become Victorians.) In poetry, nobody had appeared by 1837 to make good the losses. Tennyson and Browning, it is true, had published small volumes, but the former had had a mixed critical reception and the latter none at all. The two greatest and most popular Victorian poets would not win decisive critical recognition until 1842, in Tennyson's case, and the mid-fifties, at the earliest, in Browning's.

Although the 1830's were lacking in first-rate literary achievement (with a few notable exceptions, such as Dickens' *Pickwick Papers,* Carlyle's *Sartor Resartus,* and succeeding works by their respective authors), the romantic impulse endured across the gap, to be translated into a new idiom, partly personal and partly the reflection of a changing culture. Notwithstanding his harsh dismissal of most of the romantic poets, Carlyle—born, it is often forgotten, in the same year as Keats (1795)—kept the romantic spirit aflame. His transcendentalism, derived chiefly from German idealistic philosophy, was a new version of the romantics' pantheism. Most powerfully and influentially expressed in *Sartor Resartus,* it served, like his equally "romantic" assertion of the supremacy of intuitive feeling over the reasoning intellect, to maintain the continuity of romantic thought.

Two other great Victorians who shared philosophic sympathies and sensibilities with the romantics, John Henry Newman and John Ruskin, were on the way, but it was only in long perspective that Newman's affinities with the romantics became fully evident, and Ruskin's influential career, in which he adopted certain romantic aesthetic principles as the basis of his social criticism, began only in 1843, with the publication of the first volume of *Modern Painters.*

Some romantic elements persisted, meanwhile, in popular literature and in the social atmosphere. We find romanticism, diluted and vulgarized, in the sentimental effusions of young lady writers in the gift book annuals, complete with watered silk bindings and steel engravings, which, like the expensive coffee-table books of our own day, were a favorite status symbol in upper-class drawing rooms in the thirties and forties. But, as is true also of the deliberate imitations of Byron and Keats which genuinely talented novices like Tennyson undertook, the true passion and strength of literary romanticism were wholly lacking; the poems were paste, not gems.

In early Victorian society at large, romantic emotionalism manifested itself in numerous ways—in the rhetoric of politicians in Parliament and of Nonconformist preachers and hymn writers; in the oratory of radical agitators; in the acting style of such stars as Charles Kean and William Charles Macready; in some painters' obsession with epic-scale, even apocalyptic, subjects; in the sentimentality which governed domestic relations, the conduct of courtship, the veneration of the fireside; in the unapologetic tears shed by stalwart men when they read of the deaths of Little Nell and Paul Dombey. Lord Jeffrey, the "hanging judge" of early nineteenth-century criticism, who had torn Wordsworth's *Excursion* apart in a review, wrote to Dickens on reading the chapter of *Dombey and Son* in which Paul Dombey died, "Oh my dear dear Dickens! . . . I have so cried and sobbed over it last night, and again this morning; and felt my heart purified by those tears." The free venting of the feelings became so desirable a habit of life that people deliberately sought stimuli in the arts, including poetry and fiction, and attached an incommensurate importance to ordinary occurrences for the sake of additional opportunities to rejoice or grieve. The lugubrious trappings of woe with which the Victorians surrounded the death of a dear one—or a national hero like the Duke of Wellington—rank high among the peculiar wonders of popular culture. Side by side with this lachrymose indulgence, however, as an inevitable reaction, appeared the ideal of "manliness," according to which pain was to be concealed and grief suppressed. Reticence, as exhibited for instance in a family's reluctance to share its intimate knowledge of a distinguished relative with his would-be biographers, became part of the Victorian ethic. It was at least partially responsible for the decline in subjectivity that characterized Victorian poetic theory and practice. A true Victorian gentleman such as Browning refused, in pointed contrast with Byron, to wear his heart on his sleeve.

In many ways, therefore, the early Victorians were the heirs of the romantics. But it will not do to overstate this indebtedness, even as it is a mistake to conceive of romantic attitudes and ideas as dominating the general intellectual and social climate in the century's first quarter. For the most part, the tendencies we call by that name were subordinate rather than ascendant; their prominence has been exaggerated because they bore such marvelous fruit. However severely the romantic ideologists—the devotees of the imagination and the feelings—may have challenged it, the intellectual outlook of the Age of Reason still flourished. One need only cite the bias of the leading intellectual quarterlies, which, far from sympathizing with the romantic spirit, generally clung to the old rationalistic orthodoxy. In the early Victorian period, rationalism would acquire new authority and, even more important, immense practical influence, under the auspices of the Benthamites. John Stuart Mill, regarded today as well as in his own time as the greatest Victorian philosopher, was an enlightened rationalist. In such respects, the Victorian mind had its roots deep in eighteenth-century, not romantic, soil.

In that same soil had also been fed the familiar cluster of restrictive social values and practices attributed to the Victorians—unfairly, insofar as it is assumed that they originated them. The tastes and taboos of Victorian "prudery" and "respectability," a decalogue consisting largely of Thou shalt *nots,* began some time before the century did, in a gathering reaction against post-Augustan laxity of speech and behavior. Victorianism, in the popular sense of strict moral conduct and ethical obscurantism, existed in the court of George III, which was notorious among the freer spirits of the late eighteenth century for its oppressive virtue and sheer dullness. Dr. Thomas Bowdler's expurgated edition of Shakespeare, which has served ever since as a symbol of absurd fussiness, was published in 1818, a year before Victoria was born.

The movement for "the reformation of manners," to use the contemporary phrase, acquired greater urgency as the Georgian era was about to dissolve into the Victorian. It is worth remembering that the very span of years (roughly 1810–30) which comprises the later phase of the romantic period in English literary history is the same period which in social history is called the Regency. The Regency was an epoch epitomized by the corpulent figure and dissolute habits of the Prince of Wales, who, after having acted as regent during the last years of his insane father, George III, reigned on his own account as George IV from 1820 to 1830. The period is memorable for the attempt, on the part of the wastrel aristocracy and a contingent of imitative commoners, to revive the elegance of eighteenth-century fashionable life in a moral atmosphere reminiscent of the Restoration. Among the rich and those, no less numerous, who enjoyed unlimited credit on the strength of their expectations of inheritance, these were the years of the Beau Brummell–inspired dandy, exquisite in one mood, raffish, bawdy, and profligate in another. Regency life was characterized by expensive flamboyance of costume and by endless sessions with one's tailor, barber, and valet preparatory to attending glittering salons, gambling hells, prize fights, modish brothels, and, in extreme cases, early-morning duels.

Although the heyday of the Regency had passed, the first Victorian decade was bathed in its gaudy twilight. It was not surprising that when Carlyle sought a running metaphor to embody, in *Sartor Resartus,* his vision of a society bereft of spirituality and committed to crass and ultimately destructive materialism, he lighted upon "the Dandiacal

Body," a morally bankrupt soul clothed in the showy regalia of current fashion: clothes which, no less than rags, failed to conceal the rottenness beneath. The decay of the Regency is seen repeatedly in Dickens, whose taste in clothes as a young man was decidedly in keeping with the flamboyant style. In his novels we meet the ancient "Cleopatra," Mrs. Skewton (*Dombey and Son*), a relic of Regency bewitchment now held together only by an elaborate contrivance of cosmetic and corset; the ineffable old Mr. Turveydrop (*Bleak House*) who continues to ape dandiacal dress and manners while fantasying a fashionable status he never, in fact, enjoyed; Sir Mulberry Hawk and Lord Frederick Verisopht (*Nicholas Nickleby*), two run-of-the-Regency rakes; and impecunious young men, Dick Swiveller, Jobling, Guppy, and the rest, "gents" who on their low level emulate what they take to be the swaggering worldliness of the "swell"—the dandy gone to seed. The lingering musk and cigar smoke of the late Regency also permeate the pages of William Makepeace Thackeray, who studied his characters from life. The old rake Lord Steyne (*Vanity Fair*) was drawn from the crapulous Marquis of Hertford, and Major Pendennis is the very model of an aging Regency buck. But by then the manners, modes, and morals of the bucks and swells were giving way to the sobriety and self-conscious rectitude which had been gaining in acceptance ever since the late eighteenth century and now came to constitute the dominant ethos of Victorian society.

In the England of the 1830's the insolent luxury of the Regency was juxtaposed with the squalor and misery generated by the new industrialism. It was symptomatic of the times that the "silver fork" novels of the late twenties and thirties—fiction laid in high society and reflecting but seldom deploring its brittle glamor—were succeeded in the forties by novels of social protest, few in number but large in influence, which called overdue attention to the desperate state of the poor in factory and slum. It was at this moment that the young novelist Disraeli, himself a peacock of dan-

dies, coined—or rather, borrowed from the American
preacher William Ellery Channing—the two-word phrase
which provided a veritable text for all the subsequent Victorian literature of social criticism. In *Sybil* (1845) one of
the characters described the Queen's nation, "the greatest
nation that ever existed," as being in reality "Two nations;
between whom there is no intercourse and no sympathy;
who are as ignorant of each other's habits, thoughts, and
feelings, as if they were dwellers in different zones, or inhabitants of different planets; who are formed by a different
breeding, are fed by a different food, are ordered by different manners, and are not governed by the same laws. . . .
THE RICH AND THE POOR." The gulf was widening
year by year, and the search for the means of narrowing it
constituted the great challenge of the time.

2. *The Crystal Palace and After*

The early Victorian age, then, may be said to have begun sometime in the 1830's, when the declining superficiality
and profligacy of the Regency were accompanied by a slow,
even reluctant, coming to grips with the social crisis em-
blematized by Disraeli's two nations. It lasted to the middle
of the century. In 1851 the great event of the year was the
first world's fair, officially called the Great Exhibition of
the Works of Industry of All Nations but familiarly known
then and ever since as the Crystal Palace. Housed in the
first prefabricated public building in history, a vast construction of iron and glass set in London's Hyde Park, the
exhibition was intended to demonstrate Britain's supremacy
in design and manufacture. The design, most modern authorities agree, was atrocious; the manufacture was most
ingenious. Over half the exhibitors were from Britain and
the Empire. But the presence of impressive displays from
other nations reflected the success of Britain's new free-
trade policy. Eliminating the economic barriers between

nations, it was confidently affirmed, would guarantee not only prosperity but peace. (Prosperity was to last for twenty-five years, but peace for only three. The nation became unpleasantly involved in the Crimean War in 1854.)

The Crystal Palace celebration ushered in the "high" Victorian period, or "the age of equipoise," as the historian W. L. Burn has called it: a period of no more than fifteen or twenty years, the time we most likely see when we conjure up a mental image of the Victorian era, the time to which the old clichés about Victorianism are most applicable if they are applicable at all. It is only in the fifties and sixties that, regarding Victorianism from our vantage point of more than a hundred years, we are wholly unconscious of the eighteenth-century past on the one hand and the impending twentieth century on the other.

The short-run hopes embodied in the Crystal Palace spirit—one should add that there were more than a handful of naysayers, including Carlyle, Dickens, and Ruskin—were fulfilled. After its perilous passage through the "hungry forties" the economy bounded upward. The fifties and sixties were boom times the like of which the nation had seldom known before; Great Britain found herself incomparably the richest nation on earth, the world's foremost banker, shipper, supplier of manufactured goods, and, through her navy, keeper of the peace in the mercantile sea lanes. Batteries of statistics (it was no accident that the Victorian period saw the development of the statistical science) told the proud story. The market value of British exports quadrupled between 1842 and 1870; by 1870 British foreign trade was to be three or four times larger than that of the United States. The tonnage of ships entering and leaving British ports doubled between the mid-forties and 1860. Overseas traffic carried in British bottoms amounted to 14,300,000 tons in 1847; by 1880 the figure would be 58,700,000. The gross national income, £523,000,000 in 1851, would double by 1881. Real income increased by 10 or 15 per cent in the decades 1850–70.* The expanding middle class lived in greater comfort than it had ever done before, and a trickle of the new affluence was reaching at least some of the working class, who were thus enabled to buy an occasional modest specimen of the manufactured goods which had been so temptingly displayed under the Crystal Palace's many-acred glass roof.

With the subsidence of political agitation and social animosity, this was also an era of good feeling. In former areas of conflict, compromises had been worked out and tensions relaxed. Domestic peace and prosperity cast a rosy glow upon the future, which, in the view of those most in harmony with the temper of the times, promised simply a prolongation *ad infinitum* of present conditions, only more so. These were, in truth, sunlit years, looked back upon with nostalgia (as many accounts attest) by the people who had been so fortunate as to share in their comforts and confidence.

But the complacency that filled the air was not universal, nor did the hard-won stability last. Few important problems had been solved once for all. The forces of change and reform had merely paused to regain strength and determine new directions. In 1859 the publication of Charles Darwin's *On the Origin of Species,* shortly followed by several controversial works on theology, upset whatever illusory intellectual stasis had been reached. The nation was generating new conflicts and anxieties to replace those which either had been alleviated or had simply become outmoded.

---

* It is evidently impossible to translate Victorian money values into present-day terms with any precision, especially since there was considerable variation in the course of the century and from region to region. At a conservative estimate, the purchasing power of the pound then was between ten and fifteen times as great as now. In early Victorian England a yearly income of eight hundred to a thousand pounds was adequate for a family in good society. In that era, Browning's father, after forty-nine years as a superior clerk in the Bank of England, earned only £275, but the family of four lived comfortably enough in a London suburb.

The high Victorian era closed some time toward the end of the sixties, certainly no later than the middle seventies. If a single year may be taken to mark off the late Victorian period from the halcyon middle one, it would undoubtedly be 1867, when the Second Reform Bill doubled the electorate by enfranchising town workers. The Victorians were thereby brought face to face with an issue which had been slowly taking shape over several decades but which they had chosen not to think too much about: how to accommodate the nation's political structure and, even more importantly, its culture, to the power now within the grasp of the common man. The preceding decades had seen the middle class achieve its place in English society; now it was the manual workers' turn. Bitterly though many might deplore the advent of democracy, somehow it had to be accepted as an accomplished fact.

The national outlook was further clouded by the agricultural depression which began in 1873 and lasted, though relieved by intermittent spells of comparative prosperity, to the end of the century. A series of crop failures, the influx of cheap machine-harvested grain from the American prairies, and the introduction of refrigerator ships which brought meat from Australia and New Zealand reduced farming to a marginal place in an economy which until the last half-century had been squarely based on the land, and destroyed the balance between agriculture and industry which had made possible the prosperity of the middle years. One momentous result was that the large landowners finally had to surrender most of the political power to which they had clung despite the inroads of industrialism.

The shift in political balance caused by the decline of agriculture and the ascendancy of the workingmen's vote was but one of the many tendencies which complicated and in many ways darkened the later Victorian decades. The economic decline revived labor unrest. Trade unions, strengthened by legislation passed in the seventies, promoted strikes in many industries, and the socialist movement was re-invigorated after many years of suspended animation. It was increasingly obvious to social observers like Ruskin that the nation's wealth was not being distributed equitably; in fact, the prosperity of the sixties and early seventies had meant growing disparity. While there was more rhetoric than fact in the claim that the very rich were growing richer while the very poor were growing poorer even faster, it is true that there were more in each of these extreme classes, and that although some of the workers did share modestly in the nation's wealth, the rest slipped farther behind.

Meanwhile, Britain's pre-eminence as a financial and shipping power, and even as "the workshop of the world," was threatened as Germany and the United States—the latter recovering from the economic disruption attending the Civil War—gained competitive strength. When Disraeli bestowed upon the Queen the additional title of Empress of India in 1876, her country was approaching the height of its influence and achievement as an imperial power, but the involvements and responsibilities this position entailed would complicate political life for the rest of the century. The seemingly incurable Irish problem, which had festered throughout the reign as it had for centuries earlier, became the nation's most pressing domestic issue as the militant nationalists' demand for Home Rule took the form of dynamiting and murder.

Most important for its effects upon the literature produced in those years, intellectual life was troubled by the breakdown of the verities that had lent the fifties and sixties an air of stability. The church's influence over men's minds declined as decisively as did its influence over society and state. The confrontation of religion and natural science produced an atmosphere of secularism and skepticism. The Ruskinian "morality of art" (Chapter VIII) lost its authority and was succeeded by an attitude toward aesthetic experience which had nothing to do with morality. The intensified campaign for women's rights raised insistent and often uncomfortable questions about the place of women in society and the relation of the sexes. The unorthodoxy, the habit of incisive criticism which had earlier characterized the thought of some of the nation's greatest literary figures now spread from the prophets to some of the people.

The generation who witnessed the Queen's passing settled nothing. They handed down their restless spirit of quest and questioning to the Edwardians who succeeded them. The concerns of those last Victorian years were not so much the unfinished business of the past as the steadily more urgent issues of the future. For these reasons among others, modern historians argue that the Victorian age proper came to an end about 1880; at least one would move the date back to 1870. Thus, while it is usually exhaustion or lack of time which induces teachers of college courses in Victorian literature to put off considering post-1880 works to some dim future occasion, there is an arguable historical reason for doing so. Later Victorian literature speaks with a quite different voice, echoing the contemporary mood in which values were being drastically re-ordered and intellectual energies were set working in new directions.

II

THE VICTORIANS: ACTORS

AND AUDIENCE

1. An Evolving Society

ONE OF THE MOST distinctive features of Victorian literature is its social orientation. From the classes to be described in this chapter were drawn the prototypes of the men and women who figure in the age's fiction. More important, it was their respective characteristics and ways of life that formed the principal concern of the many observers whose acute social criticism lent Victorian literature what has proved to be perhaps its most enduring interest. And among these classes were the hundreds of thousands of readers who constituted the audience for the fiction, prose of ideas, and poetry the Victorian age produced, and who thereby largely determined the nature of that literature.

The chief preoccupation of the major novelists, as it was a leading one of other prose writers, was the structure, internal movement, and moral atmosphere of contemporary society. The novelists, Thackeray above all but closely followed by Anthony Trollope and by Dickens in his later books, were especially concerned with the anxieties, envy, insecurity, snobbery, and kindred psychological malaises that stemmed from the ambiguities of rank and wealth in a time of social flux. The proper study of mankind in Victorian fiction often took the form of a study of men and women in a given class and their efforts to maintain their status against outside pressures or, more often, to improve it.

The Victorians had inherited Edmund Burke's organic view of the political state and of society. Just as the state was an organism with internal principles of growth which were not to be interfered with by artificial instruments and innovations, so society was made up of well-defined social strata, the living result of centuries of tradition, and was endowed, as a result, with a near-mystique. The belief that the hierarchical structure based on hereditary privilege had something sacred about it survived into an age of increasing social fluidity, and not alone in stuffily conservative minds. In Victorian England the concept of "deference"—willing acknowledgment that the people in the classes above one's own were justly entitled to their superiority—was so strong that it was proof against all the subversive and disintegrating forces which were brought to bear against it.

Down to the end of the eighteenth century, the caste system had served England well, social friction being harmlessly drained off, for the most part, by the universal safeguards embodied in the law, which was itself a product of long and gradual development. But the complications attending the Victorian economic, social, and political revolution shattered the relative simplicity of the older social structure, and the population was fragmented into many interest-groups, partly social, partly religious, partly occupational, partly demographic—rural as against urban. The emergent groups were often mutually suspicious, sometimes overtly hostile. Throughout the era, those on the lower rungs of the ladder entertained toward their "betters" much resentment, and at certain junctures undisguised rancor. And yet, thanks to the deep-seated habit of deference, these attitudes never kindled into anything resembling class warfare. Repeatedly, in national emergencies or on occasions of national mourning or rejoicing, the intricate pattern of a pluralistic society divided both vertically and horizontally was obscured in an onrush of universally shared sentiment. The compelling idea of "Englishness," transcending considerations of superiority or inferiority, proved one source of the country's salvation during the Victorian years.

Another saving factor was the theory of an open society. The dissolving of the traditional hierarchy into numerous smaller constituent groups continued to reduce the rigorousness with which, in a feudalistically derived society such as England's, each individual was confined for life to his inherited social position. The health of the social system rested, as it had since Tudor days, in the idea of "removable inequality." Theoretically there was nothing to prevent a man fired by praiseworthy ambition from rising as high as his talents and exercise of the appropriate prudential virtues allowed. In practice, the odds were against it, but now they were not as long as they had been. The possibility, as the spectacular careers of any number of self-made Victorians testified, was there. And unquestionably the general social movement was upward, even if most gains were modest.

The diversity and (to a degree) the instability of the social pattern were complicated by sectional differences. Although improved communication tended to impose a certain uniformity upon the country's social attitudes, in such matters as the relative standing of the various classes and occupations, the distinctions of rank, and social mobility there were still noticeable regional variations. Few generalizations hold for the entire country. For example, details of social organization and individual expectations in the agricultural south, where vestiges of the feudal pattern of degree and deference lingered, were quite at variance with those in the north, where the common people were less heedful of social distinctions and therefore were more blunt and independent in manner.

2. The Aristocracy

Near the top of the social pyramid, directly under the pinnacle occupied by royalty, was the aristocracy which had governed the nation since Tudor times—the families of blood, wealth, and venerable name, some three hundred of them in the early Victorian period, who had continually strengthened their position by intermarriage and by playing commanding roles in political life. They constituted the core of the "landowning interest," which derived its wealth from the nation's agrarian economy—a security to be threatened by the new economy based on industrial production and world trade.

In the first half of the nineteenth century their already large estates were extended still farther by the enclosure system. Hitherto, in most parts of the country (some of the southern counties had undergone the process in earlier centuries), agriculture had been conducted on a subsistence basis, small tenants and their laborers tilling their allotment of detached oblong strips into which the open fields were divided, and communally owning and using the "commons" —meadows and wasteland—for pasturage and wood-gathering. Now, under hundreds of *ad hoc* acts passed by Parliament between 1760 and 1840, the open fields and commons were bought up and consolidated into hedge-enclosed acreage that was suitable, as the former layout had not been, for the scientific methods of agriculture that had begun to be developed in the mid-eighteenth century. At the beginning of the Victorian era, no aristocratic landowner possessed less than 10,000 acres; by 1883, twenty-eight noblemen owned estates of over 100,000 acres each.

But now, in addition, some fortunate families acquired new wealth from the rental of London real estate (which increased spectacularly in value as the metropolis grew ever larger and busier) and from mineral rights, especially the royalties from coal mines worked under their land. They were the families to be envied when the bottom fell out of agriculture in the 1870's. In the last decades of the century, the old-established nobility's resistance to the incursion of outsiders gave way as new fortunes accumulated in manufacturing, business, and finance equipped their parvenu possessors with the kind of credentials that were most to the point in a period when bank balances were coming to weigh more heavily than acreage owned. To the names familiar to Englishmen since the sixteenth century were added those of newly-created peers whose presence in high society, though far from universally approved, was inevitable in a nation devoted to industrial capitalism. The last phase of the "vulgarization" of the old aristocracy by the infusion of plutocratic blood—aureate rather than blue—occurred under the auspices of the Queen's eldest son, the Prince of Wales (later Edward VII), whose circle came to include suitably wealthy Jews and Americans.

In earlier centuries, the families of great landed wealth and supreme social position had formed the oligarchy which, whether behind the scenes or publicly in Parliament and the offices of government, had determined the nation's course. They had also constituted a cultural leadership which had been largely responsible for the flourishing of English civilization from the time of Elizabeth I to that of George III. But in the nineteenth century the threat to their domination which was posed by newly rich middle-class industrialists and financiers was accompanied by complaints that they had abdicated their social responsibilities. Carlyle, Mill, and Arnold, to name only three of their critics, attributed many of society's ills to the wastrel habits of the aristocracy (Carlyle's "idle, game-preserving dilettantes"; Arnold's "barbarians"). These social parasites whiled away their days shooting huge numbers of pheasants in their well-guarded preserves and lounging, during the fashionable London season, in town houses resplendent with the kind of ostentatious bad taste that only unlimited money can buy.

There was plenty of reason for discontent. In a time

when millions of their fellow-countrymen were barely keeping alive, the great families sank fortunes into building stately sham-Gothic mansions or adding wings, often in conflicting architectural style, to their ancestral homes. The Duke of Devonshire's conservatory at Chatsworth, "one mass of glass, 64 feet high, 300 long and 134 wide," as an admiring visitor, the Queen herself, described it, was the model for the justly praised Crystal Palace. At Petworth, Lord Egremont stabled three hundred horses. Entertainment was on a princely scale; guests were constantly coming and going, their needs attended to by companies of gorgeously attired footmen, their slumbers ended in the morning (at least at Belvoir, seat of the Duke of Rutland) by the military band belonging to their host's regiment.

Some noblemen went in for drinking, racing, foxhunting, and gambling—and occasionally philandering—on a scale appropriate to their wealth and the dignity of their house. The last Marquis of Hastings, one of the richest peers in England, started betting at sixteen and died, a ruined man, at twenty-six. In six years (1839–44), a combination of lavish entertaining, the expense of several great houses and game preserves, and association with the underworld which battened on incautious nobility enabled the second Duke of Buckingham to amass a debt of a million pounds, some of it at 15 per cent interest. By 1847 the interest exceeded his annual income by £20,000, and the next year his magnificent mansion at Stowe was sold at auction, lock, stock, barrel, and 60,000 ounces of gold and silver plate. The Duke died in 1861, dependent on his son's charity.

But these were notorious individual cases. While financial bankruptcy did occasionally overtake a titled spendthrift, the charge of moral bankruptcy preferred against the governing class as a whole was not well founded. By no means the majority of the noble families turned their backs on their obligations to their inferiors or lived other than sedate and inoffensive, though admittedly extremely comfortable, lives. The general sobriety of habit which the

Evangelical moral code (Chapter V) had introduced into middle-class life reached upward as well. Notwithstanding Carlyle's accusation of an idleness endemic to a whole class, men of commitment were as numerous in the Victorian social register as they had been in any period, though none was the equal of Lord Ashley (later the seventh Earl of Shaftesbury); Ashley's devotion to causes he believed in and his tenacity in pressing them made him one of the age's greatest humanitarians and reformers. In addition, the majority of posts in every cabinet down to 1874 were occupied by members of the nobility and the closely associated higher gentry, and many of them were not figureheads by any means. Most of the nation's domestic and foreign policy-making was in the hands of what could fairly be called a working aristocracy.

That the nobility was as conscientious as it was in discharging its social responsibilities owed something perhaps to the Young England movement, initiated in the early forties by a group of Tories led by Benjamin Disraeli, just beginning the political career which would lead finally to the prime ministership. In his novel *Coningsby* (1844) Disraeli expounded the idea of *noblesse oblige*—derived partly from Scott's portrayal of chivalry in his fiction, partly from Coleridge's and Carlyle's social theory—which envisioned a modern aristocratic party dedicated to serving society. His solution for the "two nations" problem, then in its most acute stage, was to unite the workers and their noble protectors against their common enemy, the commercial middle class, which Disraeli's rival, the Tory leader Sir Robert Peel, himself the son of a self-made mill owner, was trying to attract into the Tory camp. Young Englandism did not have the practical effect Disraeli had contemplated—no such unlikely alliance of Tory aristocrats and subservient calloused workmen was ever achieved—but during its brief life it did provide an ideal of disinterested service, on a semi-feudal model, which motivated a few noblemen at a time when the aristocracy as a class needed fresh inspiration.

Although feudalism no longer prevailed, the landowners' presence in the countryside was always felt, and in many ways. They led the fox hunts in which lesser neighbors might join; they exhibited at local agricultural fairs. The father of the aforesaid Duke of Devonshire declared that the proudest moment of his life was when his pig won first prize at Skipton Fair. A local magnate might entertain hundreds of his tenants at a feast on his son's twenty-first birthday or some other notable occasion. He might, on the other hand, summarily evict those tenants, as the Duke of Newcastle evicted two hundred residents of Newark who in 1829 failed to vote for his parliamentary candidate. "Have I not a right to do what I like with my own?" he asked, invoking Matthew 20:15. The remark was widely disliked, and we find it echoed for several decades in literature critical of the upper classes; but it merely expressed, in rather too blunt a way, the basic principle of English representative government before the Reform Bill of 1832 (below, pp. 85–88). Hundreds of landowners "owned" parliamentary seats. Some of these seats were for rotten boroughs—depopulated districts where the few remaining voters could be controlled either by pressure or by bribery. The member of Parliament for Bossiney in Cornwall, for example, was elected by precisely one voter. The rest of the seats at the disposal of the large landed proprietors were for pocket (also called "nomination" or "close") boroughs, whose electors, however numerous, also could be relied upon to obey the magnates' will. Unless such an owner wished to reserve the seat for a relative, he was free to advertise it in the newspapers as available to the highest bidder. In 1812 the Duke of Bedford sold a Cornish borough, complete with a dozen or so complaisant voters, for £32,000.

The way each elector voted was public knowledge, because not until 1872 was the secret ballot introduced in national elections. Interested parties therefore had no trouble finding out whether or not the voter was faithful to whatever bargain had been struck. The partial elimination of rotten and pocket boroughs in 1832 was counterbalanced by the increased corruption that marked elections thenceforth. The farcically riotous Eatanswill election in *Pickwick Papers,* like a number of later elections in Victorian fiction, accurately represented the spirit and action of many "beer and mob rule" contests. To get their man into Parliament, local magnates or their agents used virtually every device of persuasion and coercion known to the art of representative government. Qualified voters were treated to unlimited food and drink; the first time William Ewart Gladstone, the future prime minister, stood for office he was billed £2,000 for meals and liquor consumed at a single inn. In some districts, votes brought a price ranging from £15 to £100. A voter, having cast his oral ballot, got a receipt, passed it into a hole in a nearby wall, and collected the agreed-upon sum at another. Sometimes, with the connivance of the authorities, men not only voted early but voted often; sometimes, too, dead men voted from the grave; on still other occasions, candidates hired hoodlums to make sure that voters who were unpurchasable in their behalf did not get to the polls to vote for the opposition. In the years 1832–54 alone, the corruption in seventy-seven elections was so blatant that the winner was unseated by act of Parliament and the constituency deprived of representation until the next election. Such was the case at Beverley, Yorkshire, in 1868 after Trollope ran unsuccessfully on the Liberal platform.

3. The Gentry and the Middle Class

Just below the aristocracy, sharing many of its privileges and sympathies and often connected with it by birth or marriage, was the gentry, or "squirearchy." This class included the younger sons of peers, whom the law of primogeniture barred from succeeding to the family fortune, and baronets (possessors of hereditary knighthoods), who, as a character in Disraeli's *Sybil* observed, were a blend of "the nobles of whom they are the popular branch [and] the people who recognize in them their natural leaders." Other important members of the gentry bore simply the title of "gentleman." To these the ordinary people of the countryside continued to owe customary, if not explicitly legal, allegiance. Unlike medieval serfs, tenants and laborers were no longer bound to the manor, but upon meeting his squire the countryman pulled his forelock as a gesture of deference, even as his ancestors had done. In many cases the squire possessed the right of selecting the clergyman who (nominally, anyway) ministered to the parish's spiritual needs, and he also often had one or more parliamentary seats in his pocket. But his most direct and constant effect on the community stemmed from his powers as magistrate. Until the Municipal Corporations Act of 1835, the first step in overhauling a system of local government that had been patched together across the centuries, he, his fellow landowners, and their appointees governed the boroughs near which they lived, supervising such matters as the care of the poor, road repair, and the removal of "public nuisances" (night soil, dung heaps, garbage, and such). Even after the administration of boroughs was transferred to elected officials, the rural areas, where most men did not receive the vote until 1884, remained under the authority of the squire sitting as justice of the peace and meting out sentences to poachers, fathers of illegitimate children, housebreakers, and similar offenders. For various political and economic reasons the squirearchy, as innumerable Victorian novels testify, set the tone of rural and small-town society, sometimes to its benefit and sometimes to its detriment. Along with the aristocracy, it supplied a valuable element of continuity in a time of rapid social change. It also supplied much of the resistance to that change.

Several major Victorian writers came from the gentry. Elizabeth Barrett Browning, for example, belonged to a "county family" with an estate in Herefordshire, and Algernon Charles Swinburne's father, an admiral, was the second son of Sir John Edward Swinburne, sixth baronet of Capheaton. And Victorian literature presents squires of every type: Mr. Brown in Thomas Hughes's *Tom Brown's School Days,* Mr. Holbrook in Mrs. Gaskell's *Cranford,* Sir Leicester Dedlock in Dickens' *Bleak House,* the leaky-minded Mr. Brooke in George Eliot's *Middlemarch,* and Sir Aylmer Aylmer in Tennyson's "Aylmer's Field."

Below the gentry, and ambitious to join them, lay the middle class, whose expansion and rise to power was the great phenomenon of nineteenth-century social history.* Pre-eminently, until then, the class of merchants, shopkeepers in a prosperous way of business, and professional men, it had been growing since Elizabethan days. The Protestant Reformation and the Puritan Revolution had both been middle-class movements, and much of the spirit behind them survived, with necessary modifications brought about by changed conditions, in the Victorian era.

The industrial revolution, beginning about the middle of the eighteenth century and gaining momentum as the century drew to a close, brought unprecedentedly numerous recruits, many of them of new breeds, to the middle class— first the manufacturers and then those who served as supporting troops for the economy as it shifted from land to factory: commodity brokers, financiers, foreign traders, providers of consumer goods and services to an increasingly wealthy home market. Every one of the many occupations associated with industrial capitalism required and rewarded the skills, shrewdness, and enterprise that had traditionally characterized the commercial middle class.

The class multiplied itself in the course of the nine-

* In a nineteenth-century context, it is considerably more accurate to speak of the "middle *classes,*" because this was the most pluralistic part of an increasingly pluralistic society. But the singular form, while it oversimplifies, is more convenient.

teenth century, but no one knows how many times. Contemporary students of society never agreed, any more than the people involved did, on its upper and nether boundaries, which had never been very clear and which became increasingly indistinct as time went on. At one extreme, sufficient wealth and aggressiveness enabled men at the top of the middle class to insinuate themselves into the gentry, often to their subsequent secret discomfort as well as that of their new "equals." A rich banker or manufacturer might do so by purchasing a landed estate, the first requisite of gentility, from an impoverished gentleman-by-blood. Tennyson's grandfather, a successful provincial lawyer, strengthened his social position by that means, as had many similarly circumstanced men in the eighteenth century. At the other extreme, highly skilled artisans, independent and perhaps themselves employers of labor, clung to the lowest middle-class rung of the social ladder and looked hopefully upward. Middle-class values and appurtenances had a powerful attraction for the artisan class. The prospect of enjoying some of the physical comforts associated with middle-class life and, no less important, the feeling of status that those possessions brought with them, was the most effective upward stimulus the age knew. This was what had motivated Sir Roger Scatcherd, in Trollope's *Dr. Thorne,* to struggle from the humble position of stonemason to the superficially exalted one of landed proprietor, a climb that resulted only in disappointment and an addiction to brandy.

It was the middle-class orientation and code of values that lent the Victorian social climate its distinctive flavor. Its moral ideology, to be explored in some detail in Chapter V, embraced the values to which most Victorians, even including some aristocrats who could have afforded better ones, subscribed. In another sphere, in contrast to the traditionalism of the land-based Tories, this commercially oriented society was the seat of liberalism, the cluster of attitudes that were widely interpreted as most faithfully representing, for better or worse, the temper of the new, forward-looking age.*

Since the middle class regarded itself as the moral heart of Victorian society, a conviction assisted by the shift of the economic center of gravity in its direction, it took the understandable position that what was good for it was *ipso facto* good for the nation. This was dogma which, on the whole, was believed in as devoutly as even the existence of a Christian God or the sacredness of the British Constitution. The venerable aristocracy might disagree, but there was little it could do in the face of such self-assurance backed by figures.

As with all large social groups, the Victorian middle class was divided into numerous smaller bodies, according to income, occupation, education, and religion. (Again, there was no uniform national pattern: the distribution and nuances of distinction varied from region to region.) The term "middle class" covered a wide range of groups and subgroups, from cotton brokers, brewers, and ironmasters to self-employed artisans who lived in the large permanent gray area where social ambiguity was most pronounced.

The breadth of the middle class as well as some of the distinctions of rank it maintained is well illustrated by the social origins of a number of Victorian authors. Newman's

---

* Because the word "liberal" occurs in varying contexts in Victorian discussion and its meaning sometimes differs from today's, its Victorian uses had better be clarified at once. In the political-social vocabulary it was the rough synonym of watered-down Benthamism (see Chapter IV), including suggestions of free-trade economic theory, cautiously democratic sympathies, belief in reason and progress, intellectual tolerance, and moderate reformist impulses. In early Victorian times it also became the name of the erstwhile Whig party. In religious thought it referred to the subordination of church to state, the minimizing of creedal differences, and open-mindedness toward new (and often disturbing) intellectual tendencies affecting faith. Later its connotations of rationalism and skepticism drew it closer to "free thought," but the two were by no means identical. On the whole, the word has lost none of its resistance to exact definition in its passage from the pre-Victorian era down to ours. On the Victorian meaning of "radical," see page 115, note.

father was a partner in a London banking house, whereas Browning's was only a clerk in the Bank of England. Ruskin's father was a partner in a leading firm of wine importers. Both Carlyle and Hardy were builders' sons. George Meredith's grandfather was a successful Portsmouth naval tailor, but his father, after reverses, lapsed into the ignominious status of a journeyman in the trade, and as a consequence the novelist, who expertly anatomized social distinctions in several of his books, was always reticent about his family background, although he included much autobiography in *Evan Harrington.* William Morris' father was a businessman who struck it rich in shares of Cornish tin and copper mines. Thackeray was something of a special case: he belonged to the "nabobs," English families whose heads had acquired wealth and social standing as administrators, businessmen, professional men, or military officers in India and then returned home to form a closely knit social community of their own. Of all the major Victorian authors, Carlyle possibly excepted, Dickens' credentials were perhaps closest to the borderline of respectability, because his father was merely a pay clerk at naval stations.

In some groups—doctors, clergymen, and teachers, for example—there were superior and inferior grades, which depended on numerous factors such as family lineage, education, professional success, and the social standing of their clientele. A London society physician, such as Dr. Lydgate in *Middlemarch* eventually became, was separated by an almost unbridgeable gulf from the small provincial practitioners, such as Mr. Gambit the midwife, who had been his resentful former colleagues. An even wider abyss separated a classics master, B.A., M.A. Oxoniensis, at aristocratic Eton, and a slum-born London schoolteacher like Bradley Headstone in Dickens' *Our Mutual Friend.* The comparative ratings of various occupations shifted in the course of the era. Professional men generally rose in status, with the establishment of organizations intended, among other things, to prescribe and enforce standards of preparation and ethical codes.

New professions, of unquestioned importance, had to be placed. Where did civil and mechanical engineers, actuaries, analytical chemists fit in—above or below physicians (who by common consent were higher than dentists), above or below solicitors (who were lower than barristers)? The sheer gentility of an occupation elevated it above those closer to the streets: a lawyer's clerk necessarily assumed he was the superior of the publican who served him his beer, and a male assistant in a retail shop outranked a skilled wheelwright. Employers of labor, likewise, were a degree above self-employed craftsmen.

Certain occupations increased in size as the requirements of society changed. Commercial clerks, working for banks, railroads, insurance companies, and manufacturing concerns, came to comprise one of the largest middle-class groups. Civil servants, too, became much more numerous as government activities multiplied on both the national and local levels.

Religion made much difference in social standing. An Anglican mill owner ranked as far above a Nonconformist * mill owner of identical income as a parson in his neo-Gothic church ranked above a Methodist minister saving souls in his brick and mortar chapel in a dreary Manchester slum. The worst social handicap an ambitious member of the middle class had to labor under was a double one—being a Dissenter and earning one's money "in trade," that is, in any kind of commercial occupation producing or selling goods, especially at retail, as distinct from finance, foreign commerce, the professions, or moneyed leisure. It was a ticklish problem of current social values which is reflected, in all its

---

* The virtually interchangeable terms "Nonconformist" and "Dissenter" designate members of religious denominations which, beginning in the seventeenth century, broke away from the state ("Established") Church of England. "Nonconformity" refers to their refusal to conform to the Anglican Church's ritual, "Dissent" to their disagreement with the Church's doctrines. In the nineteenth century they combined with a portion of the Anglican Church to form the Evangelical movement (Chapter V).

nuances and manifold personal consequences, in innumerable Victorian novels. Too close contact with money con-
taminated one; it was quite another matter to receive a large
income through an intermediary such as an estate agent (the
occupation of George Eliot's father) or a solicitor.

One reason why Dissenters formed so large and influential a segment of the commercial class—they were certainly more numerous than Anglicans—was that since the
seventeenth century they had been more or less segregated
from the main current of English life. Only in 1828 had
the repeal of the Corporation and Test Acts (passed in 1661
and 1673 respectively) allowed Dissenters to hold public
office, including seats in Parliament, without requiring an
ex post facto dispensation through an annual Act of Indem-
nity passed for the purpose. Because until 1854–56 they
could not take degrees at Oxford or Cambridge (until then,
Oxford barred them from even matriculating), they were
prevented from entering the learned and "gentlemanly"
professions. The intelligence and prodigious energies of the
non-Anglican members of the middle class therefore had to
be channeled into materialistic pursuits; hence their historic
identification with "trade."

Dissent was a socially stigmatized religion just as
trade was a socially stigmatized pursuit. To be a Nonconformist when the best people for centuries had been
Anglicans was, at the very least, in dubious taste. And to be a
Methodist in particular was to be classed as an "enthusiast"
—a person of coarse religious manners bordering on fanaticism, a follower of field preachers, a constant Bible-quoter
and participant in mass conversions. As a result, despite the
gradual remission of their disabilities, Dissenters, no matter
how wealthy, formed a somewhat separate community
throughout the nineteenth century. Association with ledger
books, cash drawers, and chapels named Shiloh, Ebenezer,
Bethel, or Zion made a man and his family socially suspect
in the eyes of people conditioned to revere old values and
churches named for Christian saints.

How could the disadvantage of trade and Dissent be overcome? There were two ways, neither being wholly efficacious without the other. A man could, as we have seen, buy a landed estate and thus possess the physical evidence of gentility. Without land, one was nobody. But even a plethora of acres was not enough; it was migration to the Church of England that finally certified one's fitness to mingle in the best Victorian circles. Only communion at the Anglican altar could remove the taint of having earned one's fortune in trade.

Probably the most comprehensive single account of such social distinctions and prejudices is *Middlemarch*. Although it explicitly describes the social structure of a provincial town (Coventry) in the early 1830's, in many respects it is also an authentic picture of conditions as they continued to exist in the early seventies, when the novel was published. Trollope's fiction, the Palisser series in particular, offers a similar panorama of social organization and dynamics on a generally higher level.

At a rough guess, 90 per cent of the characters in the Victorian fiction which is read today belong to the middle class and the gentry. The estimate would have to be revised in the case of individual authors; members of the lower classes are more numerous in Dickens than in, say, Thackeray or Trollope. If (unthinkably) a sociological analysis were made of all the more than 40,000 novels the Victorians are estimated to have produced, still another distribution might appear. The incidence of nobility and higher gentry in the silver fork novels and later in the confections of the best-selling authoress "Ouida" (Marie Louise de la Ramée) is much higher than in Victorian fiction as a whole.

4. *"The Lower Orders"*

"Folks," observed Jorrocks, the well-to-do Cockney grocer in Robert Smith Surtees' popular novels about foxhunt-

ing, the sport that often brought noblemen and commoners together in a common pursuit, "talk about the different grades o' society . . . but arter all's said and done
there are but two sorts o' folks i' the world, Peerage folks
and Post Hoffice Directory folks." Although the statement
accurately reflected a widely held social opinion, it was, of
course, wrong: for below the middle class, whose names
were duly listed in the Post Office Directory, lay what was
by far the largest portion of the English population.

In earlier centuries, it was called simply "the poor."
Now it was "the masses," "the million," "the working class,"
"the lower ranks," "the laboring population," "the industrious class," "the inferior orders," "the laboring poor,"
and, increasingly, "the people," although at first this term
was normally confined to the middle class in its broadest
aspect. These were the laborers in the fields and factories,
the unskilled and semi-skilled as well as those more expert
in their occupation, who were a group apart, because their
work was steadier and in good times they could earn twice
as much as the unskilled. (The frequently met term "me-
chanic" was originally applied to skilled industrial workers,
including machine builders and repairmen, but later was
downgraded to become almost synonymous with "machine
tender.") Menial domestic servants, of whom there were no
fewer than a million in 1851 (as compared with 1,790,000
in agriculture and 1,670,000 in the textile industry), belonged to the working class, but farm stewards and house-
keepers—positions Dickens' paternal grandparents had had
at Lord Crewe's Staffordshire home—ranked higher. Although historical sources and fiction provide much less evidence on the point than exists for the middle class, the
workers seem to have had their own informal system of distinctions. A skilled handloom weaver like Silas Marner,
though out of work, as more and more of them became,
clearly outranked a comparatively well paid but rough
"navvy" (itinerant construction worker, member of the gangs
that built canals and railways). A consumptive piecework

tailor employed in a sweatshop still was better than a road mender.

"The million" claim attention in these pages for two reasons. One is that working-class life was the subject of a particular genre of fiction, especially prominent in the 1840's and fifties (the industrial novel) and again in the eighties and nineties (the novel of proletarian London life). The other reason is that in the nineteenth century life among the masses became for the first time a serious concern of the classes above them. The fundamental questions of human values it raised engaged the minds of numerous Victorian social critics. The workers' emergence into startled, often horrified view, in all their ignorance, squalor, frequent brutality, and pathos, after centuries of relative obscurity, reverberated in every corner of Victorian life—its politics, social creed, culture, and, not least, its literature.

There had been plenty of misery among peasants when they were tied to the land. Country laborers in every period were accustomed to living from hand to mouth. Their homes were hovels built of mud, lath, and plaster, with floors of dirt or stone, and rafters instead of ceiling under the leaky thatch. Domestic fowl and animals such as pigs shared these dark, damp, sparsely furnished quarters with the family. There was no sanitation, and often there was no adequate heat. It had been a hard, grim life, whose only purpose, year after year, was somehow to extract the bare essentials of diet and clothing from field and pasture. It was lightened only by the occasional holidays and fairs that punctuated the march of the seasons and by an oral folk culture of stories, songs, and superstitions. The "merrie England" conjured up by Christmas cards and popular art is a figment of sentimental sociology, for which some Victorians, in their understandable desire to dramatize present misery by contrasting it with past contentment, must be held responsible. There never was a rural English society in which snug honeysuckle-covered cottages, plum puddings, fresh-faced village maidens, and hearty, rubicund squires joined to form a picture of utter bliss. Arcadia must be sought elsewhere in the annals of the race.

In the nineteenth century, largely because of the spread of the enclosure system, farm laborers were apparently worse off than they had been for several generations. From time beyond reckoning, they had had the free use of commons where they grazed a pig or cow and fed a few fowl, and of strips of arable land where they grew crops for their household needs. Now deprived of meat and vegetables, the rural family's diet became even more scanty and monotonous, consisting only of bread, potatoes, and tea. The landowners did not raise wages to compensate for this loss of the common land, so there was widespread destitution. Seven or eight shillings were all that the drudgery of six long days could earn. There were no prospects for improvement, because the supply of labor was more than adequate, especially in view of the fact that children did not have to go to school— if there were any school in the vicinity.

The consolidation of farms into large estates under a single owner meant that many independent farmers (yeomen), undercompensated for selling their freehold, had either to become tenant farmers or, failing that, to lapse into the wretched condition of common laborers. The decline of the yeomen as a class was among the most regrettable developments that drastically changed the nature of rural society, for it was they who, in George Eliot's words in *The Mill on the Floss,* "dressed in good broadcloth, paid high rates and taxes, went to church, and ate a particularly good dinner on Sunday, without dreaming that the British constitution in Church and State had a traceable origin any more than the solar system and the fixed stars." For centuries the yeomen had represented solidity, prosperity, decency, independence; they had been beholden to no man; in time of national crisis, their courage made them the very personification of the English "hearts of oak." Now, dispossessed of their acres, they were joined by other disemployed workers, village craftsmen, principally spinners and weavers, who had been thrown out of work by machines. All shared a common demoralization but it was perhaps worst among the field laborers, whose loss of what had hitherto been property for communal benefit deprived them of such small but important sense of self-sufficiency as they had enjoyed.

Again there was much regional variation in the size of the labor force and the wage scale. In some areas, such as the Midlands and the north, where factories, iron works, and coal mines paid better wages, farm hands could make double the sum they could earn in less competitive regions. They could also afford to be slightly more independent. But irrespective of what they earned when the sun shone, nobody made anything when the weather was bad or the season wrong. The Victorian countryman's lot was unenviable, to say the least. One of its few redeeming features was the occasional solicitude of the landowners, whose main form of philanthropy was replacing some of the ruinous habitations with cottages that were neater, more spacious (two rooms up and two down), and healthier. Dorothea Brooke in *Middlemarch* occupied her leisure drawing plans for such "model" cottages.

Even palatial housing, however, would not have reduced the countryman's bitterness toward his squire on the matter of poaching. When the common land was lost, the obvious substitute for the food formerly raised there was the partridges and hares abounding in the hedges and copses. But, by an exercise of property rights even more arbitrary than enclosure, the landowners made poaching one of the most heinous of crimes. Since their position as magistrate enabled them to act as judge as well as prosecutor, the poachers they convicted received stiffer sentences than did men guilty of much graver offenses. A hungry cottager caught with a net at night could be transported (sent to a penal colony in Australia) for a long term of years. Some of the most severe hazards and penalties, it is true, were removed before the Victorian age began: the deadly mantraps and spring guns, for example, devices which could mutilate or kill anyone unlucky enough to trip them, were made illegal in 1827, and the law limiting the shooting or catching of game to the squire and his eldest son was repealed four years later. But enough game laws remained in force, and the memory of the others was sufficiently fresh, to make the poaching issue a lasting source of enmity between classes. The continued existence of a black market in protected game tempted many a countryman to join one of the numerous poachers' gangs or to take a pheasant or two on his own. Whatever rich men's delicacies he caught, he could stealthily barter for his own table's necessities.

Apart from figuring in the newspapers as convicted or injured poachers or as participants in radical demonstrations, rural laborers were the forgotten people of the era. George Eliot, to be sure, was praised for her portraits of life among the country people, and such somewhat earlier novels as Disraeli's *Sybil,* Kingsley's *Alton Locke* and *Yeast,* and Mrs. Gaskell's *North and South* had paid at least tangential attention to the pervasive "agricultural distress," but Thomas Hardy was the first major novelist to portray in realistic detail the life of the humble rural laborer. Yet in the middle of the century more than a quarter of all Englishmen over the age of twenty worked on the land. Wretched as they were, it was not their condition but that of the workers caught in the toils of industrialism which aroused the early Victorian social conscience.

5. Factory and Slum

The factory system dated from the latter half of the eighteenth century, when the old system of cottage labor (handicraftsmen and their families doing piecework at home with materials usually supplied by their employer) was gradually supplanted by small-town workshops in which a number of craftsmen worked side by side with their employer. In due course these "manufactories" adopted such inventions as the power loom, flying shuttle, and spinning jenny, and were accordingly relocated along the streams from which they got their motive power. To help tend these primitive machines, the mill owners imported wagonloads of orphans from cities like London and Edinburgh. The parish authorities who were responsible for their upkeep were only too glad to be rid of them, especially as it was not unknown for employers to agree to the authorities' throwing in one idiot or crippled child for every twenty whole ones they supplied. It was these hapless so-called apprentices who were the first victims of the industrial revolution.

The adoption of the steam engine, beginning about the turn of the century, marked the decisive movement away from small factories, adjoining equally small communities of workers' houses, to great mills, powered by steam and situated near the sources of iron, coal, and cheap adult and child labor. Here, initially stimulated (until 1815) by wartime demand for its products, the factory system flourished. The smoky blight from its chimneys was cast not merely across the contiguous landscape but across all English society. By 1884 Ruskin had transformed it from fact into metaphor, "The Storm-Cloud of the Nineteenth Century" becoming a capacious symbol for the whole state of modern man, poisoned, choked, and blackened as he was, body and soul, by the industrial system.

The human toll it exacted became a matter of general concern in the early thirties. Because of the sensation the early revelations caused, there is a tendency to assume that most of England's workers were then suffering in the ways described in the first of the long series of "blue books" (voluminous collections of statistics and evidence gathered by the two kinds of official fact-finding bodies, "select committees" of Parliament and royal commissions) and in the reports of private philanthropic organizations investigating local conditions. Actually, the particular conditions which most stirred the national conscience affected only a minority of the laboring population, the textile mill workers. That they should have received an amount of publicity out of proportion to their actual numbers was only natural, because, for one thing, their industry was at the very center of the national economy. England now was importing more raw cotton than any other commodity, and finished cotton products were her largest export. Conditions and events in the textile trade affected all Britain.

The well-documented historical fact is that in the early and mid-Victorian periods, taking all industries together, the preponderance of English labor continued to be made up of handicraft workers, not machine hands, who lived in small towns, not the sprawling factory cities of the Midlands and the north. And even in those big towns, factory hands were in the minority. It was not until late in the century that factory-employed "operatives," as distinct from hand workers, became so numerous as to account for something like half of the whole labor force engaged in industry. Even in the cotton trade, which was in the vanguard of industrialization, less than half the total number of workers were employed in mills as late as 1850; the rest were old-fashioned hand workers. The woollen and hosiery industries were slower to mechanize, and most other industries—metal, leather, wood—lagged still farther behind.

Although the handicraftsmen did not receive the publicity their machine-tending fellows did, they were no better off. The misery of the hundreds of thousands who still worked by hand was as great as that arising from slavery to the machine and imprisonment in the slums that speculators threw together in the shadow of the mill. (In one way their situation was worse, because as the mills took over more and more of their trade, employment steadily became less certain and wages decreased.) All together shared, if not in the specific evils of factory and factory-town life, then in the general misery of the times. The regional differences that existed were merely differences in the degree of wretchedness.

But it was the malign combination of town life *and*

factory life that produced the conditions which horrified the
more concerned portion of the nation when they were
finally brought into the open. The industrial revolution, not
the mechanization of the textile trade alone but such other
developments as the railroads' sudden demand for rolling
stock, rails, bridge materials, and other iron products, had
packed workers into towns totally unprepared to house
them. The population of all the major industrial conurba-
tions, Manchester, Leeds, Bradford, Birmingham, Liverpool,
and Sheffield, gained an average of 50 per cent in the single
decade 1821–31, and the rate of increase in the following
decades was only slightly smaller.

This jamming of hordes of wage earners into what had
once been quiet country towns was something new. Until
now, the evidences of poverty and social injustice, though
numerous, had been out in the open, in town and country
alike. People were accustomed to seeing them and, if so
moved, to applying a small poultice of charity to the victims.
But with the coming of the factory town, the most acute
suffering was largely hidden from public view. A stroller
along the main thoroughfares of a city like Manchester (or
for that matter London, which, though not a major industrial
center, had its own abundant portion of urban misery)
was unaware that only a few hundred yards away, down
dark alleys and courts, festered slums unfit for human habi-
tation. When, eventually, their existence became known to
people in the classes above, the shock of sudden discovery
was all the more acute.

Moreover, whereas the old kind of deprivation and
suffering was diffused, the new kind was concentrated and
its effect upon the beholder intensified. Individual cases,
thousands upon thousands of them, coalesced into a mass of
misery. No ordinary exercise of private philanthropy would
suffice to relieve it. Its magnitude was such that only a concerted effort on an unheard-of scale would have any hope of
success. But history offered no guidance; the conditions to
be remedied were the result of novel causes, yet the remedies

had to be such as could be applied through existing institutions.

This was the nub of the "condition of England question" that confronted the nation in the forties. As Carlyle showed in the passage in *Past and Present* which made the term a popular catch phrase, it was a question that affected all of Britain, not the laboring poor alone. It was as infectious and malign as the typhoid in his real-life parable of the poor Irish widow in Edinburgh who went with her three children from charity to charity,

helped by none;—till she had exhausted them all; till her strength and heart failed her: she sank down in typhus-fever; died, and infected her Lane with fever, so that "seventeen other persons" died of fever there in consequence. . . . The forlorn Irish Widow applies to her fellow-creatures, as if saying, "Behold I am sinking, bare of help: ye must help me! I am your sister, bone of your bone; one God made us: ye must help me!" They answer, "No; impossible: thou art no sister of ours." But she proves her sisterhood; her typhus-fever kills *them:* they actually were her brothers, though denying it!

The steam-powered mills were manned by displaced hand workers and by refugees from the hopeless penury of life on the land, where, as we have seen, there was now an excess of labor. Swelling the labor force were hundreds of thousands of Irish, whose presence in the English towns and cities generated social friction and prejudice not unlike that produced in our time by the influx of people of other colors. The Irish, driven from their native land by endemic poverty and, in particular, by the catastrophic famine of 1845–47, were casual labor. They did the heaviest work (as navvies and stevedores) for the longest hours and often the lowest pay, and their squalid living conditions and drunken, brawling habits earned them, among the native English poor, the reputation of filthy savages.

During the decades when factories went unregulated, men, women, and children worked at monotonous tasks, the forerunner of the twentieth century's production line, for as many as fourteen or even sixteen hours a day, six days a week. They were deafened by the noise of the steam engines and the clattering machinery and stifled in air that not only was laden with dust but, in the absence of ventilation, was heated to as high as eighty-five degrees. The workers were driven to maximum output by strict overseers, fined for spoiling goods, dozing off, looking out the window, and other derelictions, and forever imperiled by unguarded shafts, belts, and flywheels. Industrial diseases and those caused simply by the proximity of many unwashed, chronically ill human bodies conspired with accidents to disable and kill them. There were no effective industrial unions until the seventies (although the movement began in the twenties), and no unemployment benefits, workmen's compensation funds, or social security. A sick, crippled, or merely worn-out employee was an unregarded casualty of the system, cast out to suffer and die.

At night these weary laborers crept home to slums in which they existed as no large communities of English people had ever before been forced to live (except in the noisome rookeries of London, which long antedated Dickens' Tom-All-Alone's and Jacob's Island). Their warrens—a most suitable word, with its English countryman's connotations of tight packing and prolific breeding—were long rows and blocks, newly built with the cheapest of materials, or subdivided old houses, all designed to cram the most people into the least space. In Liverpool as late as the sixties, there were 66,000 men, women, and children for every square mile. Speculative builders never had to worry about construction regulations or zoning ordinances, nor were the landlords oppressed by housing codes, for such hindrances to free enterprise were as yet inconceivable. These teeming slums were the sites of almost unimaginable degradation. Large families, even two or three families, occupied a single room. As many as seven or eight persons—children and adults of both sexes—slept in one bed (or, more likely, on a filthy collection of rags), a practice that frequently resulted in incest, just as it did under similar conditions in the countryside. Many, especially the Irish, lived in gloomy cellars where the only light came from a grating at street level and the walls and floor were perpetually wet with foul seepage. In Manchester alone, in the 1830's, between 40,000 and 50,000 persons lived in cellars. Even street-level rooms had little light, because, until the repeal of a seventeenth-century law in 1851, every window over a certain number in a dwelling place was subject to taxation.

The jerry-built houses shared a common back wall, so that there was no ventilation and no space for even the most minuscule garden. Many slum blocks were thickets of courts, which, because they were outside municipal jurisdiction, were cleaned even less often than the public byways; that is to say, never. A single communal privy, itself never cleaned, might serve as many as forty multi-family dwellings. Cesspools, where they existed, constantly overflowed. Efficient sewer piping had not yet been invented, and even if it had, there was no supply of continuously flowing water to carry away the waste. Open-air drains therefore sent the walkways and unpaved streets awash with filth, thus creating monstrous enlargements of the disease-breeding conditions which had prevailed in towns ever since the Middle Ages. The stench, indoors and outdoors alike, was of a vileness which the euphemistic language of contemporary accounts ("noxious effluvia," "offensive odors arising from excrementitious matter") did nothing to sweeten.

If water was available at all, it came from a common tap in the courtyard which drew on a supply that was turned on only an hour or so every day, and it was usually the runoff from the drains and cesspools, reused without the intermediate benefit of recycling. In the middle of the century, half of London, whose population had doubled since 1801, got its drinking water from a reach of the Thames into which more than two hundred sewers flowed. Epidemics of typhoid and cholera—outbreaks of the latter killed 16,437 people in England and Wales in 1832, and some

16,000 in London alone in 1849—joined with diseases induced by malnutrition, exhaustion, and "vice" (a conveniently vague catchall term, with particularly strong connotations of alcoholism and illicit sex) to further increase the death rate, which in these conditions was several times the national average. One out of every two babies born in the towns died before the age of five. Life was as cheap at home as it was at work.

This purgatory was both fetid and dark. Its streets were unlighted at night, and unpoliced at any time. (Municipal police forces, replacing the useless old-time watchmen, were introduced only in the forties and fifties, following the successful establishment of London's Metropolitan Police in 1829.) Many such slums lay in low ground along streams swollen by human sewage and industrial waste; sometimes the pollutants were so thick that land birds could ride on the surface. And over all hung a cloud of sulphurous smoke, the delusive sign of prosperity. When the chimneys billowed and the very rain was dirty, people were "in work." A similar evidence of prosperity in the iron industry was the slag heaps that spread, acre by acre, over what had hitherto been green fields.

The effluents from the chimneys laid waste whole tracts of countryside. Not without reason was the region around Birmingham called "the Black Country," the name it deservedly retains today. But this meant little to the slum dwellers, because the more the cities grew around them, the less chance they had to flee, on a Sunday or holiday, to open spaces. There were no parks or playgrounds until the middle of the century, and the only places to which they could repair for recreation of a sort were the taverns, gin shops, brothels, occasional cockfights—and, oftenest of all, the mean streets themselves.

This was *The Condition of the Working Class in England in 1844*. The words form the title of a book written by the German-born Friedrich Engels, who had come to Manchester to learn the cotton trade in a mill owned by a company in which his father was a partner. The book was based on his personal observations and on the blue books which had lifted the lid in the previous decade. In time—it was first published at Leipzig in 1845, the first English translation appearing only in 1892—Engels' book, in all its sickening but verifiable detail, would become part of the classic Marxist literature of protest against the enslavement of the masses by the capitalist bourgeoisie. (In 1848 Engels joined his close friend Karl Marx in publishing the *Communist Manifesto.*)

The most immediately resultful of the blue books upon which Engels and other polemicists drew were those which documented in graphic text and pictures the conditions under which women and children slaved in mines and factories (1842–43). A shocked England learned, among other things, that tiny children worked side by side with adults in the narrow corridors of coal mines; that five-year-old boys and girls were kept in solitary darkness, twelve hours a day, opening and shutting the doors upon which the miners' safety depended; and that in those same stifling mines other children and half-naked women, some in the last stages of pregnancy, worked on all fours, straps between legs, hauling loaded carts to the surface. Other human beasts of burden, male and female, climbed steep ladders, with heavy bags of coal slung on their backs. As a direct result of the publication of the blue book on women and children in the mines, Parliament passed Lord Ashley's Act of 1842 which forbade the employment of women in mines and restricted children's labor there to those over ten. But some mine owners smuggled women and children underground nonetheless.

Meanwhile, the first effective Factory Act, containing the all-important provision for enforcement through inspection which had been lacking in several earlier, toothless measures, had been passed in 1833. Restricted to the cotton industry, its provisions, considered drastic at the time, suggest the magnitude of the evils to be remedied. No children under nine could work in the mills; those between nine and thirteen were limited to eight hours a day, six days a week; those under thirteen had to attend school in the factory two hours a day. (Compliance in many factories was limited to setting up a classroom in the boiler room and appointing the stoker, a crippled former mill hand, or some other illiterate to do the teaching. In other mills, forged certificates of attendance concealed wholesale violations of the law.) The Factory Act of 1844, retrogressive in that it lowered to eight years the permissible age of children's employment, cut their daily working hours to six and a half, and set the maximum for women at twelve. The most bitterly opposed of the series, the Ten Hours Act of 1847, limited women and children alike to ten hours a day and thus, in effect, imposed a similar maximum on men, because they could not work without the help of the others. Similar legislation was extended only gradually, over a period of several decades, to other industries. As late as the eighties, working conditions and hours in some smaller industries were still entirely unregulated.

It is impossible to tell how much the fiction and, to a smaller extent, the poetry of the period, in conjunction with such philippics as Carlyle's *Past and Present,* had to do with arousing the nation's conscience. As the sequence of events shows, the initial reforms, at least, were accomplished before men and women of letters addressed themselves to the condition of England question. But by adding their often eloquent humanitarianism to the message contained in the blue books and in the news accounts of constant strife between labor and management, they unquestionably gave greater impetus to the cause. A series of novels protested the human cost of industrialism and sometimes suggested ways by which the interests of employer and worker could be reconciled: Disraeli's *Sybil* (1845), Elizabeth Gaskell's *Mary Barton* (1848) and *North and South* (1854–55), Charlotte Brontë's *Shirley* (1849), and Dickens' *Hard Times* (1854). The publicity given to laboring conditions extended to sweatshops and other non-factory enterprises as well. Thomas Hood's "The Song of the Shirt" (*Punch,* 1843) stirred indignation against the exploitation of women in the needlework trade; Elizabeth Barrett's "The Cry of the Children" (1844) was the most notable poetic protest against child labor; and Charles Kingsley's novel *Alton Locke* (1850) was in part an exposé of sweated tailoring shops.

With the curbing of the worst abuses in some portions of industry and the return of prosperity in the late forties and early fifties, the lot of some workers—by no means all, or even a majority—became a bit more endurable. The appearance of a few public parks, beginning about 1850, and the introduction of cheap excursion fares on the railroads enabled them to escape briefly from their depressing habitats. But the habitats themselves remained largely what they had been. In 1842 Edwin Chadwick's monumental report on *The Sanitary Condition of the Labouring Population* turned the nation's stomach but resulted in what amounted almost to an intellectual craze, "the sanitary idea"—zeal for eliminating the worst breeders and transmitters of disease. Never before had so much earnest public discussion (lightened once in a while by a bit of *Punch*-type humor) been devoted to subjects like cesspools, sewers, and the quality of the water supply. The disease-breeding properties of old burial grounds came in for particular attention: the four acres of Bunhill Fields, in the middle of London, held 100,-000 bodies, and elsewhere as many as fourteen fresh corpses were crammed into a single grave. The subject of what the *Times* called "consecrated cesspools" formed a theme of some importance in *Bleak House.* At that time, medical opinion generally favored the theory that diseases like typhoid and cholera were spread through the atmosphere by malign gases from decomposing organic material. Only in the early eighties was this etiological theory displaced by the one that attributed disease to specific living organisms present in food and water.

Meanwhile, however, pioneers of public health such as

Chadwick and John Simon, advocating right measures for wrong reasons, made some headway against the environmental sources of infectious diseases and the vested interests that resisted sanitary reform. The reappearance of cholera in 1848 led to a Public Health Act that prodded local authorities to devise and enforce building codes and institute sanitation measures. But the towns' response was uneven, and not until the seventies did the national government force the issue. In the interim, pending municipal action, the campaign against mass disease was aided by such innovations as the cheap, washable clothing made possible by the mechanization of the textile industry, the cheapening of soap, and the gradually increased availability of relatively pure water.

For various reasons, after the middle of the century the evils of the factory system itself ceased to be a leading theme of social commentary and fiction. But toward the end of the century the issue of how people lived, or were forced to live, was revived in a new locale, the East End of London, where the foul conditions of slum life aroused the conscience of a new generation. Surveys showed that fully a third of the population lived on or below the bare margin of subsistence. Again there was agitation for reform, and again fiction found a theme in the life of the workers. George Gissing was the most prominent of the realistic novelists who wrote more or less Zolaesque accounts of the London slums and the limbo of the plebeian who was hardly better off than the irregularly employed and ill-paid docker or the sweated tailor.

By that time, the problem of the masses had entered a new phase. Compassion had somewhat ameliorated the conditions in which they toiled and lived, but they still were a race apart. Now (1867, 1884) they were receiving the vote. How could this numerically preponderant section of the population be assimilated into the fixed fabric of English society and culture? Many traditionalists, wedded to the idea of an oligarchical government and an élitist culture, viewed the development with alarm and despair. Others, more sanguine and sympathetic and less frightened by the prospect of drastic change, looked upon it with hope. A democratized society might or might not be a happier, more contented society. Much depended on the intangibles of the spirit, for man does not live by factory and public health acts alone. His body might well be relieved of some of its suffering by governmental action, but what of his mind? The quality of life, though dependent in the first instance upon a reasonable degree of bodily health, extends far beyond it. What chance did contemporary conditions of factory and city life offer for the expansion of the intellect, the gratification of one's sense of beauty? This was the great question, intertwining man as a private creature with man as a member of society, which superseded those that had preoccupied the first social protest novelists. To writers like Carlyle, Ruskin, Morris, and Arnold, as we shall see in later chapters, they became the supreme issue facing English society.

6. "The Weaker Sex"

Meanwhile, there were the women, who in the nature of the case must be considered separately. Their status in Victorian society and the roles they assumed had much to do with the form and content of fiction as well as with the moral atmosphere that permeated much other literature.

Upper- and middle-class women were sedulously set apart from the worlds of commerce and, generally, of intellect. This represented a marked reversal of attitude and custom. In the seventeenth century, aristocratic ladies had actively managed their family's household and estates. In the eighteenth, there had been plenty of middle-class businesswomen, engaged in a variety of occupations from fanmaking and hairdressing to catering, and, as widows, often carrying on their husbands' trades, whatever these might have been—bookselling or hatmaking, building or ironmongery. But the nation's increasing wealth and the growing complexity of the mercantile economy required a special kind of managerial expertise which supposedly was a peculiarly masculine gift. At the same time, prosperity among tradesmen and skilled artisans, often accompanied by a separation of business premises from the home, encouraged the detachment of women from the money-making world, and they began to aspire to a state of gentility devoid of responsibility.

By the beginning of the nineteenth century the powerful concept of "refinement" prescribed that all women outside the working class abstain from gainful employment except in cases of extreme necessity. It was such cases which resulted in a few Victorian women becoming professional writers. Frances Trollope, Anthony's mother, was forced to take to the pen when it became painfully clear that her husband, an unsuccessful lawyer with a disagreeable personality and unstable mind, would never earn the family bread. The Brontë sisters wrote, at least in part, to supplement their father's meager income as a clergyman. Mary Ann Evans wrote books and magazine articles simply to support herself, an unmarried woman with no other income. But it is noteworthy that prejudice against women writers was strong enough to make advisable the adoption of masculine pen names. Anne, Charlotte, and Emily Brontë wrote as Acton, Currer, and Ellis Bell; Mary Ann Evans took the name of George Eliot.

The way of life led by ladies near the top of the social hierarchy, as reported in popular fiction and journalism, tinted the ambitions of women below them on the scale. At a time when the world of men was governed by the idea of utility as the supreme value, the world of upper-class women made uselessness the test of almost any activity. Theirs were lives of elaborate idleness; they worked harder at being decoratively futile than any productive occupation would have required. They passed their days indulging desultorily in the "female accomplishments" learned in girlhood, needlework, making boxes from shells collected at the seaside, sketching and watercolor painting, flower arrangement, strumming at the piano or harp. Their only faintly constructive deeds, apart from supervising the household staff, involved charity—taking blankets and basins of soup to the unfortunates on the estate, visiting the local school the family supported.

Among the aristocracy and the higher gentry, women had considerable freedom of movement. There was constant visiting back and forth among the intricately intermarried families. In the fashionable season, one occupied one's town house and was caught up in an exhilarating and fatiguing round of balls, "at homes," and dinner parties. Many families traveled about the Continent. The middle-class female enjoyed few such luxuries, although she joined her husband in dreaming of them. No family liking to think of itself as middle-class could be without at least one servant, and this was one ambition that was easily satisfied. Domestic servants were to be had for a pittance—over 10 per cent of the female population were working as maids, washerwomen, and charwomen in 1851—and with shops stocking a growing number of commodities which had formerly been produced in the household, more and more women had less and less to do. Leisure was a sign of status, and in the middle class it was occupied as unproductively, in most cases, as in fashionable society. This new leisure had an important effect upon contemporary literature, because it was responsible for a greatly enlarged female reading public. In the servant-equipped middle class, books and magazines, mostly of an undemanding nature, helped fill the matron's yawning hours when no church bazaar required her firmly guiding hand, the children were in the nursery with their governess, and the weather was too wet for her to go shopping or supervise the gardener's work.

She may or may not have wished to occupy her time so flabbily, but the Victorian woman had no choice. *Pater familias,* when he came back from the office after a hard day competing in the business jungle, reigned as lord and master at table and fireside. His wife, though supreme arbiter of household affairs, was subservient to him, a devoted (and submissive) wife and mother of often all too many children. This allotment of roles belonged as much to the basic order of things as the concept of degree which Shakespeare so memorably formulated in *Troilus and Cressida*—a passage it is easy to believe Tennyson had in mind when, in *The Princess,* he had the king declare:

> *When the man wants weight, the woman takes it up,*
> *And topples down the scales; but this is fixt*
> *As are the roots of earth and base of all;*
> *Man for the field and woman for the hearth:*
> *Man for the sword and for the needle she:*
> *Man with the head and woman with the heart:*
> *Man to command and woman to obey:*
> *All else confusion.*

Woman's serfdom was sanctified by the Victorian conception of the female as a priestess dedicated to preserving the home as a refuge from the abrasive outside world. Convention dictated a rigorously stereotyped personality. She was to cultivate fragility, leaning always on the arm of the gentleman who walked with her in a country lane or escorted her in to dinner. The woman of the well-off middle class lived, in effect, under one of those capacious glass domes which protected parlor bric-a-brac—stuffed birds, ornate shells, papier-mâché constructions, wax fruit and flowers—from dust. She was Dora Spenlow (in *David Copperfield*) and Rosie Mackenzie (in *The Newcomes*); she was The Angel in the House, to borrow the title of Coventry Patmore's hugely popular versified praise of domestic sainthood and the mystical, non-fleshly institution of marriage.

But underneath all the pretense, middle-class women had a real grievance. It was understood that, as Tennyson's neurotic hero in "Locksley Hall" put it,

Nature made them blinder motions bounded in a
shallower brain:
Woman is the lesser man, and all [her] passions,
matched with mine,
Are as moonlight unto sunlight, and as water
unto wine—

Putting aside woman's lack of sexual passion, which is clearly implied in the lines and was universally accepted as a biological fact because to assume otherwise was indecent, there was the wider implication that woman was inferior to man in all ways except the unique one that counted most (to man): her femininity. Her place was in the home, on a veritable pedestal if one could be afforded, and emphatically not in the world of affairs. In *Our Mutual Friend,* Bella Rokesmith told her husband, long before Ibsen's Nora Helmer got the idea, "I want to be something so much worthier than the doll in the doll's house." But the middle-class Victorian woman was allowed no such privilege.

Until fairly late in the century, any prospect of escape from the doll's house was made nugatory by two reigning assumptions: the female brain was not equal to the demands of commerce or the professions, and women, simply by virtue of their sex, had no business mingling with men in a man's world. "Be good, sweet maid," ran Kingsley's familiar advice, "and let who can be clever." There was something unpleasant, even alarming, about strong-willed women who insisted on using their minds. Accordingly, the education which girls of the upper and upper-middle classes received from governesses and from visiting language and music teachers was devoid of intellectual content, let alone intellectual challenge. It was limited to the polite accomplishments which were calculated to help her first to win a husband and then, after that primary goal was reached, to infuse her household with an air of the softer graces so as to maintain its separation from the gritty world of affairs. As Thomas Henry Huxley put it, girls were educated "to be either drudges or toys beneath man, or a sort of angel above him."

This severe limitation of purpose prevailed in girls' private schools as well. Miss Pinkerton's early nineteenth-century establishment at Chiswick, which Becky Sharp thankfully leaves at the opening of *Vanity Fair,* was probably better than most such schools in Victorian times; most were abysmally bad. Only with the establishment of Cheltenham Ladies' College in 1853 was the first move made toward providing girls with a secondary education comparable to that received by boys in the better public (American: private) schools. As for higher education, Tennyson spoke the mind of most Victorian men, and probably most Victorian women as well, when he assigned forthrightly anti-feminist sentiments to speakers in *The Princess* (1847). Nonetheless, the Queen's College was founded in London the next year, and in 1880 women were for the first time allowed to take degrees at the University of London. Women's colleges were established at Cambridge and Oxford in 1869 and 1879 respectively, but women could not take degrees at either university until 1920–21. A few young women of surpassing determination fought their way through medical school before the end of the century.

But these were rare specimens. It is true that their acceptance was somewhat eased by the heroic example of Florence Nightingale, a seemingly fragile gentlewoman whose ruthless resolution and efficiency, applied to the lethal field hospitals in the Crimea during the war of 1854–56, triumphed over military and bureaucratic negligence and incompetence. Miss Nightingale, "the lady with the lamp," became a cherished Victorian legend, and, more important, founded the modern profession of nursing. Nevertheless, until the last decades of the century almost the only occupation open to women of good family but reduced circumstances was teaching, as a schoolmistress (Charlotte and Emily Brontë) or, more likely, as a governess in a private family (Jane Eyre). In either case, the work was hard and the teacher's social status was as low as her pay; in most homes governesses ranked with the superior servants. But single women, disappointed in their hopes of marriage—census figures showed a surplus of females in Victorian England—perforce had to settle for "governessing slavery," as Charlotte Brontë called it, if they had to earn a livelihood. Like the spinster aunts who found haven as permanent guests in many households, they were regarded, and regarded themselves, as failures.

It was, in any event, an unnaturally sheltered and restricted existence the middle-class girl and woman led; little wonder that neurasthenia was as prevalent as the personal records of the period reveal it to have been. And little wonder, too, that at the very same time they portrayed "ideal" specimens of Victorian girlhood and womanhood, wrapped in an aura of virtue and innocence, the leading novelists, from Thackeray to Meredith and Hardy, repeatedly studied the nonconforming woman—the outsider, the prey of ambition, the man-eater—and her various motivations, pride, possessiveness, sexual hunger, intellectual aspiration, or whatnot. The revered cluster of Victorian domestic virtues served as a norm, a vulnerable assumption upon which writers frequently mounted an outright or covert attack on the unrealities and perversions of the prevailing womanly ideal, the myth of domestic accommodation and tranquility.

Life was very different in the working class. Here women, far from living under a glass dome, were part of the labor force, as they always had been in order to help their husbands squeeze out a living. The conditions under which they labored changed as the factory system replaced cottage industry; the necessity that drove them to work was more bitter than it had ever been. Their availability in large numbers enabled employers to pay the low wages which, in a vicious circle, required all able-bodied members of a family to work, irrespective of sex or (apart from exceedingly young children) age. Women toiled long hours on the land in season; they worked by their husbands' side in the handicraft shops and in the mills and factories; until public outcry more or less put an end to it, they slaved in the mines.

Except for children, women were the most exploited of all workers. Long after the factory acts had curbed the worst abuses of female labor in the textile industry, girls and women continued to be sweated in dressmaking and tailoring establishments and in such trades as nailmaking and matchmaking. The latter trade was the scene of an especially famous London strike in 1888, when the plight of the Bryant and May match-tippers acquainted the public with the ravages of "phossy jaw," a form of necrosis caused by the phosphorus they handled. Women who could not leave home often did piecework at starvation wages—boxmaking, for example, and tinting Christmas cards and book illustrations. One's pleasure in leafing through a Victorian gift album, a sporting book, or even an occasional novel is diminished by the reflection that the engravings were colored by hungry women and their small children, often working by the light of a single candle. Whether they were employed in a factory or at home, women who were tied to machine or table for long hours had little energy left to care for such homes as they possessed or for the sickly children they bore. What with the exhausting nature of their employment, the unhealthy conditions wherever they worked, the lack of medical care, and the price exacted by repeated childbearing, Victorian working women were old in their twenties.

Whatever their social rank, in the eyes of the law women were second-class citizens. Although there was sporadic discussion of the female franchise, and some mild agitation in its favor, women were at the bottom of the electoral priority list, and the only concession made to them by the end of the century was the right to vote in local elections. Only in 1918, after many years of militancy (window-breaking, mass meetings, street demonstrations, and hunger strikes when they were jailed), did women win participation in national elections, as a reward for their contribution to the war effort; even then, the franchise was limited to those over thirty.

Of more immediate concern to Victorian women were the other legal disabilities they suffered. Until 1839, a woman who was separated from her husband, regardless of the reason, lost custody of their children; in that year the law was changed to allow her to retain those under seven, and in 1873 the age was raised to sixteen. The law under which everything a married woman possessed or acquired became the inalienable property of her husband was changed only by a series of parliamentary acts in 1870–82. Until 1857, divorce, which opinion condemned except in the most intolerable circumstances, was possible only by means of an act of Parliament introduced for the individual case. The plight of Stephen Blackpool, the workingman in *Hard Times* who was married irrevocably to an alcoholic wife, was typical of many such situations. Even after divorce became available through the courts, the procedure was so expensive that few could afford it. And, as with employers in their relations with workers, the balance of justice was tipped toward the ruling party. A husband could divorce his wife on the simple ground of adultery, but a wife had to prove not only her husband's adultery but an additional offense such as desertion, cruelty, rape, or incest. As late as the nineties, less than six hundred divorce cases went through the courts in a year.

"The Queen," wrote Victoria in her regal third-person style, "is most anxious to enlist everyone who can speak or write to join in checking this mad wicked folly of Women's Rights, with all its attendant horrors, on which her poor, feeble sex is bent, forgetting every sense of womanly feeling and propriety." But the poor, feeble sex was not without its champions. John Stuart Mill's *The Subjection of Women* (1869) was the most important statement of the feminist position since Mary Wollstonecraft's *A Vindication of the Rights of Woman* (1792). It gave impetus to an emancipation movement which, by the end of the century, achieved several goals in addition to the ones just mentioned and built up so much pressure in behalf of others that they were won early in the present century. During the later eighties and the nineties "the new woman" was a familiar figure in social commentary, humorous papers, and once in a while in fiction. She sought equal moral standards, to replace such anomalies as the legal assumption that adultery was a worse offense for a woman than for a man. The adoption of more sensible clothing, coupled with the invention of a manageable pneumatic-tired bicycle to replace the clumsy old hard-rimmed "penny-farthing" machine which had jolted men's bones, gave her greater physical mobility; simultaneously she deserted the croquet lawn for the tennis court. Most important of all, she could make her own respectable living in an increasing number of occupations, not only in teaching, where the new government-run board schools afforded many more opportunities than had previously been available, but in shops and offices, in professions such as nursing, and in the civil service.

7. The Reading Public

These, then, were the people who appear in Victorian literature. They were also, many of them, the people for whom that literature was written and whose interests and tastes determined its tone and content. Although it is customary to speak of "the reading public"—singular—in connection with the audience for the printed word, in Victorian times that audience, like today's, was not really a cohesive, homogeneous unit but a whole cluster of publics, as various as the society to which they belonged.

The upper class probably read neither more nor less than it had done in earlier centuries, when it had subsidized authors through patronage and some of its members had themselves contributed to the national literature. Walter Bagehot, one of the shrewdest mid-Victorian social com-

mentators, probably was not far from the truth when he remarked, "A great part of the 'best' English people keep
their minds in a state of decorous dullness." At all events,
the upper ranks formed a negligible fraction of the Victorian reading public.

Some members of the working class read, but it is impossible to tell, except in the most general way, how numerous they were. The crucial question, naturally, is that of
literacy. As will be seen in Chapter VII, popular education
during most of the century was spotty and ineffectual,
though as the years passed it reached more and more people. The national literacy rate for adults, based on the ability
to inscribe one's name in the marriage register, rose from 67
per cent (male) and 51 per cent (female) in 1841 to
approximately 97 per cent for both sexes in 1900. But
these figures exaggerate the incidence of reading ability
among the masses. Many thousands who could trace their
names could not read a word of print. Because the figures
do not distinguish among social classes, the over-all national
rate was pushed upward by the high incidence of literacy
in the middle and upper classes, and if it were possible to
segregate the working class in these statistics, it would be
seen that the literacy rate there was markedly below the
national average. More significant figures come from local
surveys. In 1833, in an artisan-class district of London, 777
parents could read and 267 could not; in 1845, 75 per cent
of the children leaving 176 Midland schools (after an average attendance of a year and a half) were, for all practical
purposes, illiterate. Many observers reported that whatever
reading skill a child acquired during his brief attendance
at school often was irretrievably lost, through insufficient
practice while in the classroom or subsequent disuse. In the
year the Second Reform Bill was passed (1867), a house-
to-house canvass in Manchester revealed that barely more
than half the adults could read.

Living conditions were anything but conducive to the
reading habit. Long hours of strenuous work left little lei-

sure or inclination to take up a book or magazine. Crowded rooms noisy with quarreling adults and squalling children, insufficient light, poor eyesight caused in part by nutritional deficiencies and eyestrain at work—such factors discouraged reading even among those who had the ability to do so.

The gradual improvement in working conditions after the middle of the century favored the spread of reading. Wage earners worked fewer hours per week, and, if they were lucky, their wage packets contained a few pennies over what was required for necessities. On the other hand, crowding in working-class houses was not significantly reduced until the end of the century. The building of public libraries, it is true, allowed the worker bent on reading to flee from his private pandemonium to the comparatively silent harbor of the reading room. But as libraries multiplied, so did other ways of spending one's leisure: music halls, cheap theaters, sporting matches, choral societies, entertainments at church or chapel, public parks, railway excursions. The printed word had increasingly stiff competition.

Some intellectually ambitious workers applied themselves to serious books, working their way through them slowly, attentively, and *re*tentively. But the majority chose books and papers written expressly for an audience of semiliterates whose requirements were simple but demanding. Because they possessed virtually no general information, their reading matter had to be devoid of all but the most familiar literary and historical allusions; they could not be expected to waste time puzzling over any more recondite kind. And because their attention spans were short, they needed a running supply of excitements, brief and to the point, and sentences and paragraphs to match.

For these readers were published incalculable quantities of easily digestible books and papers: "penny dreadfuls" and "shilling shockers," the equivalent of the American dime novels of the same epoch; cheap weeklies featuring interminable serializations of thrilling fiction (for men and boys) and sentimental tales (for women and girls); drastic condensations of "standard literature," among them some literary classics such as Scott's romances; broadsides reporting sensational news events such as fires, murders, and natural calamities; cheap Sunday newspapers enlivened with radical politics and extensive police reports. The moral gamut ran from religious tracts to semi-pornographic ballads. There was an extensive Victorian literary sub-culture, but, except for the self-taught workmen who, in a way of speaking, read above their station, the lasting works of literature which their age produced seldom filtered down to the semiliterate audience. To us, the interest of the printed matter which they actually devoured is sociological, not literary. The tart phrase a late Victorian prime minister applied specifically to the cheap "instructive and entertaining" miscellaneous weeklies of the *Tit-Bits* type describes most contemporary working-class reading matter: "Written by office boys for office boys."

The audience for the literature which continues to be read today was concentrated, therefore, in the middle class. It was primarily there that printed matter in all its forms became a much more familiar accompaniment to everyday living than ever before, and the activity of reading occupied a notably larger portion of many persons' free time. The same modest affluence which enabled them to hire servants and artisans gave them additional pocket money to lay out for "a good read."

The middle-class market for print was divided into many interest-groups: the young, the religious, the fashionable, the educated, the ambitious, the time-killing. As each of these audiences grew, publishers catered to it by finding writers and forms to meet its peculiar requirements. But there was much overlapping. A few Victorian authors, such as Dickens and Tennyson, appealed to almost every sector of the middle-class public and had a following in the more literate reaches of the working class as well.

Many readers, furthermore, had diverse tastes; what

they read at a given time depended on their mood and what was being talked about. They read for amusement, to pass the time pleasantly and without intellectual strain. Hence the mounting popularity of fiction, which was usually regarded as entertainment and only gradually, in the course of the era, acquired a measure of critical acceptance as a serious art form. Novels had the same place in many intelligent readers' diet that detective stories and science fiction have had more recently: they relaxed the mind after its strenuous labors. Macaulay, for example, annually consumed hundreds of worthless novels, the more sentimental or incredible the better. It is a tribute to Victorian taste that some of the best novels of the time sold as well as did many of the worst.

Victorian readers also went in for inspiration. Moralized stories and biographies, sermons, religious literature of all kinds, including periodicals for Sunday reading, gushed from the presses by the ton. They were not always dull reading, by any means. The true-life and fictional narratives, whatever their tincture of moral uplift, were designed to compete with secular reading matter on its own terms, and so they contained plenty of suspense and thrilling episodes. Even the sermons—not the learned variety, but those appropriate to revival meetings and similar evangelical occasions—had some of the qualities of third-rate fiction, not least its fustian style.

The Victorians, finally, read to learn. There was an enormous literature of information, some ponderous and some lightweight, on every topic of human interest, from celestial mechanics to what might be seen under a microscope, from Arctic exploration to pinmaking, from grave social questions to pithy anecdotes. Relative to the total population, there was a much larger audience for serious writing in Victorian times than in ours. Around what would now be called the intelligentsia existed, as we shall see in Chapter VII, a large periphery of decently educated readers, not in any sense erudite, who devoted themselves in after-business hours to learning more about the world they lived in and its inhabitants. They supported, sometimes handsomely, more "quality" magazines and reviews than our modern culture can accommodate, and made it possible for commercial firms to issue innumerable books of a sort which would now be published, if published at all, by university presses.

8. *The Power of the Press*

That so many people in what were then called "the middling walks of life"—and even, to a degree, the "humbler" ones—were lifelong devotees of books is evidence of a cultural climate which stressed the value of education and ideas, and exalted books as the noblest product and symbol of civilization. To the Victorians, the printing press driven by a steam engine was, indeed, the most pregnant emblem of their achievement and aspirations. Gutenberg was virtually a culture hero, and his invention, it was thought, was the most potent instrument of social improvement ever conceived.

Victorian literature was a product of the first age of mass communication. Some, perhaps the most important part, was directed to a small minority of the total audience; but the conditions under which all of it was produced were influenced by the development of mass-media print. The expansion of the reading public was accompanied—it is impossible to distinguish cause from effect here—by technological advances which made the printed word both cheaper and more readily accessible than it had ever been before. The steam press, the stereotyping process, new papermaking machinery and the adoption of cheaper ingredients than the former staple of rags, machinery for prefabricating bindings, and, late in the century, mechanized typesetting enabled books, magazines, and newspapers to take their place among the other Victorian commodities that were cheapened by mass production and made more widely available by energetic merchandising. By the end of the century English publishing had undergone a revolution. From a sleepy, unimportant trade whose practices differed little from those prevailing in Shakespeare's time it had grown into a bustling business, as inventive, competitive, and specialized as any other branch of Victorian commerce.

In the first half of the century, however, books were something of a luxury item, despite the declining costs of production. Publishers usually sold a substantial part of an edition to commercial circulating libraries at a big discount, meanwhile keeping the retail price artificially high. Many readers therefore got their books, especially newly published ones, from the libraries, which lent them for an annual subscription. After 1850, as has been noted, free libraries began to appear in various towns and cities throughout the country; these catered to both the middle and working classes.

From the time of *Pickwick Papers* (1836–37) to the sixties, a certain amount of popular fiction, including a dozen of Dickens' own novels, four of Thackeray's, and eight of Trollope's, appeared in monthly or weekly installments over periods of up to eighteen months or two years. Publication in numbers or parts, as they were called, brought down the price to the buyer. Each monthly number usually cost a shilling and the total outlay amounted sometimes to only two-thirds the price of a hardbound novel. Like magazine serialization, number publication presented the author with opportunities and technical problems that are usefully borne in mind in any critical analysis of fiction which first appeared in installments. During the middle decades of the century part-issue existed side by side with magazine serialization, but by the seventies it was crowded out by the magazines, which had the advantage of offering the reader, at no increase in price, not only a segment of a novel but a variety of other features. Once in a while new non-fiction was issued in parts. Carlyle's *Latter-*

Day Pamphlets came out in eight monthly numbers (1850), and Newman's *Apologia* in seven weekly ones (1864).

Several times during the Victorian era experiments were made in publishing new books in cheap format, but it was not until the last decade of the century that the price of new fiction, until then inflated by the alliance between publishers and circulating libraries, was reduced to the point where most readers could afford a freshly published novel. Meanwhile, however, cheap reprints of fiction and non-fiction, in various formats including "board" bindings (the forerunner of modern paperbacks), loaded railway station bookstalls and other outlets. Apart from original editions, therefore, the average Victorian reader was well supplied with books he could afford.

This was the great age of English periodicals. In the beginning of the Victorian era, the magisterial quarterly reviews, the Whig *Edinburgh* (founded 1802), its rival the Tory *Quarterly* (1809), and the Benthamite *Westminster* (1824), shared the top intellectual level. Enjoying circulations which, in proportion to the size of the reading public, were much greater than any comparable periodical can boast today, these powerful journals were edited and written by some of the era's leading authors and public men. Most of Macaulay's essays, for example, were written for the *Edinburgh*.

The quarterlies had to share room with the monthly magazines, typified in the first Victorian decades by *Blackwood's Edinburgh Magazine* (1817) and *Fraser's Magazine* (1830). These were distinguished by lively writing, irreverence, and a partisanship which sometimes exceeded that of the opinionated quarterlies. Instead of the lengthy essays posing as book reviews which were the quarterlies' staple, each issue of the monthlies had a variety of contents, short and serialized fiction, topical articles, true narratives, satirical essays. In *Fraser's* first appeared Carlyle's *Sartor Resartus* (as well as many of his separate essays), Thackeray's *Yellowplush Papers,* and Kingsley's *Yeast.*

In the forties and fifties the miscellaneous magazines were joined by weekly papers addressed to a wider "family" audience. *Punch* (1841) was among the first and incomparably the greatest of the Victorian humorous journals, printing the work of many talented writers and artists and both reflecting and exerting much influence on middle-class opinion. Its cheaper (non-humorous) contemporaries, such as Dickens' *Household Words* (1850–59) and that paper's successor, *All the Year Round,* were edited for a still larger, less sophisticated readership. In addition to short articles on topics of current interest and chatty essays, these weeklies featured serial fiction—Dickens' *Hard Times* and Mrs. Gaskell's *Cranford* in the case of *Household Words,* and *Great Expectations,* Wilkie Collins' pioneer detective stories *The Woman in White* and *The Moonstone,* and three of Trollope's novels in that of *All the Year Round.*

A new generation of monthly magazines and middlebrow reviews in the sixties and seventies continued to refine the formula that was proving so attractive to the better educated portion of the middle-class audience. The spectacularly successful *Cornhill Magazine* (1860) serialized three minor novels by Thackeray, its first editor, as well as George Eliot's *Romola,* Trollope's *Framley Parsonage,* and Hardy's *Far from the Madding Crowd.* In the *Fortnightly Review* (1865) appeared three of Trollope's novels as well as most of Meredith's *Diana of the Crossways* and *The Tragic Comedians.* The leading novelists wrote not only for the quality periodicals but for their numerous weekly and monthly imitators, which were slanted toward a more popular audience. Trollope's novels appeared in ten magazines representing various levels, Hardy's and Reade's in almost as many.

But perhaps most interesting to the modern reader who browses in the bound files of the most distinguished periodicals is the amount and excellence of their non-fiction. The novels they serialized leavened a loaf rich in intellectual vitamins. This higher journalism—there is no better term for it—was an art indigenous to the Victorian periodical edited for the intelligent lay reader. Its forte was the treatment of a subject of interest to the educated mind, in a manner that was serious but not heavy, urbane rather than facetious or sedulously "bright." The writers in that genre discovered a happy middle way between vulgarization and pedantry, an art almost lost today because evidently there is no demand for it.

Much Victorian higher journalism was purely expository, but at least a comparable amount was devoted to stating points of view or advocating courses of public action. There was a more than coincidental relationship between the enlargement of the printed medium and the simultaneous development of political democracy. Public opinion became for the first time a decisive influence, an agent of change.

The prior association of print and political life in England had been mainly through argumentative pamphlets and books addressed to a comparative few, those in positions of power. Private influence, assisted by the "public opinion" which was, in fact, only the opinion of a select articulate group, was the motive force behind change. But the passage of the Reform Bill in 1832 over the recalcitrance of Tory landowners and Church dramatically revealed how much things had altered. It was public opinion on an unprecedentedly large scale, mobilized and directed by newspapers and pamphlets, which gave the Whigs, spokesmen for the middle class, their victory.

Actually, the role the press played in the 1830–32 crisis had been prepared for a generation earlier. The techniques of printed propaganda had been adapted for a mass audience as early as the 1790's by the radical political associations and their mortal enemies, the Evangelicals, backed by the alarmed governing class. The first great battle of the books which sought to win the minds of the common people pitted Tom Paine's radical "atheism," as it was inaccurately regarded, against the socially conservative religion of people like Hannah More, who gained much celebrity as the principal author of the *Cheap Repository Tracts,* simple stories designed to persuade the laboring class to remain loyal and docile.

The evident, though by no means complete, success of these widely circulated tracts in neutralizing Paine's "poison" during the remaining war years encouraged confidence in the press as a prime means of influencing the mass mind. But two, or any number, could play the game, and thenceforth organizations of many kinds—religious, philanthropic, political—adopted printed propaganda as the chief device in an apparatus of agitation which came also to include mass meetings, marches, "classes" (for the study of the issues), petitions, and lobbying. The later phase of William Wilberforce's long crusade to abolish slavery, which employed all these devices, has been called the most systematic and widespread program of agitation that the nation had ever seen. Like Hannah More's, it was energized by Evangelical religious passions. And after the Evangelicals with their pious presses and the native Jacobins with their subversive ones came the Methodists (who had experimented with printed propaganda in a small way much earlier), the Owenites and other radical groups of the twenties and thirties, the Chartists, the Anti-Corn Law League. . . . No important movement was without its publications section. In one year (1843) the Anti-Corn Law League distributed nine million pamphlets urging the abolition of the tariff on grain. This saturation coverage doubtless had something to do with the fact that three years later the duty was repealed.

The claim, made in 1832 and again in 1846, that "the people had triumphed" was not mere empty rhetoric. They had, thanks to a press that stirred more men's thinking than had ever been stirred before. It was not surprising, therefore, that faith should grow in the effectiveness of what

John Stuart Mill called "the collective will" as the prime influence on decision-making, and that the press should become the chief instrument of its expression.

Although little of this enormous body of printed argument and exhortation has survived as literature, it provided the matrix for the masterpieces of social discussion which are still read today. Few of the great writers on social questions, including the novelists, were affiliated with any individual movement which sought to bring public opinion to bear on Parliament or other centers of power. But their expressions of personal opinion were uttered in a spacious forum resounding to many voices, and the particular nature of their own rhetoric is best defined when it is compared with the persuasive techniques of their workaday contemporaries. A man who, like most educated Victorians, read a fair sample of the barrage of topical argument, year after year, could not avoid having his personal style and strategy affected by it when he joined the symposium.

Alongside this babel of controversial voices—propaganda in the ordinary sense of doctrinaire partisanship—existed a more disinterested kind of discussion whose subject was issues rather than causes. Here the would-be persuaders were ordinarily not zealots but men of controlled intelligence—the philosophers, scientists, government officials, lawyers, clergymen, higher journalists who were the real opinion-makers. They subjected contemporary problems and institutions to a continuous process of analysis and criticism, and they did so in a manner noteworthy for its restraint and civility. However sharply they differed from one another, they wrote like gentlemen. Rant was a method of argumentation associated with working-class radicals and Wesleyan revivalists; courtesy of discourse was the sign of the well-bred scholar. Perhaps this is one reason why they had an effect reaching far beyond specific decisions in Parliament and governmental policies. Their vigorous but mannerly discussion influenced the long-term direction of public thought and action. Even some printed government docu-

ments, indeed, had this quality and effect. John Simon's annual reports as the public health officer, first for the City of
London and then for the national government, were praised
in the *Times* for their "terse, forcible, and graphic" style,
which possessed "real eloquence, intense and fervid, reaching the climax of a deep and almost terrible earnestness."
Despite their repulsive subject-matter, their editions were
quickly sold out. There seems little question that the literary
quality of this kind of "public prose," such a far cry from
the customary jargon of bureaucrats, had much to do with
awakening the public to the gravity of certain social problems and stirring it to demand—and get—action.

Although books and magazines and newspapers echoed
with the shibboleths and cant of contemporary economic,
political, social, religious, and moral opinion, they could also
be the most formidable enemies of smugness. "If," as a
leading modern Labour Party intellectual has put it, "millions of people in Victorian Britain were complacent, there
were armies of intellectual non-conformists breaking in on
that complacency and compelling their countrymen to accept the facts of change and the discoveries of science,
ready to court unpopularity by challenging the Victorian
bishops and shattering the illusions of the Victorian politicians. . . . Victorian Britain was not a democracy—the
working class was still excluded from any real share in
government. But it was a free society in which the ideas
bubbling out of the controversy of public opinion fashioned
and re-fashioned the form of the State." [1]*

The evolving social structure described in the earlier
part of this chapter, the political revolution to be reviewed
in the next, and the economic, religious, and cultural issues
that will occupy still later ones were the chief subjects of
what might be called the Victorian literature of discussion.
Carlyle's *Sartor Resartus,* Macaulay's essays extolling the
blessings of Whig governance, Ruskin's attacks on political

* Sources of quotations drawn from modern books are given on
pages 318–319.

economy and associated evils in *"Unto This Last"* and *Munera Pulveris,* Arnold's *Culture and Anarchy,* Huxley's essays on science and education, Morris' socialistic preachments—all originally appeared in Victorian periodicals and were part of the constant debate which brought differences into the open and engaged the minds and emotions of their readers.

The press had as many voices as it had audiences. Carlyle's thunderings were echoed, at the distance of a generation, by Arnold's suave and malicious irony; and while some spoke to the select few, others addressed the multitude. It was thanks to this versatility, this many-voicedness, that the several classes came to a certain understanding of one another's positions in the fluid state of society. So long as the press kept the crucible of controversy seething, the nation's mind could not stagnate. And because the press provided at the same time a safety valve by which class enmities and other potentially dangerous differences could be vented without harm, Victorian England escaped class struggle. The Victorians had been persuaded that the press was mightier than either pulpit or cannon, and that the health of an ailing society could be restored by the reasonableness of the printed word. Insofar as the nation entered the twentieth century intact and prosperous, its mind vigorous and its freedoms unabridged, that faith was not misplaced.

III

THE SPIRIT OF THE AGE:
TIME, PLACE, AND CHANGE

1. The Coming of Railways and Cities

VICTORIAN LITERATURE IS, among other things, the record of a society seeking ways to adjust itself to conditions as revolutionary as any we face today. The Victorians found themselves living in a world whose novel demands they were wholly unprepared to meet. It was a crucial moment in modern history. "Could the people of this island," as a recent historian puts it, "and, particularly, its dominant middle class, with its energy, its moral earnestness, and its seemingly limitless resources, bring about the miracle of adjusting human life and Western civilisation to the new conditions?" [1]

No wonder the Victorians were self-conscious. When they thought of themselves as an Age, and they soon came to do so—the adjective "Victorian" was coined as early as 1851—they were deeply impressed by their uniqueness. At the very threshold of the era, John Stuart Mill began a penetrating essay on "the spirit of the age" by commenting that the phrase was

in some measure a novel expression. I do not believe that it is to be met with in any work exceeding fifty years in antiquity. The idea of comparing one's own age with former ages, or with our

notion of those which are yet to come, had occurred to philosophers; but it never before was itself the dominant idea of any
age.

It is an idea essentially belonging to an age of change. Before men begin to think much and long on the peculiarities of
their own times, they must have begun to think that those times
are, or are destined to be, distinguished in a very remarkable
manner from the times which have preceded them. Mankind are
then divided, into those who are still what they were, and those
who have changed: into the men of the present age, and the men
of the past. To the former, the spirit of the age is a subject of
exultation; to the latter, of terror; to both, of eager and anxious
interest.

This corporate self-consciousness intensified throughout the
century. The Victorians were very much aware that they
were performing in the limelight of history, and one of their
great ambitions was to do so with credit. "We are an era in
human history," they said in effect, "the farthest milestone
on the long road of man's progress. We take our role very
seriously. Will posterity applaud or deplore our performance?"

Charging the spirit of the age, lending it both exultation and terror, was the keen sense of change of which
Mill spoke. It is true that a consciousness of "improvement"
had been current before the 1780's and was the source of
a widespread satisfaction which foreshadowed the Victorians' incomparably grander one. But the modest advances
science and technology had made in Dr. Johnson's day had
not affected the surface look of his world. Although the
young American Henry Adams, arriving in London in 1858,
wrote that he found himself back in the eighteenth century,
he soon must have had occasion to think differently. A
decade earlier, in *Dombey and Son,* Dickens had described
the large-scale slum clearance and engineering operations
incident to bringing the railroad into the metropolis, and
this was but one phase of a continuous process of demolition
and reconstruction which transformed Dr. Johnson's and

Charles Lamb's London into Dickens'. Not since the Great
Fire of 1666 had there been so sweeping an alteration of
the scene.

To the Victorian mind, the coming of the railway was
the great demarcation line between past and present. "Your
railroad," wrote Thackeray in 1860, "starts the new era,
and we of a certain age belong to the new time and the
old one. . . . We elderly people have lived in that prae-
railroad world, which has passed into limbo and vanished
from under us. I tell you it was firm under our feet once,
and not long ago. They have raised those railroad embank-
ments up, and shut off the old world that was behind them.
Climb up that bank on which the irons are laid, and look to
the other side—it is gone." Between 1830 and 1848, over
5,000 miles of line had been built in an area no larger
than Georgia, Illinois, or Wisconsin. The railroad's tunnels,
viaducts, bridges, and trails of steam, smoke, and sparks
altered a landscape which, except for the checkerboard
effect of hedgerows and ditches resulting from several periods
of enclosure, had not changed since the Middle Ages. The
lumbering passenger and mail coaches soon vanished from
the roads, and the inns where they had once stopped lapsed
into drowsiness. In London, such famous coaching inns as
the White Horse Cellar in Piccadilly, where Esther Summer-
son arrived from the country (*Bleak House*), and the Sara-
cen's Head in Snow Hill, where Mr. Squeers interviewed
prospective victims for Dotheboys Hall (*Nicholas Nickleby*),
gave way to a novel species of traveler-serving buildings,
imposing yet bustling "termini" (the elegant Latin is characteristic of the time), often with large hotels under the
same roof.

As they appeared in other large cities, these massive
structures, their train sheds often imitating in iron the lofty
naves of cathedrals, became at once the focal point, lord-
ing it over town hall, churches, and business buildings.
Railroads brought the life blood of commerce and crowds

into population centers, some old, some recently transformed from country towns. In 1800 there had been but one British city of over 100,000 population (London, with 865,000); at mid-century there were nine; in 1891, twenty-three. About 80 per cent of the total increase in population across the century occurred in cities and towns. Greater London grew from less than a million in 1801 to over four million at the end of the century.

The compact town of the past, where no street was more than a few minutes' walk from open fields, gave way to cities in whose centers ugly banks and looming warehouses covered the sites of artisans' shops. Each city had its fashionable neighborhoods—and more than its share of slums huddled near the mills and engineering works and the railway lines and rivers that had determined their location. The Victorian city was noisy, not so much with the raucous cries of hawkers, though these persisted from olden days, as with the clatter of horses, carriages, drays, omnibuses, and, later, trams. It was also dirty, the stone of its new public buildings and venerable churches alike blackened with soot and pitted and eroded by fumes from the factory chimneys. The chimneys themselves, poking up thickly alongside the old towers and spires in distant prospects of the city, were an ever-present reminder of how much the world had changed in a few years.

The symbolism was not lost upon the onlookers. The English had always been a country-dwelling race, and these dense concentrations of buildings and men were new in their experience. In fact, the special form urbanization took in the Victorian era was new in human experience. Never before, probably, had half of any nation's people lived in towns and cities, as the English did as early as 1851. And although large cities as such were no novelty, neither Rome nor Paris nor Vienna nor Berlin had been dominated at any time by industry as most British cities now were. The problems of adjusting human living to limited space that are dealt with in modern urban studies had their origin in these

Victorian cities which grew without any consideration of their effect on people.

The city, like the railroad, had a profound impact upon sensibilities. It was at once the supreme triumph of civilization and civilization's most catastrophic mistake. It was overwhelming, no matter in what light one was disposed to look at it. Some, like the younger Dickens and, many years later, Henry James, found it exhilarating in its complexity and contrasts of scene and people. They saw a fearful beauty in its sheer mass, and discovered less imposing but still striking qualities, ranging from the picturesque to the grotesque, in its smaller dimensions. They were fascinated by its kaleidoscopic movement, its perpetual restlessness, the changes being wrought by wreckers and builders—changes which, unlike those long familiar in the country, were unrhythmic and unrepetitive, never doubling back on themselves. In the nineties, guided by James McNeill Whistler's painterly eye, a young generation of impressionistic poets and craftsmen in prose discovered fresh beauty in cityscapes, unexpected glamor in streets and taverns, music halls and mist-softened bridges.

But if the spectacle enthralled, it also appalled. The city's density and expanse bred a sense of captivity, of helplessness, of claustrophobia. Its ugliness finally obscured its grandeur; the wretchedness of most of its inhabitants mocked the luxury of the few. In the workers' quarters it was a sink of vice and disease. And, perhaps worst of all, it was crowded with rootless, anonymous strangers, indifferent to their fellows' fate, bent only on surviving the competitive turmoil of what the Victorians, following Wordsworth, often chose to call "the monstrous ant-hill." Paradoxically, the closer people were brought together physically, as in mill or slum, the farther apart they drifted in any social or spiritual sense; in the midst of crowds they were alone. The only bond that held society together was the economic one, and that was both tenuous and sterile. There was grim appropriateness in the fact that Gustave Doré, having done a set of illustrations for the *Divine Comedy,* should have gone on to portray mid-Victorian London in terms powerfully suggestive of Purgatory and Hell.

In many ways, cities were in truth unpleasant places for men to live. Yet the sensitive Victorian's denunciation of the city was also a convention inherited from Rousseau and the romantic poets and, by way of the eighteenth-century Augustans, from Virgil's Rome—the assumption that the city was inherently evil and the countryside idyllic in its lovely innocence. A candid examination of the way people lived in the Victorian countryside (or for that matter any countryside) might have led some believers in the superiority of *rus* over *urbs* to think differently. Kingsley, for one, was not deluded. "Those picturesque villages," supposedly the epitome of "fertility, loveliness, industry and wealth," were "generally the perennial hotbeds of fever and ague, of squalid penury, sottish profligacy, dull discontent too stale for words." But literary myth often wields an authority disproportionate to its realistic truth.

While Ruskin and Wordsworth were denouncing its desecration of the Lakes, the railroad claimed a good measure of acceptance on social grounds. It was, for one thing, a patriotic symbol, the nineteenth-century British equivalent of ancient Rome's military roads and aqueducts. Its financing and the engineering which converted company shares into lines of iron rail were accomplished on a scale unmatched in history. In the mid-forties—the height of the "railway mania," although 15,000 more miles of track would be laid before 1889—Britain realized for the first time how vast its capabilities were if its economic, material, and human resources were efficiently mobilized. The existing 6,600 miles contributed much to the Crystal Palace euphoria.

It was fitting that the spreading network should have brought most of the visitors to London in the summer of 1851, but the railroads had other, less festive, social uses. They had added a disturbing new element to the political situation in the forties. They made it easier for radical

crowds to assemble at vulnerable spots; it would be interesting to know how many of the Chartists who flocked to
London on several occasions between 1839 and 1848 traveled
at least part of the way by rail. By the same token, the
government could rush troops to trouble spots within a few
hours, as it did in 1842 when it sped trainloads of soldiers
from London to Manchester to put down mill hands' riots.
If faster transportation meant that radicals and their sympathizers could work more closely together and that civil
disturbances could escalate more quickly, it also meant that
they could be quelled with equal dispatch. It is hard to
tell which side benefited more from the early railroads, the
militants or the law-and-order forces. Certainly the danger
of sudden and possibly bloody confrontations was increased.
It was lucky that the nation's political temperature sub-
sided before the new mobility could be put to a definitive
test.

The railroads' other effects were just as double-edged.
They and the cities they helped build meant the end of the
regional cultures and economies into which Britain had been
divided so long as bad roads discouraged all but the most determined travel and the most essential communication. (Except for the new macadamized toll roads, which were
perfected just as the railway arrived to make them obsolete,
the roads were scarcely better than Macaulay described them
as having been in 1685.) Each section of the country had
had its own dialect, its own mores, its own cultural heritage;
each, furthermore, had been a relatively self-sufficient economic entity, consuming most of what it produced and having only a limited trade with the rest of the country. Within
a generation, provincialism give way to national cohesion.
The commodities and services of any given area were inte-
grated into a single large economy, with great gains in
efficiency and cheapness. Newspapers printed in London
reached the most remote parts of the nation within a few
hours, the result being that the best—and the worst—that
was said and done became overnight the possession and

concern of the whole country. Cheap fares enabled common people, few of whom had ever been more than a few miles from their birthplace, to move considerable distances at will. Their horizons were broadened beyond the narrow confines of the parish and the town marketplace.

This was all to the good, although critics of cultural parochialism like Matthew Arnold understandably required much more to be done. But the breakdown of the old regional structure had its less happy results. The village and small country town declined in economic importance. Local artisans and tradesmen lost their livelihood as people could travel farther for what they required and as, conversely, food and manufactured goods could be brought to them from the larger centers. The cottage industries, supplying their respective trades through the entrepreneurs who brought down raw materials and returned with finished products, were finished; the railroads joined with the factory system to concentrate manufacturing in relatively few centers. Even building materials ceased to be distinctive, as stone had been in the Cotswolds and brick in the north. Now they were moved by rail wherever they were wanted, and the former pleasant harmony of landscape and architecture using indigenous materials was at an end. Cement and red tile were cheaper, even when brought from afar. But perhaps the hardest blow of all occurred when a thriving village was missed by the railroad, often in response to the village's opposition or that of the local landowner. In many instances it preserved its tranquil picturesqueness at the cost of its economy.

In other respects, however, change bypassed the countryside. The political reforms initiated in the Benthamite era were confined to the towns and cities; as we saw earlier, until late in the century rural areas were still governed by obsolete and anachronistic laws and authorities, many of which could be traced back to feudal times. Despite all the advances in transport and communication, the conservatism that characterized rural attitudes persisted. The effect was that in Victorian England two societies lived side by side, their interests and viewpoints frequently conflicting: the cautious, stratified, tradition-bound rural society, and the liberal, ongoing, relatively flexible town one, infatuated with the idea of progress. Or, to put it another way, on the one hand there was a closely interlocked aristocracy and gentry, living as they had done for centuries on the proceeds of their landed estates; on the other, a rising middle class and a more populous working class, both coming to be based more and more in new-style industry and commerce. The landowners wished, naturally, to cling to their inherited position and prerogatives; equally understandably, the middle class and the workers demanded a voice in political affairs commensurate with the ever larger contribution they were making to the nation's wealth.

2. The Rising Tide of Democracy

A sixty-year stretch of Tory rule, briefly interrupted on only two occasions, had solidified the power of the landed class, whose interests the Tories faithfully served. The Whigs, whose late seventeenth-century origins lay in the opposition of certain great families to the royal domination of Parliament and who, although equally aristocratic, were therefore committed to a wider and balanced distribution of political power, were the obvious party to promote the interests of the commercial middle class. But most of that class were excluded from the franchise, because the nation's electoral system, a patchwork of wildly dissimilar local laws, had gone unrevised since Tudor times and thus contained little provision for them. Economically the class was gaining strength as its mills and mines multiplied; politically it was almost impotent.

Beginning with the popular London movement for "Wilkes and liberty" in the 1760's, there had been a certain amount of agitation for political reform, especially for widening the franchise beyond the small, select fragment of "the superior orders" who then constituted the electorate, and for modernizing an antiquated parliamentary system which was constructed to favor the few. But the outbreak of war with France quieted the stir except among native sympathizers with the Revolution, who, brandishing radical propaganda like Paine's *The Rights of Man,* called for enfranchising all men, not merely those of the middle class.

Until these last years of the eighteenth century, the working class had remained what it had always been, a constant on the social scene, composed of the Biblical hewers of wood and drawers of water, the people who did the hard, monotonous, ill-rewarded toil without which human life could not be sustained. Not all middle-class Englishmen, of course, regarded them as, in Burke's notorious phrase, the swinish multitude. But until now their importance in society had been clearly limited. They were valuable as an inexhaustible fund of cheap and docile labor. They might engage the compassion of a handful of philanthropists who dispensed Christian succor to the orphaned, penniless, infirm, and aged, and a modicum of instruction to the young. And they were also the potential source of mischief or actual revolt. Outbreaks of extreme discontent were infrequent, but the dangerous possibilities inherent in mob action had been demonstrated from time to time, most alarmingly in the "No Popery" riots in London, led by the rabidly anti-Catholic Lord George Gordon (1780), and readers of Gibbon, schooled in the destructive achievements of the Roman rabble, were quick to see an analogy.

Then, in the era of the French Revolution, the common man moved into unwonted prominence. Poets like Burns and Wordsworth and novelists like Scott celebrated the natural simplicity of his humble, unlettered existence. The poet George Crabbe, more realistic, described its hardships. Political theorists like Jeremy Bentham looked forward to the day when, his reasoning faculty suitably honed, the workingman could take his place among the councils of the nation. Radical agitators following in Paine's fiery wake exhorted him to claim "the rights of man" (i.e., his due share in the affairs of government). But although the advocates of unqualified democracy made a great clamor, it is likely that the masses of workers were as yet indifferent to the seductive vision of political power. In such a situation, however, it is noise that counts, and what they heard struck fear into the hearts not only of conservatives but of many moderates as well. The whole idea of democracy was identified with Jacobinism (the uncompromisingly egalitarian philosophy of the party that conducted the Reign of Terror), and it acquired virtually treasonous implications during the decades when Britain was fighting first a revolutionary and then an imperialistic France. If any lesson could be drawn from the convulsion across the Channel, it was that the masses, aroused by sloganeering demagogues, were capable of precipitating civil war, even anarchy. In a ferocious outburst of revolutionary mindlessness they could destroy the fabric of society. If it could happen in Paris, it could happen in London.

The prevailing uneasiness was intensified by the Luddite riots in the Midlands and Yorkshire in 1811–12, which figure in Charlotte Brontë's *Shirley* (1849). Taking their name from one Ned Ludlam, a youth who was reputedly among the first to break stocking frames, although his was a mere act of personal pique against his master, roving bands of hosiery knitters raided scores of mills, destroying their machinery. Their depredations were intended to pressure their employers to enter into collective bargaining on various grievances and were not, as it appeared at the time, a protest against mechanization *per se,* because simple machinery had been used in their craft for almost a century. Nor did the riots have any direct political significance. But memories of them lingered for years and added to the apprehension felt when the war ended with Wellington's victory at Waterloo in 1815, the customary post-war economic depression set in, and newly returned veterans increased the already large number of unemployed.

Having successfully dampened the radical fires for twenty years, the reactionary Tory government confirmed its resolve to put down dissidence in any form, however mild and whatever its causes. It soon had occasion to do so. Radical sentiment spread through the working class, now aroused by a new generation of inflammatory orators and journalists undeterred by the suspension of habeas corpus and the heavy punishment meted out to those convicted of sedition and other crimes against the state. In St. Peter's Fields, Manchester, in 1819, an orderly meeting of some 60,000 men, women, and children, gathered to listen to a radical speaker, was broken up by nervous, ill-disciplined militia summoned by the local authorities. Between ten and fifteen people in the crowd were killed and hundreds wounded by sabers, trampled, or half-suffocated during the ensuing panic. "The Peterloo Massacre," to give it the name immediately applied to it by a local radical paper, became to the working class and a sympathetic segment of the middle class the abiding symbol of tyranny, as Shelley's poem, "The Masque of Anarchy," attests. Among the rest of the population, the memory of Peterloo served as a constant reminder of the peril offered by a restive working population. It was this event, more than any other, which conditioned men's attitudes, their fears and desperate hopes, as the era of the First Reform Bill drew near.

This was the very time when the social problems generated by the factory system were becoming acute in the new industrial towns, the centers of infection. The country's first necessity was to find ways of adjusting its institutions to the new conditions. Instead, all official energies, intensified and focused after Peterloo by a new set of stringent laws (the "Six Acts" of 1819) abridging freedom of speech, assembly, and the press, were devoted to crushing the workers' protest movement. These efforts were only partially successful. Despite hundreds of prosecutions, which contributed to the atmosphere of a police state, the radical press refused to be silenced. A more important reason why the reform fever declined among the working people in the early twenties was somewhat improved economic conditions, which for the moment took the edge off their grievances. But at the same time, the dissatisfaction of the unenfranchised portion of the middle class was mounting. Its goal, like the workers', was the destruction of the Tory-landowner domination of government—"Old Corruption," as the radical journalist William Cobbett, whose influence approached its peak during these years, was fond of calling it.

In 1828 the Duke of Wellington's government relaxed its obduracy enough to repeal the Test and Corporation Acts, thus legalizing Dissenters' participation in government; the next year the Catholic Emancipation Act removed a similar disability from Roman Catholics. But far from quieting the liberals and radicals, these reluctant concessions merely strengthened their determination. Admitting Dissenters and Catholics to public office was a step in the right direction, but it did not touch the heart of the issue, which was that in England and Wales, with an adult population of about seven million, only 435,000 could vote. Of 658 members of Parliament, moreover, only some 234 were elected by any sizable body of voters; the rest were hand-picked by the aristocratic owners of pocket and rotten boroughs. In Old Sarum, most notorious of the latter, seven inhabitants sent two members to Westminster. Yet the new industrial cities— Manchester with its population of 182,000, Birmingham (146,000), and Leeds (123,000)—were wholly without representation.

By 1830, the cry for reform united more sections of the population than had ever been brought together by a single issue. Manual laborers, clerks, artisans, businessmen, even country gentry in places free of aristocratic control joined voices. The three-day July revolution in Paris, which dethroned a Bourbon king and replaced him with the bourgeoisie's man, Louis Philippe, increased the English middle class's determination. If their French counterparts could achieve their goal through a bloodless—almost respectable —revolution, so, as a last resort, would they.

When the new Parliament elected after the death of George IV met in the autumn of 1830, the issue of reform was laid squarely before the Duke of Wellington, still the prime minister. He declared that the present system was perfectly adequate. It was a most inopportune moment for him to do so, because fearsome memories of the marauding Luddites of twenty years earlier were stirred by the violence sweeping a dozen counties in the form of an agricultural workers' uprising led by a mythical "Captain Swing." Haystacks were burned by the hundreds, farmers' houses sacked, their implements broken up, and the countryside terrified. Although the cause of the disturbances was the workers' demand for a decent wage, it was inseparable from the reform fever, and political considerations obviously affected the rioters' punishment. Nineteen were hanged, 644 jailed, and nearly five hundred transported to Australia for long terms of penal servitude. And while haystacks flamed in the counties encircling London, suggesting to the already nervous inhabitants of the capital that they were in a virtual state of siege, town workmen were arming and drilling in the north.

Wellington having resigned on an issue unconnected with reform, a coalition ministry was formed under Lord Grey, a Whig. It promptly introduced a reform bill (March, 1831). The bill passed the House of Commons by one vote, and then ran into trouble in committee. As a consequence, Parliament was dissolved and a new campaign waged, with reform almost the sole issue. The free electors returned an ample majority of members sympathetic to the bill. But this time the House of Lords rejected it by forty-one votes. Now new troubles broke out across the nation. There were riots in London, Birmingham, and elsewhere, and mobs burned the central section of Bristol as well as Nottingham

Castle, property of the tenant-evicting Duke of Newcastle, who owned a number of pocket boroughs. To add to the tension, the dreaded cholera was appearing in the ports.

By May, 1832, the great coalition of pro-reform factions was organizing runs on banks; factories were shutting down while employers and employees alike attended mass meetings; the newly reactivated radical press spread news of every instance of protest; the nation's troops were alerted. Throughout the country there was acute fear that a spark would ignite the whole explosive mixture and tear Britain apart.

After further political maneuvering, ending in the Duke of Wellington's failure to form a government, Lord Grey returned to office and received William IV's promise to pack the House of Lords with newly created peers, favorable to reform, if it persisted in its refusal to pass the bill. The Lords capitulated without suffering their numbers to be increased, and the First Reform Bill became law in June, 1832.

Bonfires of rejoicing replaced burning haystacks across the country; in Lincolnshire, Alfred Tennyson and his sister rang peal after peal on their church bells. But to the Tory landowners who had fought reform every inch of the way, the end of the world was at hand. The Established Church was about to fall, the monarchy was to be dethroned, the House of Lords abolished, and private property confiscated. "The barriers of the constitution are broken down," announced Wellington; "the waters of destruction have burst the gates of the temple."

It was not quite that bad. The First Reform Bill enlarged the electorate in England and Wales from 435,000 to 652,000, an increase of approximately 50 per cent—which meant that five out of every six adult males still had no vote. It also abolished the most flagrant of the rotten and pocket boroughs, although several scores were preserved; despite much redistricting, the size of constituencies still varied greatly, and the one man, one vote principle was far from realized. After hysteria on all sides, relief on the one hand—the Tories discovered that the sun still rose in the morning—and disillusionment on the other. The workers had been encouraged by their middle-class sympathizers to expect that they would themselves receive the franchise; that, after all, was part of what their own campaigning had been about. In their case, nothing was changed. They could not vote before 1832, and they could not do so now. And while a third reaction, contentment with the gains accomplished, characterized those of the middle class who now received the vote for the first time, there was widespread middle-class disappointment as well. Only a fraction of the class, perhaps half, was now enfranchised, and in the redistribution of seats the big industrial towns were conspicuously overlooked, receiving but token representation. The main beneficiaries were the smaller, rural boroughs, especially those in the agricultural south.

The fact was that, stripped of all the resplendent rhetoric and appeals to high principle that gave it the appearance of a crusade dedicated to winning the vote for the common man, the feverish agitation of 1830–32 had simply been waged in behalf of a long-overdue adjustment of the balance of power between the Tories and Whigs. The Tories' possession of some two hundred "safe" seats had virtually guaranteed their permanent control of Parliament. The chief practical fruit of the First Reform Bill was that by redistricting and setting up uniform electoral requirements it divided the representation somewhat more equitably between the two parties, both of which remained essentially aristocratic in composition and interest. The old claim that the First Reform Bill put the middle class into power is now universally discredited. What happened in 1832 was that the commercial, "town" interest *began* to play an effective role in politics, breaking the monopoly hitherto enjoyed by the great landowners. The social complexion of the House of Commons was little changed, because the newly enfranchised part of the middle class evinced a rather touching inclination to elect sympathetic men of inherited wealth and rank as its representatives. In the first reformed Parliament sat over two hundred sons of peers or baronets. Genuine businessmen and industrialists were sufficiently rare in the new House of Commons as to be regarded as curiosities.

In the Victorian period, therefore, middle class measures were enacted by Parliaments still heavily peopled by men of the upper class, and they were administered by cabinets the majority of whose members, down to the last quarter of the century, were noblemen. The middle class influenced the tone and temper of Victorian society more than it influenced politics.

For a few years after the passage of the Reform Bill, once the initial reactions had worn off the predominant feeling in England was one of sheer relief—relief that such (relatively) drastic changes had been made in the electoral processes with scarcely any bloodshed and no damage to the Constitution or to revered national institutions. This mood, however, was replaced in the later 1830's by one of growing tension and unrest. The ensuing decade, which coincided with Victoria's first ten years on the throne, was the most harrowing and dangerous of the entire century.

Times were worse than they had been in living memory. There was a general economic depression, with factories closing or working part time as unsold goods piled up in warehouses. The labor market, already swollen by seasoned workers thrown out of employment, was glutted with new recruits, for machines had displaced additional tens of thousands of hand workers. There was a series of bad harvests, and cholera reappeared in some towns, where every condition was present for its encouragement.

The popular bitterness against the political establishment, which, though somewhat "reformed," remained largely indifferent to crisis conditions, found its expression in Chartism, the first sustained, inclusive working-class movement in modern English history. The name referred to the People's

Charter, an electoral bill of rights which, delivered to an unresponsive—in fact, openly derisive—Parliament in the form of a petition in 1839, 1842, and 1848, demanded the reforms that had failed to materialize in 1832. The six-point program called for universal manhood suffrage, the secret ballot, payment for members of Parliament, abolition of the property qualification for members, equal electoral districts, and annual elections.

The assumption was that if Parliament could be made truly representative of the people, it would somehow magically transform the economy. A democratically elected legislature, purged of the hated Tory landowners who had miraculously survived the whirlwind of 1832, would bring prosperity for all. This was the same naïve assumption which had led a motley assortment of radical factions to pool their strength under the banner of reform in 1830–32. Now history repeated itself, the People's Charter replacing the Reform Bill as the holy grail. But far from being truly dedicated to a single cause, the Chartists were nothing more than a loose federation of disaffected working people with a variety of grievances. Though all were called Chartists for convenience—it was their brush to begin with, and the frightened middle and upper classes did not hesitate to tar them with it—most cared nothing for ballots so long as they could find something to put in their bellies. Among them were hordes of technologically unemployed handicraftsmen, such as handloom weavers and stocking-frame knitters—perhaps the most numerous of the factions, as their prospects were the most bleak; skilled London craftsmen, aristocrats of labor who had formally initiated the movement; protesters against the new Poor Law; northern textile mill hands on short hours and shorter wages; even followers of Cobbett, who saw salvation in a retreat to a benevolently ruled peasant society devoid of machines. If their alliance had been tighter and their leaders more of one mind, national security in those years would have been in even greater peril than it was.

Concurrent with Chartism, whose fortunes waxed and waned as economic conditions fluctuated between bad and not quite so bad, was the largely middle-class campaign to repeal the Corn Laws. This all too obvious piece of class legislation had been enacted in 1815 to protect the agricultural interests from the economic shock attending the conclusion of the long war, specifically the revived competition from foreign grain. As amended in 1828, the law provided for a sliding-scale tariff: the lower the domestic price of grain fell, the higher the duty. The operation of supply and demand kept the domestic price high, since the supply was artificially limited while the demand was growing as the population increased. The workers consequently could not afford bread. Although they saw the situation in a different light than did the manufacturers who subsidized the propagandist and lobbying Anti-Corn Law League—the latter wanted bread made cheap so that they could keep wages down and thus, in turn, keep the prices of their products competitive—the Chartists were as vehement as their masters in denouncing the laws.

"Slowly," wrote Tennyson in "Locksley Hall," published in 1842, "comes a hungry people, as a lion creeping nigher, /Glares at one that nods and winks behind a slowly-dying fire." The fear of violent social and political upheaval, which had dominated the national mood during the years of the French Revolution, had begun to fade in the Napoleonic era; but it had been revived, in a new, close-to-home context, to stir the apprehensions of a new generation, by the alarms, hysterical words, and often violent events attending the agitation for the Reform Bill. In these Chartist years the freshly intensified fear was of a completion of the rush to catastrophe, as it appeared to men of conservative inclination, which had been so narrowly stemmed in 1830–32. Did not the Chartists' marches, pamphlets, orations, and petitions in behalf of political democracy foreshadow the cataclysmic last act of the drama that had begun with England's revulsion at the Reign of Terror? Carlyle's *His-*

tory of the French Revolution (1837), therefore, was of the utmost timeliness. So, four years later, was Dickens' *Barnaby Rudge,* which depicted London at the mercy of a pillaging, burning mob during the Gordon Riots of 1780. Both authors could trust their readers to discern the parallels between the historical events and the present peril. The fear of revolution had almost become part of the collective unconscious. As late as 1869, when Bertrand Russell's maternal grandfather, Lord Stanley of Alderley, lay on his deathbed, he "heard a loud noise in the street and thought it was the revolution breaking out, showing that, at least sub-consciously, the thought of revolution had remained with him throughout long prosperous years." [2]

But it was not only the vestigial dread of Jacobinism and more recent memories of the Reform Bill tumult that fed anti-democratic feeling in the Chartist era. More important, perhaps, was the conviction that the old political and social structure had served so well in the past that it could somehow support the nation now, no matter how radically conditions had changed. The romantics' veneration of the common man did not wear at all well with most intellectuals of succeeding generations. The egalitarianism of the American experiment was not for them—the rough social manners of the Jacksonian era were particularly repellent—and when men of good will went out from England to see for themselves, many came back disillusioned. Dickens was one such. He left England with high expectations, and on his return he scarified the raw republic both in the American phase of *Martin Chuzzlewit* and in *American Notes,* the travel book he assembled from the extensive letters he wrote as he toured. Many years passed before the Americans forgave him.

In spite of everything, however, the common man slowly came into his own, beginning with the commercial middle class. In 1846 Sir Robert Peel, the Tory prime minister whose party had always looked after the landowners' interests, even as his wing of it sought a *rapprochement* with business, dramatically reversed himself and committed the Tories, now increasingly called Conservatives, to repealing the Corn Laws. (The immediate occasion was the failure of the Irish potato crop, which made necessary the unrestricted importation of grain. "Rotten potatoes have done it all," grumbled the Duke of Wellington. "They put Peel in his d——d fright.") With this event, free trade triumphed; it was the industrialists and foreign traders, not the farmers, whom the nation's economic policy was henceforth to serve. But notwithstanding the renewed prophecies of doom that were heard in 1846, improved farming methods and an increasing population kept the landowners prosperous until the middle seventies, when a series of bad harvests and the tariff-free importation of vast quantities of foodstuffs presaged the imminent end of the agrarian economy.

Two years later (1848) Chartism precipitated its climactic emergency. In a season when Europe was being swept by liberal revolutions, the leaders of the several Chartist factions decided upon a mammoth demonstration in London as a preliminary to handing to Parliament their third petition. The metropolis braced itself for a siege. Wellington commanded military preparations; between 170,000 and 200,000 citizens were deputized as auxiliary policemen; and the government offices were barricaded with bound volumes of the *Times, Hansard's Parliamentary Debates,* or bulky files of official papers—a point on which the historians differ. The result was a fiasco. After parleying with the police, who refused to let the assembled Chartists cross the bridges to Westminster after their mass meeting on the other side of the Thames, the leaders agreed to transport their petition to the House of Commons in a procession of cabs. They might have saved their fare: the petition, which was alleged to bear 5,706,000 signatures, proved to contain only two million, and many of these were forged, fictitious, and/or facetious ("Victoria Rex," "The Duke of Wellington," "Sir Robert Peel"). For the third and last time, Parliament threw the Charter out. For all practical purposes, Chartism died on that April day.

In retrospect, the event and the fortunate outcome could not have been better timed. As throne after throne was (temporarily) overturned on the Continent, England's remained secure; militant radicalism had spent its force. Now, finally, even those most fearful of a proletarian takeover began to concede that it probably would not happen here. The clinching proof came three years later, when throngs of workingmen and their families, among them many erstwhile Chartists, poured into London to see the Crystal Palace. Despite predictions of rampant crime and disorder, nothing untoward happened; "the people," enjoying a holiday sponsored in some instances by their employers, proved to be orderly, sober, and good-humored—anything but revolution-minded.

It was in a comparatively peaceful atmosphere, therefore, that the march toward political democracy resumed. The franchise had not been altered since 1832. The remaining half of the middle class and all the workers were still without the vote, and therefore much ground remained to be won. In the sixties renewed popular sentiment was rallied in great mass meetings. Only in London, where workers caused disturbances after having been denied permission to hold a get-the-vote assembly in Hyde Park, was there any violence. In 1867, after years of partisan maneuvering, the remainder of the middle class was enfranchised along with most town workers. Almost a million men were thereby added to the electoral rolls. An accompanying redistribution of seats gave the large cities the representation withheld from them in 1832. In 1884 the third and final reform bill extended the vote to two million agricultural laborers and so made possible locally elected governments in the rural areas.

The debate preceding the passage of the 1867 bill was not stilled when the bill became law, as the publication of Matthew Arnold's *Culture and Anarchy* in the *Cornhill Maga-*

zine (July, 1867–September, 1868) testifies. Fundamental questions of social and political philosophy were involved, for now the nation had to face squarely the possible consequences of so broad a franchise. Although some upper-class sympathizers welcomed the *de jure* democratization of Britain's political institutions, others were unreconciled to what they anticipated would be the *de facto* consequences. The former fear of armed revolution was now replaced by a no less anxious apprehension of ballot-box democracy. The by now professionally pessimistic Carlyle likened the Second Reform Act to "shooting Niagara," and others, invoking a phrase as old as Rabelais and Hobbes, described it as "a leap in the dark." At least, fears that the government would be radicalized proved unfounded. The next election brought in no more revolutionary a party than the Liberals (as the Whig party had come to be called), under the leadership of the impeccably pious, middle-class Gladstone. The alternation henceforth between Liberal and Conservative governments showed that the newly enfranchised workmen were content for the time being to operate within the old two-party system. Today's Labour Party was still far in the future, although its eventual presence was foreshadowed by the growing political activity of the trade unions in the last three decades of the century.

After the violent talk and deeds of the thirties and forties, the conversion of England into a political democracy had been completed without bloodshed and without any shattering of traditional institutions. In 1832, notwithstanding the pipe dreams the middle class encouraged among the workers, to most Englishmen the notion of the laboring class helping to elect Parliament was unthinkable; to many it was nothing short of a nightmare. Seventy years later, not only did almost all the workers have the vote but men from their own class were actually sitting in Parliament. They were curiosities but no longer absolute rarities. The old order had changed indeed, yielding place to new. But little had Tennyson conceived, when he wrote those words ("Morte d'Arthur," 1833–34), how revolutionary that change was to be.

3. The New Sense of Time

"The silent social revolution" had not happened overnight. Different though the political order had become, the change, marked by the three milestones of the Reform Acts of 1832, 1867, and 1884, had been spread over more than fifty years, and the results of the first act, as we have seen, were far less sweeping than the furor attending its passage had suggested. More immediately evident was the physical transformation that came with the city and the railroad. But it was the new concept of time which had the most profound effect upon the Victorian spirit. And here again the railroad played a principal role.

In a supersonic age it is hard to imagine the psychological adjustment required when the maximum speed to which people had been accustomed, fifteen miles an hour at the outside for fast coaches—De Quincey, in "The English Mail-Coach," timed the London-Glasgow mail at twelve—gave way by mid-century to the express train's forty or fifty. The railroad did more than any other Victorian innovation to infiltrate the national consciousness with the idea of speed. Turner's painting *Rain, Steam and Speed*—a train hurtling through a downpour—is more than a work of art: like the numerous exclamatory descriptions that adventure-some early riders wrote in their diaries and letters, it is a historical document.

Hitherto, time had been measured by the slow progress of a summer day, or, even more rudimentarily, by the growth rate of the countryside—a season for a crop to mature, most of a generation for a row of trees to reach full height. (The traditional conservatism of landowning men could doubtless be attributed to the time-sense acquired in a lifetime of watching things grow; the impatience ascribed to political radicals, their demand for reform at once, was incomprehensible to farmers accustomed to the slow evolution of plants.) Now the shadow creeping across a sundial was replaced by the minute hand of a pocket watch as its owner anxiously compared it with a railway timetable.

A steamship now could cut the Atlantic crossing time by one-half. In steam-powered factories, vast quantities of goods were produced in a small fraction of the time it once took to fabricate them by hand. Beginning in the middle forties as a railroading device, the electric telegraph sent messages across hundreds of miles in a few seconds. Newspapers, with their up-to-the-minute coverage of events made possible by the telegraph and, later, the submarine cable, and by steam presses turning out tens of thousands of copies within a single hour, contributed still more to the feeling of immediacy. Even art ceased to be long as the invention of photography made possible instant portraiture of people and scenes.

No wonder, then, that Matthew Arnold, among others, complained of the "sick hurry" of modern life. The Victorian man of affairs was constantly on the go (Arnold himself, a government school inspector, spent much of his working life on trains). There was no chance to savor the true quality of life, no leisure to acquire wisdom. Even English prose was affected. Whether or not the age witnessed the decline of the English sentence, as is sometimes alleged, there was a world of difference between the expansive style of, say, a Ruskin or a Meredith and the economical one of an H. G. Wells or an Arnold Bennett, trained in the school of popular journalism. The Victorian audience consisted more and more of those who read while they ran. Paradoxically, the more time technology saved man, the less time he had.

Yet he still had plenty. We look back with justifiable envy upon the spacious days and evenings the Victorians had in which to read. Most of their great novels are far longer than today's average, and while it is true that some were published in installments over many months, it is also true that their readers were reading much else concurrently. And those who wrote were no less amply supplied with time. Ruskin's total output occupies thirty-nine bulky volumes, and even so, writing was but one of his many occupations. William Morris turned out immense narrative poems as a sideline to his careers as interior decorator, versatile craftsman, and socialist organizer; he wrote almost literally with his left hand, because he wove tapestry and composed verse simultaneously. As we read Dickens' letters, of which over 12,000 (presumably a mere fraction of the total) have been preserved, we are forced to believe that his days must have been forty-eight hours long, because in addition to writing a long series of novels and editing (in many cases extensively rewriting) the contributions to his weekly journals, he was active in public causes, in amateur theatricals, and as a platform reader. Trollope wrote some fifty novels, many of them while working full time as a post office inspector. His mother had set him a good example—she wrote thirty-four. But her record was far eclipsed by other women later in the century: the best-selling Mary Elizabeth Braddon turned out eighty novels, and her contemporary Margaret Oliphant wrote more than one hundred, as well as some two hundred contributions to *Blackwood's Magazine* alone. If time fled faster than ever before, such people wrung from it every minute it contained.

Perhaps it might be said that the Victorians lived their everyday lives according to two times, the old leisurely one and the new headlong one. As for their larger concept of time, it too underwent a revolutionary expansion, one which affected the very heart of their world outlook. At the beginning of the century, the scope of time, which meant essentially the duration of mankind's occupation of earth, was defined by the chronology reckoned by a seventeenth-century bishop of Armagh, James Ussher. Using Scriptural evidence such as the ages of the patriarchs and the lengths of kings' reigns, Ussher worked backward to establish that

God had created man, along with his universe, in seven days during the year 4004 B.C. (In a later refinement, another theologian pinpointed the moment of creation at 9 A.M. on October 23 of that year.) This meant, therefore, that cosmic time was a matter of some 5,800 years. Long as this span was as compared with a single human life, and therefore hard to conceive of, it still was one which the ordinary human mind, given a bit of imagination, could live with.

But even in Bishop Ussher's time, a few men were tempted to believe that the world was unimaginably older than the received Biblical scheme allowed. And in the eighteenth century, a number of English and French scientists, theorizing independently on the significance of the fossils and geological formations they were discovering, began to perceive the vast vista of prehistoric time. The progress of geological and paleontological studies in the first half of the nineteenth century, climaxed by Alfred Wallace's and Charles Darwin's simultaneous announcement of the theory of biological evolution (1858)—matters to which we will return in Chapter VI—made it evident that "the past" had to be measured not in centuries or millennia but by geological ages stretching back hundreds of thousands of years. The nebular hypothesis of the origin of the solar system—that the sun and its planets resulted from the cooling of superheated gaseous masses in space—had a similar effect. Although the hypothesis itself, the product of eighteenth-century speculation, now was rejected by most astronomers, it continued to have a powerful impact on the popular mind. The human imagination had to adjust itself to staggering new concepts of time derived not only from the age of the earth but from the even more immense spans involved in the nebular process.

The adjustment profoundly affected the Victorians' view of their own place in the cosmic sequence. The Bible and classical sources had, of course, transmitted knowledge of contemporaneous civilizations in the Near East, and this knowledge was now being greatly amplified by the excavations conducted by the archaeologists, a new breed of scientific inquirers, at the sites of Nineveh and Babylon, and elsewhere. But other archaeological discoveries in the mid-Victorian period revealed that, over the millennia, several other brilliant civilizations—pre-dynastic Egyptian, Sumerian, Mycenaean—had flourished and then vanished, leaving only mutely eloquent ruins attesting to the heights they had once reached. Their command of technology, for example, was almost awesome. It was ironic that a society which regarded itself as the unique climax of civilization should have sponsored the diggings which shattered that comfortable illusion.

The cultural stream to which the Victorians belonged was merely one of history's many, and perhaps not even the most accomplished, let alone the most enduring. Certainly Judaeo-Christianity could no longer be thought of as having continuously occupied the center of the world stage; it was a mere incident in a complex drama reaching back over long ages. The cave paintings discovered in southern France and northern Spain in 1878–79 were relics of a culture which throve in the wake of the last ice age, twenty thousand years ago, some fourteen thousand before the Biblical Creation. To replace Adam with a race of Upper Paleolithic men, or with Neanderthal men (discovered in 1856) from a much more remote age—estimated at the time to be between 150,000 and 180,000 years ago—required a drastic alteration of historical perspective, to say nothing of an equally drastic revision of modern man's view of his place in the vast process which science was now revealing to him.

Apart from the humbling effect, the consequences of this expanded awareness of time were felt in several ways. It widened the scope of the historical relativism which had been characteristic of the romantic mind: different times and cultures meant different values and viewpoints. The rise of the study of comparative religions, for example, called for a candid reexamination of the assumption that ultimate truth resided exclusively in the Western tradition. It could be argued that truth of equal intellectual and spiritual validity existed in any of the other religions and, indeed, in any of the other secular cultures which were now being opened to view. Those Victorians who were not bound to the old exclusive reliance on Christian revelation found compelling principles of life and order in history itself. Carlyle, for one, after he could no longer accept the Calvinistic theology in which he had been reared, discovered a substitute in the belief that God's purpose could be read in all the events of human history.

The sense of history also had a liberating effect, which the Victorians eagerly embraced. Now that the physical and social environment was being transformed, the present seemed to be separated from the past by a much more formidable barrier than Thackeray spoke of in connection with the railroad. But the widening and deepening sense of history opportunely reinforced the sense of continuity that was being weakened by the disappearance of physical links with the past. Time, so to speak, gave the Victorians a spacious place to live, a refuge from the narrow confines of the immediate moment.

For all their pride in the present, they had an ineradicable feeling—the word "nostalgia" does not do it justice—for the past. Although in one mood they valued the innovative, the liberal, and the rational, their affinity with the romantic temper nourished an equal sympathy with the antiquarian, the conservative, the emotional. The latter were qualities to be desired, for they could moderate and enlighten the hectic temper of the new day. It says much of the Victorians that when they put up a new building of any importance, its architectural style was intended to make it look old from the moment it was finished. Victorian architecture was, almost by definition, backward-looking; there was no contemporary, indigenous style. The only considerable building that was an exception to the rule was the

Crystal Palace, and it was so far in advance of the times that contemporaneity never caught up with it. It burned down in 1936, before the modern glass-and-steel mode it had presaged established itself.

Of the several revivals—Greek, Gothic, Renaissance, and, late in the century, bogus Queen Anne—which the Victorian age witnessed in architecture and the decorative arts, by far the most important, and the only one which had a marked effect upon literature, was the Gothic or, more generally, the medieval. Here again the Victorians were the romantic age's heirs. The vogue for old ballads and for erecting artificial ruins of nonexistent castles and abbeys on country estates, the interest in the supernatural, the Gothic novel, and, in a very different mode, the Waverley novels with their evocation of the atmosphere and ideals of the age of chivalry—all these had been romantic phenomena. Medievalism, however, or what passed for it, was more deeply embedded in the Victorian spirit, doubtless because the need for some such tie with the remote (and supposedly preferable) past had become all the more pressing with the advance of materialism and secularism.

In the second half of the eighteenth century, the Gothic look had been applied solely to genuinely medieval cathedrals and churches that had suffered an overlay of other styles, and to mansions and villas seeking to imitate, on a reduced scale, Horace Walpole's famous "folly," Strawberry Hill (1750–76). During the Regency, domestic architecture went increasingly neo-Gothic, and of 214 edifices erected during a great wave of church-building, 174 were in a style confidently described as Gothic. As the fashion spread in Victorian times it also was applied to railway stations, town halls, banks, hotels, schools, lunatic asylums, lodging houses, jails, public baths, public libraries, and public houses. Even the Crystal Palace, the monument to modernity, had a "medieval court" displaying stained glass, encaustic tiles, and other freshly manufactured reminders of a departed age.

Innumerable old churches and not a few cathedrals were damaged by the rage for "restoring" their fabrics and furnishings according to what an enlightened age thought Gothic should be. Despite the even earlier (Saxon or Norman) origins of some, they were ruthlessly Gothicized in the interests of respectability and up-to-dateness. Young Thomas Hardy participated in the operation to the extent that, as an apprentice architect in Dorchester, he made many drawings of the churches his firm was commissioned to refurbish. The well-meaning but ill-conceived vandalism that went on for many years in the misapplied name of restoration had, perhaps, something to be said for it: it did result in many buildings' being rescued from the total destruction, through neglect and sheer deterioration, that would otherwise have been their fate, and at the same time, it provided valuable lessons in the science of architectural preservation. But the frequent tastelessness and disregard for historical authenticity that marked the process stirred William Morris and others to apoplectic wrath and resulted in their founding the Society for the Protection of Ancient Buildings. This organization, familiarly known as "Anti-Scrape" because it opposed the practice of chipping off weathered stone from the buildings' exteriors, was the prototype of similar ones in our own day, among them an English society dedicated to preserving the most notable examples of nineteenth-century Gothic.

The medieval craze had its comic side. In 1839 a twenty-six-year-old sportsman, the thirteenth Earl of Eglinton, got the notion of holding at his Scottish estate a magnificent chivalric tournament, complete with chain-mailed jousters on caparisoned horses, a court of noble women attending the Queen of Beauty, and the pageantry and (preferably) bloodless combat proper to medieval entertainment. The cream of British society was invited and spent a huge sum—in a year of great economic distress among the people—equipping itself with gorgeous medieval costumes, armor, and all the correct accouterments. The host himself laid out £40,000. On the opening day, there was a thirty-mile traffic jam on the Ayr-Glasgow road that led past Eglinton, and the grounds were crowded with 100,000 commoners, some of whom had come great distances to see Scott's romances brought to life. But within a few hours a raging storm sent them struggling homeward through morasses of mud, and the blue-blooded cast of hundreds, finding that jousting under umbrellas was impractical, retreated into tents and other temporary structures that spouted water at every crevice. There, from under medieval hairdos now become sodden and lank, they beheld their armor beginning to rust and the noble ladies' gowns stained with mud and shrunken. To keep their hand in, some of the knights tilted with mops and brooms in the waterlogged ballroom, and when the sun eventually reappeared the ladies made parasols by sticking arrows through their programs. The press had a field day of its own.

Hilarious as the ill-fated Eglinton Tournament was, it was also symptomatic. Its glamorized medievalism anticipated Disraeli's Young England movement with its theory that the revival of chivalric *noblesse oblige* was the solution for the nation's social ills, and it bore a certain oblique relationship to the Oxford Movement (below, pp. 208–15) as well. And it found its way into literature, most notably in Disraeli's *Endymion* but also in the mock tournament Browning satirized in "The Flight of the Duchess" and in an episode in Tennyson's *The Princess.*

But these last were light variations on what was otherwise a serious Victorian theme. Tennyson wrote a number of poems on medieval subjects, "The Lady of Shalott" and "Sir Galahad" as well as the long *Idylls;* Arnold and Swinburne also took up the Tristram story; the three poets associated with the Pre-Raphaelites adopted medieval themes as often as did the painters. Rossetti, Swinburne, and Morris retold (or invented) medieval narratives, most frequently in ballad form. Sometimes the poets simply shared the fondness the romantics had felt for the picturesque or for the pleasing mystery attached to remoteness. Others, most notably Morris, portrayed medieval scenes and episodes with a hard realism far removed from sentimental fancy. But there was a more pressing reason for this recurrent evocation of the Middle Ages: the wish to discover there a society more stable and equitable, an intellectual temper more unified and free of doubt, than the Victorian age was capable of. The faster the rate of change and the more bewildering their orientation became both physically and intellectually, the more some Victorians longed for a fixed order. The Middle Ages, they persuaded themselves, had provided such a spiritual *terra firma* for the people who had lived then. Change was so slow as to be negligible; cathedrals took centuries to build.

Such was the case also (or so the Victorians liked to think) with the other civilizations whose romantic memory they invoked. Thus poets like Swinburne dwelt upon the serenity of ancient Greece, and essayists like Walter Pater and John Addington Symonds found a refuge in the Italian Renaissance. Attitudes such as this constituted what one might call a preferential view of history, but the Victorians' psychic need for such resting places in the past over-ruled their realism.

The result was one of the period's most favored artistic devices, the use of chronological contrast. Robert Southey had shown the way in his *Sir Thomas More; or Colloquies on the Progress and Prospects of Society* (1829), in which, with More as a mouthpiece, he contrasted sixteenth-century society with that of the nineteenth, to the latter's considerable disadvantage. Seven years later the newly converted Catholic architect, Augustus Welby Pugin, published *Contrasts; or a Parallel between the Noble Edifices of the Fourteenth and Fifteenth Centuries and Similar Buildings of the Present Day, Shewing the Present Decay of Taste,* an album in which pairs of facing engravings compared medieval buildings, the product of a society at peace with itself and God, with scenes in the modern city, whose ugly buildings were emblematic of dehumanization and wage slavery. This comparative technique, recalling Hamlet's command to his mother, "Look here, upon this picture, and on this," was used by Carlyle in *Past and Present,* in which he re-created the twelfth-century Benedictine abbey of Bury St. Edmunds, ruled by the strong but benevolent Abbot Samson, to place in bitter juxtaposition with it the drifting, leaderless condition of England in 1842. In *Idylls of the King* Tennyson revived Arthurian legend to read his contemporaries a lesson on their materialism and sensuality. Throughout their careers as social critics, Ruskin and Morris used the Middle Ages as the very exemplar of the good society, medieval art bearing witness (so they argued) to the contentment of the individual worker in a society to which he *belonged.*

Nearly all the Victorian writers who used the past-and-present device found in favor of the past age, whatever it may have been: the Middle Ages in the case of Arnold's "Stanzas from the Grande Chartreuse," the seventeenth century in that of his "Scholar-Gypsy," and Periclean Greece in that of his cultural criticism. Even when specific comparison of the unhappy present with the self-fulfilled past was not intended, Victorian writers often achieved a distancing effect by transferring a Victorian situation to some earlier era. Thus Browning, in a group of poems, "Caliban upon Setebos," "An Epistle . . . of Karshish," "Cleon," and "A Death in the Desert," commented obliquely and sometimes with mordant irony upon modern religious thinking. Each of his characters, the half-man, half-beast Caliban, two contemporaries of St. Paul, and the last surviving apostle, is of his own age, but what he says is implicitly addressed to the present: *de te fabula.*

4. Progress?

The Victorians' expanded apprehension of time and history, therefore, not only was psychological and metaphysical but involved questions of social value. Time and change obviously were inseparable; Heraclitus' dictum "All is flux" was constantly before them. That they lived in the midst of change was undeniable. It was not a matter of faith but of common observation. But flux in what direction?

To the typical Victorian mind, sanguine in temperament and materialistic in its values, the answer was a confident "Forward." However fatuous and shallowly grounded may have been their faith that change meant progress, the Victorians were lucky they had it. It gave them what they most needed, a dependable source of strength to cope with problems so large and complex that they often seemed insuperable. The eighteenth century derived satisfaction from the status quo; the Victorians derived theirs from the very lack of one.

The immediate source of their confidence was the great strides man had lately taken toward fulfilling his oldest dream, the conquest of his physical environment. Man and nature had always been at strife, and now at last, thanks to the advance of scientific knowledge, man was winning, bringing nature meekly to heel. In the course of the century, such fields of scientific inquiry as electromagnetics, organic chemistry, bacteriology, thermodynamics, and astrophysics were opened for exploration. Although in some fields practical applications necessarily lagged far behind theory, technology had already constructed ample proofs of science's benefit to mankind. In fact, the national genius for empiricism had produced a race of inventors a century in advance of the pure scientists such as James Clerk-Maxwell and John Tyndall who were to come into prominence during Victoria's reign. It was native technology which had made Britain the birthplace of the industrial revolution, with all the benefits that that implied. Macaulay spoke for his pragmatic generation when he exalted the edible fruits of Bacon's natural philosophy over the showy but useless flowers of Plato's intellectual hothouse. No Platonist had ever invented a steam locomotive, gas lighting, the electric telegraph, chloroform, or any of a hundred kinds of machine tools.

Though focused on material improvements, the Victorian confidence in progress extended to the less tangible aspects of life, to social relations and even morality. The brain which had bridged chasms, driven tunnels through mountains, and sent steamboats to defy adverse winds was just as capable of solving the problems of society. "Human engineering" was a term unknown to the Victorians, but it well suggests the logical leap by which the methods that promised total mastery of the physical environment were thought to be applicable to society. Somehow—and here the formula suddenly became nebulous—the conquest of the material universe would be accompanied by man's mastery of himself. But understanding of the processes of the mind and of social dynamics was far in arrears of the physical sciences. Hope for the millennium was based on something called "moral progress," the premise that human betterment was a built-in concomitant of material progress. By a happy arrangement of Providence, cosmic tendency and the Victorians' ambition coincided; the spirit of the universe was on their side. Which is but another way of saying that they were so convinced of the definitiveness of their moral and social values that, by a singular exercise of anthropomorphism, they read their aims into the process of change itself.

Although many Victorians in places of intellectual as well as political authority gave bracing voice to a doctrine which uncounted numbers of lesser men accepted as a description of world purpose, belief in progress was by no means universal or unqualified. There was, for instance, the troublesome possibility that progress in one area might well be canceled out by retrogression in another; the various kinds of process were not necessarily compatible, merging into a single forward thrust. Dickens, in many ways a typically bustling middle-class Victorian, began to have his doubts as early as *Dombey and Son* (1846–48), and in successive novels, to the very end of his life, his vision of society and its prospects grew steadily gloomier. The greatest prophet-voices of the age, Carlyle, Arnold, and Ruskin, rejected the easy assumption that man was generously fated to live in a world that, with appropriate assistance, was getting better and better. And in sharp contrast with the romantic poets in their perfectibilian fervor—Shelley in the final movement of *Prometheus Unbound,* Keats in *Hyperion* —the Victorian poets did not celebrate the idea of progress with any great conviction. Occasional traces of the assumption can be found in Tennyson's early political poems, "Locksley Hall," and some of his laureate pieces. Swinburne's political rhapsodies looked forward to a happy consummation for mankind, but they were devoted to the prospects of the race at large under proper management and seldom had anything to do with the immediate idea of English progress in the nineteenth century. Browning was convinced that man as an individual could progress and improve through sheer moral determination, but he said little on the outlook for humanity. Arnold's poems certainly lent no comfort to the optimists. And in "Locksley Hall Sixty Years After" (1886) the aged Tennyson, echoing the spirit that was then being expressed by men much younger, cried out in all-embracing disillusionment, "Let us hush this cry of 'Forward' till ten thousand years have gone."

The fly in the ointment, then as now, was the pointed question: Do "improvements" such as Macaulay hymned in his essay on Southey's *Colloquies* really bring "happiness" (however defined) or even contentment? As Coleridge pointed out as early as 1829, concentration on means rather than ends was the besetting sin of the times. The age created its own metaphor for itself. Separated by a generation, Carlyle (in "Signs of the Times," 1829) and Arnold (in *Culture and Anarchy,* 1867–68) both seized upon the metaphor of "machinery" to epitomize the innovations in modern life which so fascinated their contemporaries that they failed to ask the eternally pertinent question, "To what purpose?" Machinery, in the literal sense, was one of the main exhibits in the vanity fair of Progress: it was steam engines and all the machines they drove which sped Victorian England toward an ever more prosperous and comfortable destiny. Figuratively, machinery was the predominant symbol of the age's harnessing of nature, and by easy extension it was also a symbol of social and political innovations. But no newly invented machine, however ingenious or impressive, was a good in itself; what mattered was its product.

Wealth? Comfort? Knowledge? Freedom? Democracy? These were instrumentalities, not final results; they might or might not conduce toward good. "Your middle-class man," Arnold wrote in *Friendship's Garland,* "thinks it is the highest pitch of development and civilisation when his letters are carried twelve times a day from Islington to Camberwell [two dreary inner suburbs of London], and from Camberwell to Islington, and if railway-trains run to and fro between them every quarter of an hour. He thinks it is nothing that the trains only carry him from an illiberal, dismal life at Islington to an illiberal, dismal life at Camberwell; and the letters only tell him that such is the life there." All the machinery in the world—express trains, steamships, the secret ballot, representative government, free trade, a cheap and independent press, religious toleration, universal education, mass-produced wallpaper—is worthless unless it somehow contributes to the enrichment of an individual human being's existence. Statistics of gross national product, the increasing volume of foreign trade, and greater life expectancy say nothing about the quality of life as a whole.

On such grounds as these, the more thoughtful Victorians challenged the identification of change (process) with improvement (progress). Some rejected the assumption that, irrespective of destination, process worked in a straight unending line. They pointed instead to historical evidences of other kinds of movement, none of which supported the idea of progress. There was, for example, the cyclic alternation of ebb and flow, thesis and antithesis, decay-death-rebirth which in former times had been figured as a pendulum or wheel, right-left, up-down, and therefore, from the human point of view, good-bad. The fate of a given society depended on which of the two alternating phases of process it happened to coincide with. Here again the archaeologists delivered a sobering message to the prideful Victorians. The testimony of excavations and prehistoric caves was that, over the millennia, numerous civilizations had risen and fallen, and that between the ruin of one and the rise of the next there had been long centuries of barbarism and cultural sterility. Far from being the first great cultures, Greece and Rome had been preceded and accompanied by others of comparable achievement, not merely in the Mediterranean and Near East but in Asia and central America. And every one had fallen into utter oblivion. Thus the "ebb and flow" image in Arnold's "Dover Beach" was a peculiarly appropriate symbol of the sensitive Victorian's awareness that for every mile of progress there might well be a neutralizing mile of retrograde action.

The direct antithesis of progress was sheer decadence, a retrograde action *not* accompanied by the more or less consoling prospect that in the natural course of things the movement was bound to reverse itself. This ancient interpretation of cosmic process, the basis of the Golden Age myth without its hopeful modern addendum that good times will come again when conditions are right, received support in the middle of the century from the theoretical physicists. According to the second law of thermodynamics, announced in 1850 and immediately adopted by Dickens for the running imagery of *Bleak House,* the irreversible conversion of energy to heat in the cosmos will ultimately turn it into a lifeless mass of incandescence. According to some geologists, similarly, the earth, having passed through the creative phase in which mountains and seas were formed, now had entered the final stage of process, "decrepitude" or disintegration. In the face of this postulation of universal and irreparable decay, the Victorians' confidence in the ongoing, divinely ordained improvement of man's estate could not but seem shallow, narrow, and petty—not to say ill-founded. Combined with the parallel tendencies of evolutionary theory, these intimations of cosmic mortality contributed to the somber hue of some late Victorian poetry and of fiction like Hardy's.

As with the universe, so with contemporary society. From time to time, Victorian poets struck the mutability note familiar in Elizabethan literature and now all the more melancholy because of the contrasting background. In "A Toccata of Galuppi's" Browning evoked the decadent spirit of late eighteenth-century Venice, with its proud, beautiful women and its confidence that the joy of living would never cease. But eventually "the kissing had to stop," and in the ruins of Venetian grandeur a cricket creaks, "Dust and ashes!"

"I feel chilly and grown old": so did Victorians other than the speaker in Browning's poem. To them, the robust health attributed to their society was illusory. Poets like Arnold repeatedly used images of bodily and mental disease to describe what it felt like to live in mid-Victorian England: "sick fatigue," fever, numbness, infection. Carlyle, in *Past and Present,* alluded to disease enveloping the whole of society: "fever-fits," "chronic gangrene," "social malady," the plague. Most moral diagnosticians agreed that it was fatty degeneration of the soul which had put English society on what they were convinced was to prove its deathbed unless stringent remedies were applied. But what remedies? Carlyle laughed mirthlessly at the quack nostrums the politicians vended, calling them "Morrison's pills" in allusion to the "vegetable universal medicine" which earned a fortune for the man who concocted it. Arnold complained that the "hourly anodynes" prescribed by others were no better than laudanum—or, in our day, aspirin—which temporarily killed the pain of existence but did nothing toward removing its cause.

At the end of the century, on the occasion of the Queen's diamond jubilee (1897), Kipling's "Recessional" struck an unwelcome discord in the martial music and imperial pageantry:

> Far-called, our navies melt away;
> On dune and headland sinks the fire:
> Lo, all our pomp of yesterday
> Is one with Nineveh and Tyre!
> Judge of the Nations, spare us yet,
> Lest we forget—lest we forget!

It was a far cry from Macaulay, attesting sixty-seven years earlier, in the pages of the *Edinburgh Review,* his serene confidence in the progress of a society deriving its impetus from the factory system and laissez-faire economics. It had also seemed a far cry from Nineveh and Tyre, and the vanished civilization of Ozymandias, to a proud nation on whose flag the sun never set. But perhaps the distance was to prove not so great after all.

IV

THE UTILITARIAN SPIRIT

1. Benthamism

TWO IDEOLOGIES molded early and mid-Victorian social and cultural life: Utilitarianism and Evangelicalism. Together they were responsible for much that was unappealing—to some Victorians as to us—in the age's thought and manners, as well as for social reforms which slowly mitigated the curse the industrial revolution had laid upon people's lives. As a distinctive religious party, Evangelicalism (the subject of Chapter V) peaked, as we say, about 1830; Utilitarianism in its practical applications had its maximum impact two decades later. But both left their ineradicable imprint upon the whole of the Victorian period.

The remarkable thing about the two ideologies was not their differences, which were many, but the number of ways in which, beginning from different premises and often by sheer accident, they collaborated toward the same ends. "Both," writes a modern historian, "are poles apart in their intellectual postulates, but in their methods of thought and in their practical results they are very much the same. In each case a hard dogmatic position is chosen and adhered to without the slightest concession to the fact that it is necessary sometimes to respect other people's opinions, and the implications of that position are put into effect remorselessly and coldly. They were fit creeds for a period of emotional tension and fanaticism." [1] In time, their original rigidity softened and they took on a more humane quality. In most of the literature in which their ideas are reflected or attacked, however, they are represented as still possessing the full measure of that rigidity.

Utilitarianism, the secular member of the pair, is also called "Benthamism," a virtual synonym, but in strict usage referring to the pure form of the philosophy held by the doctrinaire enthusiasts who gathered about Jeremy Bentham. Another alternate name, most often used to designate the creed of the Benthamite members of Parliament and their supporters, is "Philosophic Radicalism." * In ordinary practice, all three terms were used almost interchangeably, as they are in modern historical writing and will be in these pages. Most broadly and loosely applied, they refer to the socio-economic-political ideology and set of values held by the Victorian middle class—to the entrepreneurial mentality which dominated the period and adopted these tenets to rationalize its actions and aims, habits and prejudices.

By whatever name it is called, Utilitarianism was a hybrid philosophy partaking equally of eighteenth-century French rationalism and eighteenth-century English materialism. It was introduced into the mainstream of post-Napoleonic thought by Jeremy Bentham, a rich, amiable, eccentric bachelor whose lifelong occupation was devising master syntheses of economic, political, and social thought.

---

* It should be pointed out here that in the Victorian vocabulary "radical" was what Ruskin would have called a chameleon word. As today, its meaning and connotation varied with the users' sympathies. In contemporary writings, its application has to be ascertained from the context. In general, it referred to (a) the Philosophic Radicals —in practical usage, the "philosophic" was often dropped—who advocated Benthamite principles inside and outside Parliament, as well as their frequent allies, liberal but non-Benthamite businessmen and politicians; and (b) popular (working-class) movements agitating for basic political, social, and/or economic reform. The latter's objectives changed from period to period; if any common goal persisted through these shifts, it was that of universal manhood suffrage.

Into this grandiose ideology were absorbed many of the leading concepts of the French *philosophes* as well as those of Hobbes, Hume, Locke, Hartley, and Priestley, among their British counterparts.

Bentham's first major work, his *Introduction to the Principles of Morals and Legislation,* had been published as early as 1789, the year the Bastille fell. There could scarcely have been a less opportune moment. During the ensuing decades of war with France and loathing of revolutionary doctrines, any proposal to cope with the problems of society through the use of reason (and, what was worse, to subject all existing institutions to a hard, fresh look) was regarded as sheer Jacobinism. Bentham, the "great questioner of things established," as John Stuart Mill called him, therefore wisely kept his great schemes to himself.

But by the end of the war he was equipped with a corps of disciples ("Benthamites" in the strict sense) gathered by his near neighbor in Westminster, a personally unattractive Scotsman named James Mill. Their word-of-mouth enthusiasm atoned for the handicap Bentham's literary style laid upon the dissemination of his ideas. Never especially graceful, by this time it had degenerated into a jagged, impenetrable prose which led Hazlitt to observe, "His works have been translated into French—they ought to be translated into English." But Bentham's friends served him well, and despite the suspicion under which it still labored, his ideology made its way into the forefront of theoretical discussion in the twenties. Its proponents emerged as a force in practical politics in 1832, the year of Bentham's death at the age of eighty-four. Between fifty and 120 inner-circle Benthamites and sympathizers were elected to the first reformed Parliament. For the next decade they constituted a vocal and sometimes influential pressure group, aspiring to but never achieving the strength and status of a full-fledged party. As proponents of long-range, sweeping reform, they resisted any formal affiliation with the Whigs, whose reform impulses were sporadic and at all events moderate. But their occasional support of Whig stopgap measures (on the principle that half a loaf is better than none) gave them the illusory appearance of being aligned with that party and of lending theoretical support to measures whose true motivation lay in the exigencies of old-fashioned partisan politics.

The tag phrase indelibly associated with Utilitarianism, "the greatest happiness for the greatest number," was borrowed from Joseph Priestley, the late eighteenth-century Unitarian theologian and discoverer of oxygen. Its Hobbesian assumption was that self-interest is the prime, in fact the only, motivation behind human conduct, and that the achievement of pleasure and the avoidance of pain alone constitute that self-interest. It subscribed, as Nassau Senior, a leading exponent and apologist, put it with disarming candor, to "an arbitrary definition of man, as a being who invariably does that by which he may obtain the greatest amount of necessaries, conveniences and luxuries, with the smallest amount of labour and physical self-denial with which they can be obtained in the existing state of knowledge." Utilitarianism was, therefore, wholly hedonistic; it made no allowance for the promptings of conscience, or for the humane impulses of which the Shaftesburyan ethic had made so much a century earlier—the forces of generosity, mercy, compassion, self-sacrifice, love. Benthamite ethics had nothing to do with Christian morality.

The only determinant of personal or social action, in any given situation, was the demonstrated preponderance of "good" results over "bad" results. The demonstration was mathematical, by means of what, in the Benthamite argot, was known as the "felicific calculus" or "moral arithmetic." *

---

* Had it been available to them, the Benthamites would have happily fed all their questions of moral and social choice into a digital computer. They almost had one. A single-minded contemporary named Charles Babbage spent sixty years and £20,000 of his fortune as well as £17,000 of government money trying to perfect a calculator, and he nearly succeeded. Parts of the two machines he constructed are in the Science Museum in South Kensington, London.

The formula for deciding whether or not to adopt a given choice of action, be it an individual deed or a law affecting millions, was simplicity itself:

$$\text{PLEASURE} \qquad vs. \qquad \text{PAIN}$$
$$a + b + c + d + e + f \qquad\qquad a + b + c + d + e + f$$

where the letters represent six categories of anticipated effects: intensity, duration, certainty, propinquity (the closeness of the effect to the person(s) involved), fecundity (the degree to which the primary effect will be followed by secondary effects of a similar kind and extent), and purity (the absence of undesirable side-effects). These six qualities were to be taken into account in deciding any individual's best course of action; when a body of people was involved, a seventh quantity, the number affected, was added to the computation. The "good" results, or pleasure (defined by Bentham as "*profit, . . . or convenience, or advantage, benefit, emolument, happiness,* and so forth"), were compared with the painful results ("*mischief, or inconvenience, or disadvantage, or loss, or unhappiness,* and so forth"). When the correct weightings were assigned each factor and the balance struck, the heavier side of the scale determined the action. The sole criterion was quantitative, the arithmetical relationship between units of "pleasure" and units of "pain." Neither the quality of the supposed effects nor the possibility that individuals might differ in their notion of happiness or the degree of their altruism affected the Benthamite calculation. Presumably every human being on earth prized nothing but material values. Nor was any account taken of the happiness of those who did not belong to the greatest number. They doubtless had to accept their sacrificial position on the scale's high beam with whatever disinterested resignation they could muster.

But how was a social group to decide what constituted the greatest happiness for the greatest number? The answer was government by a representative legislature. For this reason, the Benthamites advocated universal suffrage as well as the five other Chartist principles, all of which, as a matter of fact, Bentham had advocated. They regarded the First Reform Bill as an initial step toward the far-off day when Parliament would be an infallibly accurate mirror of the wisest wishes of all the people. But they recognized that, for the present, the voters and their elected representatives would be far from agreeing on the best course of action in a given situation. The felicific calculating machine was a sure guide only if it were accurately programmed, and it could be so programmed only if every man whose personal interests were fed into it knew what they really were and what relation they bore to the interests of society. That final insight into self-love vis-à-vis social welfare could come only with universal education, which would teach every man how to define his motives through the use of reason. Pending the comprehensive reconciliation of self and society, the carrot and stick had to be provided, as we will note later on, by legislation.

The system of moral arithmetic illustrates the pedantic dependence on formula, the confidence in the universal and uniform operation of theoretical moral forces, which ruled the Utilitarian mind. Not the least of the anomalies associated with Benthamism is the fact that an ideology advocating inveterate skepticism toward all the institutions and practices of organized society made no provision for self-criticism. And nowhere is Utilitarianism more characteristic of the century in which it originated than in its unquestioning belief in the existence of immutable laws of human behavior. Benthamism was Newtonian mechanism applied to ethics. It was not accidental, then, that Benthamism played an important role in the early history of what came to be known as social *science*. The claims to scientific authority which came to be advanced by the branches of learning gathered under that name were largely derived from the Benthamite assumption, supported by similar assumptions in contemporary French thought.

2. *Political Economy*

Inseparable from Utilitarianism—for most practical purposes the two schools merged into one about 1830—was classical economics, or, to use the common Victorian designation, which often served as a further loose synonym for Utilitarianism, "political economy." The political economists, practitioners of what Carlyle called "the dismal science," held that there were economic laws which were as sovereign in that field as the law of gravity was in physics, or the pleasure-pain principle in Benthamite ethics. Their system was fixed and incontrovertible, and like Utilitarianism, it bore the cachet of mathematical as well as philosophical authority.

The first of the iron laws on which political economy rested was that enunciated by the Reverend Thomas Malthus in his *Essay on the Principle of Population* (1798): that the supply of food increases in arithmetical progression (2:4: 6:8:10:12 . . . or any series in which a constant number is added) while the population increases in geometrical progression (2:4:8:16:32:64 . . .). Malthus thus threw cold water on the dreams of such perfectibilitarians as the French philosopher Condorcet, the radical English theorist William Godwin, and Godwin's son-in-law Shelley, by arguing that the Utopia they so confidently expected could never materialize so long as the population was fated to exceed the food supply. The blunt fact was that a considerable part of the human race was doomed to a life of sickness and starvation leading to early death, for this, like war, was necessary to narrow the gap between ravenous mouths and food in a state of eternal scarcity.

In the much-revised second edition of his *Essay* (1803) Malthus struck a somewhat brighter note. A more humane expedient, he had decided, was available: "moral restraint." Perhaps the masses of people, who bore the brunt of the hunger that was built into Creation, could be educated or coerced to limit their own numbers and thus dispense the Four Horsemen of the Apocalypse from the necessity of doing the job for them. Although "Malthusianism" later became a Victorian euphemism for birth control, this misrepresents Malthus' intention; for by "moral restraint" he simply meant continence, especially by delaying marriage and so reducing the number of fertile years a marriage would have. If enough people would voluntarily abstain from procreation, perhaps the dreams of the radical political philosophers could be realized after all. But Carlyle, whose stubborn Scottish realism sometimes triumphed over his German metaphysics, knew better: "Smart Sally in our alley proves all-too fascinating to brisk Tom in yours: can Tom be called on to make pause, and calculate the demand for labour in the British Empire first? . . . O wonderful Malthusian prophets! Millenniums are undoubtedly coming, must come one way or the other: but will it be, think you, by twenty millions of working people simultaneously striking work in that department . . . ?"

Malthusianism, collaborating with Benthamism, made its greatest impact on Victorian life and thought in connection with the bitterly controversial Poor Law Amendment Act of 1834. Nowhere was the effect of the new "scientific" ways of regarding social problems better illustrated. Under laws dating back to Elizabeth I, each parish—the basic local political unit from the time of the Reformation—was responsible for the care of its own indigent and unfortunate. Although the system had been devised to suit the specific conditions of sixteenth-century rural society, no attempt had been made to adapt it to the radically altered social and economic conditions of later days. Beginning in 1795, some parishes adopted the plan devised in that year by the magistrates of Berkshire, meeting in the village of Speenhamland. This was a primitive guaranteed minimum income scheme by which low wages were supplemented from public funds, the dole being scaled to the size of the family, so that, as in modern welfare practice, each additional child meant extra money—in this case, eighteen pence a week. As the principles of political economy gained adherents, this was regarded as a most unsatisfactory way of dealing with the problem of the poor, because it was inefficient and wasteful and put a premium on anti-social fecundity and immorality. "Moralists complained that too often no distinction was made between legitimate and illegitimate offspring; pictures were drawn of the virtuous village maiden working early and late for a scanty wage, while the bold hussy, the mother of half a dozen bastards, lived in idleness and sluttish abundance on the parish allowance which she received for her ill-gotten progeny." [2] These pictures, of course, were exaggerations, but in their very overstatement they were typical of the thinking behind many proposed reforms.

To do away with this tax-supported, irresponsible breeding, Parliament in 1834 decreed the limitation of outdoor relief to those who were unable to work because of age or infirmity, and directed that, in general, able-bodied paupers and their families be sent to workhouses. In accordance with the Benthamite principles of efficiency, economy, and uniformity, the system of workhouse unions, initiated in 1782, was extended throughout the country. Several adjacent parishes joined to erect one capacious, cost-cutting workhouse or union, as it was called—the latter word serving for the individual building as well as the inter-parish consortium. Among the poor, the workhouse at once acquired the appellation of "Poor Law Bastille," an indication of the hatred the new system attracted not only from its present and prospective clients but from all who regarded the new Poor Law as proof that the stony-hearted Benthamites were out to victimize the destitute.

Despite an initial impression that went so deep as still to be preserved in some modern books, there never was any intention of eliminating outdoor relief. But many people believed there was, and that the workhouse was therefore designed to be a multipurpose catchall for the unfortunate as well as the feckless. Into it, according to the popular conception, would creep the sucklings and the senile, the robust and the crippled, the energetic and the lazy alike. The fact was that only a minority of those receiving public assistance got it in the workhouse. In 1839, for example, there were only 98,000 inmates, as against 560,000 receiving the dole in their own cottages. But the myth was powerful enough to generate a class bitterness that would not subside for many years.

Whatever the exaggerations, the reality was bad enough. The Bastilles were not misnamed, because they were not merely built to look like prisons. In effect, they were prisons. Inmates had to wear distinctive garb, as old Nandy does in Dickens' *Little Dorrit;* they were allowed few visitors; until 1842 they had to be silent at meals; and they were subject to strict discipline. But the term "workhouse" was not misapplied, either, because everyone except the hopelessly incapacitated had to work for his bread, often by stonebreaking, grinding corn, or picking oakum (pulling apart the fibers of old rope, used in caulking the seams of ships).

The workhouses were conducted on the assumption, widespread among the middle class, that poverty was the result of laziness alone, not of misfortune caused by hard times or other circumstances beyond the individual's control. The alternative to earning an honest living on one's own therefore had to be made so unattractive that the poor would be *forced* to find work outside rather than submit to the semi-starvation and indignities of the workhouse. Far from encouraging idleness, as the Speenhamland system was thought to have done, the new system made sure that the price of poverty to be paid in the unions was a scale of living lower than that enjoyed by the poorest-paid laborer outside. To achieve this without killing the inmates took considerable skill on the part of the overseers and staff. As several scandals revealed, they were not always successful in this delicate undertaking. Furthermore—and here the philosophy was pure Malthusianism—the workhouse required separation of the sexes. A condition of the meager succor it afforded was the breakup of the family. To those who still managed to retain a shred of self-respect, admission to the workhouse was the final blow. The Speenhamland system had been demeaning enough, because by using tax money to absolve the landowner from paying a living wage, it had required even the most willing worker to become a charity case to make ends meet. Now, entering the workhouse branded one a failure, because supposedly only the "idle," a damning word in the Victorian social vocabulary, sought that last refuge; the industrious poor somehow managed to cope—or were expected to.

To proponents of the new system, Christ's "The poor always have ye with you," rightly interpreted, added religious sanction to the fatalism inherent in all political economy, not merely Malthusianism. Those who were poor would always be poor; in the nature of the case, there was no hope of better times to come. As for St. Paul's celebration of charity as the crowning Christian virtue, when Parson Malthus confronted the apostle, Malthus won hands down. The poor might always be with us, but their prolonged survival, as encumbrances to an earth with a perpetually limited yield of food, did not have to be encouraged by charity, nor their numbers increased on the assumption that charity, in behalf of the heaven that was warranted to provide, would always be around to reward their animal-like fertility. A hard doctrine, but there it was. Little wonder, then, that the poor were so hostile to the new, efficient method of punishing them for being prone to misfortune.

They were not alone in their anger. The new Poor Law was the first of the many social abuses that would animate Dickens' satirical pen. In *Oliver Twist* the two systems were mingled; between them, in Dickens' view, there was not much to choose. Almost thirty years later he renewed his attack in his account of old Betty Higden's determination to save enough so that she would not have to die in the workhouse and be buried in a pauper's grave (*Our Mutual*

Friend). Carlyle, Disraeli, and Kingsley joined Dickens in denouncing Malthusianism and its clever solution of the welfare problem. Dickens not only inveighed against the principle, but, like Mr. Micawber, he defied it: he fathered ten children.

By mid-Victorian times, Malthusianism had quietly become a dead issue. The population of England and Wales doubled in 1801–51 and almost did so again in the second half of the century, but the predicted catastrophe did not occur. On the contrary, the nation prospered and the people were better fed. Improved farming practices at home and the opening of the vast food resources of the American plains and the Antipodes—developments which Malthus, erroneously assuming a fixed rate of production, did not anticipate—removed one specter from the Victorian scene. But of course it has reappeared in our own day, in a shape more frightening than anything Malthus' most convinced followers could have envisaged because it is now stripped of the former comforting assumption that only the poor need be affected.

Intimately associated with Malthus' law in the creed of political economy were David Ricardo's theories of the distribution of wealth, expounded in his *Principles of Political Economy and Taxation* (1817). As the population grew, a steadily increasing amount of sub-marginal land had to be put under cultivation to feed it. Regardless of the reduced yield, the rent the landowners got remained the same, and they thus received an "unearned increment" on their property. But higher food prices also meant a widening discrepancy between the workers' money wages and their real wages. Merely to maintain life at a subsistence level became more and more difficult. And if the workers were paid higher wages to compensate for this shrinkage of purchasing power, their employers' profits decreased. Hence there was a three-way antagonism between landowners, industrialists, and labor. As far as the latter two were concerned, the crux lay in how the "wage fund" (the amount left after the landowners got their share of the nation's wealth in the form of rent) would be divided among the producers. The increase in population meant that the supply of labor normally would exceed the demand. It was possible, therefore, for the employer to pay low wages and so safeguard his profit margin. The more workers there were to share the available wage fund, the smaller the portion each could expect. If, on the other hand, wages were increased, the workers would raise larger families and so aggravate the initial problem; for it was an axiom of political economy that the more the masses prospered, the more prolifically they bred. By doing so, they made it ever more certain that they would never rise above the subsistence level.

Here was support, from another angle, for the Malthusian argument that society should limit its numbers. If the population were reduced, by whatever means—moral restraint, disease, slow starvation, industrial accidents, "vice" —the labor force would diminish in turn, and, theoretically at least, the survivors could enjoy a slightly larger share of the limited wages available. Like Malthusianism, this principle strengthened the determinism which permeated political economy. The employer, fortunately for his conscience, found himself helpless to raise wages. To do so would be to disrupt the delicately balanced laws which nature had ordained.

"Nature"? Yes: in fact, God. Because, in literal truth, the laws of classical economics, including Adam Smith's, Malthus', and Ricardo's, were attributed to Divine Providence. The line of thinking that resulted in this reconciliation of Mammonism and theology is traceable most immediately to the Reverend William Paley's *Natural Theology, or Evidences of the Existence and Attributes of the Deity Collected from the Appearances of Nature* (1802). In this classic treatise on a familiar line of argument in eighteenth-century thought, Paley had sought to demonstrate that the physical attributes of natural creation, from the most microscopic insect to towering man, bore universal witness to God's infinite benevolence. How else could one account for the genius by which every creature was adapted to his environment? From young shrimps cavorting on the beach in sheer joy at their adjustment to crustacean life, to man with his beautifully calculated muscular arrangements, secretions, alimentary tract, blood vessels, and intricately designed organs of perception—"The examination of the eye [is] a cure for atheism," Paley declared—all living nature witnessed the merciful wisdom and supernal ingenuity of God's contrivance.

So did political economy. The connection between Paley's divine science and the dismal one was forged by, among others, the contributors to the series of *Bridgewater Treatises* (1833–36), an endowed symposium dedicated to proving "the Power, Wisdom, and Goodness of God, as manifested in the Creation." More than one of these writers argued that political economy was part of God's plan, of which Malthus and Ricardo were but the appointed expositors. The cosmos, living creation, and the affairs of men, including their buying and selling of goods in the marketplace, were subject to dovetailed laws all emanating from the same source. It was Providence, no less, that arranged that men should be in eternal peril of starvation, because this would teach them a wholesome lesson. As a modern student of this strange alliance between theology and economics sardonically puts it, "Let us glorify God that the means of subsistence are insufficient to sustain the population, because only His benevolence could have devised so infallible a system for impressing upon man the necessity, and hence the virtue, of prudence, industry, self-denial, thrift, and forbearance." [3]

But praise was not ordinarily lifted to God, a practice which was felt, in such a context, to be somehow improper. Instead, eighteenth-century usage had sanctioned "nature" as a synonym for the Supreme Being, and this was a—one might almost say providential—windfall for those who preached what might be called evangelical economics. At a single stroke, the real culprit could be decently concealed and yet His authority invoked. No one could be offended by the citation of "nature" as the lawgiver regulating supply and demand, but neither could anybody who understood what nature really meant fail to realize how solemn were His economic ordinances.

3. Laissez Faire and the Sacredness of Property

Over the preceding pages has hovered the as yet un-explored idea of laissez faire. Half a century earlier (1776), in *The Wealth of Nations,* the Scots philosopher Adam Smith had propounded the doctrine that society is but the sum of its members, each of whom is motivated by self-interest, of which he is himself the best judge. "Led by an invisible hand," not further described by Smith although every deist knew whose hand it was, the free pursuit of that self-interest cannot help benefiting society at large. Thus the key to social dynamics—or at least to those of economics, which was Smith's main concern—is a natural community of interest. In a world whose economic operations are governed by this supreme and inflexible law, the only sensible course is not to act counter to it. Government, therefore, has no right to interfere in the individual's economic relations with others.

The centuries-old policy of the English government had been to regulate certain large phases of domestic trade through Crown-granted monopolies and patents royal. Foreign trade, similarly, was controlled through the Navigation Acts (the last of which were not to be repealed until 1849) and other measures such as those which, in the very year *The Wealth of Nations* was published, had impelled the Americans to free themselves of economic restraints and taxation from abroad. Rejecting the controls of the mercantile system, Smith argued that the market should be protected from all kinds of intervention in order that economic laws might have free play. The competition generated by every man's effort to serve his self-interest—the profit motive—automatically controlled prices. Thus the free market was self-regulating; it neither required nor could tolerate outside interference.

Thanks to Smith, the industrial-commercial interests had seemingly irrefutable theoretical grounds for their crusade against the Corn Laws in the thirties and forties. The agrarian protectionism the Corn Laws implemented was anachronistic, the very antithesis of the free trade a manufacturing economy required. Unrestricted competition was the key to the common wealth, in the original sense of the term. The secret of the comforting attraction laissez faire had for the early Victorian mind lay in the premise that somehow "nature" had arranged that the prosperity of the individual—he who won out in the eternal competition of the marketplace—would automatically result in the public good.

But in this period, laissez faire became as much a social as an economic doctrine. That it was invoked so often and so successfully against proposals requiring state intervention in behalf of the common good was due to the so-called Manchester School of businessmen and politicians, an outgrowth of the Anti-Corn Law League under the same leadership of John Bright and Richard Cobden. Venerating free trade as the veritable key to the heavenly city—even today, Manchester's main auditorium is called Free Trade Hall— and invoking as well the other pertinent shibboleths of the political economists with whom they were often identified, the men of the Manchester School became hard-line advocates of laissez faire as the prime determinant of social policy.

Their rationale of laissez faire was Smith's rather than Bentham's, for pure Benthamism allowed for a substantial amount of legislation in the interests of the people at large. Bentham's theory diverged from Smith's in that Bentham was aware of man's present imperfection and the likelihood that, if left to consult his own preference, he would take advantage of his fellows in his own self-interest. Smith maintained that a man's recognition that his interests were identical with those of society's was natural, or intuitive. Bentham argued that a man would recognize it only if he were forced to do so by education and legislation. He therefore saw the need for some external means of diverting the individual's naturally egoistic activities into socially beneficial channels. Laws, in other words, had to be enacted to protect society from its individual members; legislation would harmonize the self-seeking of the parties involved into action which would be of advantage to the greatest number. The state had to act as a buffer among the conflicting atoms and parties that comprise society, an umpire to regulate competing or conflicting forces, a safeguard against anarchy. Theoretically, indeed, there were no limits to state interventionism. The national welfare and security could be safeguarded only if, as circumstances required, legislation were enacted to prevent surpluses and the resultant unemployment (the immediate cause of the crisis of 1842), set minimum wages, and provide such welfare state benefits as health insurance and old age pensions.

But such Benthamite ideas naturally were anathema to the Manchester School. They interpreted laissez faire as covering not merely the individual's freedom to buy and sell goods on the best terms he could obtain, but his right to hire, pay, and discharge workers in the same manner in which he dealt with other commodities, and to determine the conditions under which they worked. Even more: in their view, laissez faire denied that conditions of life outside the places of employment—housing, sanitation, consumer protection, educational provision—should be a concern of the state or of anyone not immediately involved. How far should government intervene, if at all? Macaulay's answer sounded as if it were brought down from Mount Sinai: "Our rulers will best promote the improvement of the nation by strictly confining themselves to their own legitimate duties, by leaving capital to find its most lucrative course, commodi-

ties their fair price, industry and intelligence their natural reward, idleness and folly their natural punishment, by main-
taining peace, by defending property, by diminishing the
price of law, and by observing strict economy in every department of the State. Let the Government do this: the People will assuredly do the rest."

By "the People" Macaulay obviously meant those who
were devotees of political economy, and, more generally,
the enlightened middle class. But, as the Manchester
School's opposition to social reform proved, "the rest," such
as the amelioration of working and living conditions, depended entirely on considerations of gain and loss. It was
a question not of humanitarianism but of pounds, shillings,
and pence. The governing consideration was the health of
the economy. If bettering the lot of the working people
would disturb the economy or (what amounted to the same
thing) put the employers out of pocket, it was not to be
thought of. In fact, it would harm the very people it was
supposed to benefit. If government interfered with the operation of laws like Malthus' by prolonging the lives of the
poor, it would merely mean that more people would go
hungry. To attempt reform in the shape of decent housing,
unpolluted water, saving women and children from the exhausting rigors of too long working hours and everyone from
mutilation by unfenced machinery, would invite disaster.
The death rate would decline; the labor force would be increased; the law of supply and demand would force wages
down; the people would be worse off than before. Laissez
faire, in short, sanctioned the policy of benign neglect which
perfectly suited the convenience of bustling entrepreneurs.

In the short view, the clear advantage lay with laissez
faire. "Why can't they leave it alone?", the querulous cry of
Lord Melbourne, the Queen's first prime minister, was the
watchword of the moment. But here it must be emphasized,
because some older accounts are misleading on the point,
that even when its influence was greatest, from the 1840's
through the fifties, laissez faire never wholly prevailed.

There never was a solid parliamentary bloc committed to it. Members could be individualists on one issue, interventionists on another. In voting on social legislation such as the Ten Hours Bill, members often were torn between the pragmatism of political economy and the humanitarianism of the bill's (mainly) Evangelical sponsors. In this case, it was "the self-same House of Commons that repealed the Corn Laws in the name of laissez-faire [which] passed the Ten Hours Bill in flat defiance of that doctrine." [4]

Much depended on whose ox was gored. Of all capitalistic enterprises, the railroads were most notably free from government interference. The wildcat speculation and wasteful duplication of routes that accompanied their building went almost entirely uncontrolled by the state, and such safety measures as the railroads adopted in the early days were the result of informal governmental cajolery rather than of the enforcement of such few weak laws as Parliament brought itself to pass. On the other hand, laissez faire was suspended when proposed legislation responded to prejudices which transcended economics, as was the case with the Obscene Publications Act of 1857, or which was too plainly in the common interest to be opposed by any reasonable person (the act of 1860 which curbed the widespread and scandalous adulteration of food and drink). There was no concerted opposition to the laws of 1840 and 1864 regulating chimney sweeping, an occupation whose misery and inhumanity William Blake had assailed as early as 1789; the "climbing boys' " masters had no such formidable lobby as the mill owners, railroad companies, and colliery operators possessed. But there was more than one way to skirt inconvenient legislation, as experience early in the century with the first factory acts had shown. In the case of the chimney sweeps a tacit conspiracy of householders and local officials, concerned more with clean flues than with such humane motives as eradicating the disease peculiar to the occupation (cancer of the scrotum), winked at the law and let laissez faire in by the back door. An effective law was finally passed in 1875.

Meanwhile, despite their theoretical acknowledgment that social legislation might sometimes be required by circumstances, the Benthamites did little to promote it. The only major exception was their consistent advocacy of state-supported and state-inspected elementary education. It was not until 1870, however—long after the Manchester School had, so to speak, ended its term, and after the waste of countless intelligences and talents that might have been cultivated in childhood had the various contending parties been able to agree on a scheme—that Forster's Education Act put into law the fundamental Benthamite principle of state-*provided* education, the national treasury supplying not only the necessary money but buildings and teachers where present provision was lacking or failed to meet government standards.

If the passage of other legislation looking toward the betterment of social conditions owed little to Benthamite votes, it owed much to the Benthamite exertions which prepared public opinion to demand it. Most of the landmark social reform legislation was preceded by large-scale investigations of the conditions which required remedy, and certain leading Benthamites, with their scientific turn of mind, were expert and indefatigable fact-gatherers. Blue books issued by the committees to which they belonged or which they served as staff played decisive roles in dramatizing and publicizing the need for remedial legislation.

Transcending the issue of laissez faire was one principle upon which landowning Tory and industrialist Whig, Benthamite and business-oriented Evangelical found no difficulty in agreeing: property was sacred. If any one value defined "happiness" according to the Utilitarian form of reckoning or "success" according to the popular philosophy descended from it, that value was the possession of material wealth, either in kind or in the form of bank deposits and lucrative investments. "Proputty, proputty, proputty" went the hooves of the cantering horse in Tennyson's "Northern Farmer: New Style," an admirable poetic summation of this crass side of the Victorian ethos.

Property not only was the visible measure of a man's social worth; it was, among other things, the criterion of his citizenship. The First Reform Bill in general limited the new franchise to ten-pound householders (owners or tenants of property worth an annual rent of £10 or more) and, in the rural regions, to the owners of property worth forty shillings' annual rent. The Second Reform Bill (1867) also related the franchise to property, although this time the terms were so liberal that nearly all men who owned or rented town domiciles of any kind, including lodgers paying £10 or more a year, were covered. In the Third Reform Bill (1884) these qualifications were extended to rural voters as well. Until 1858, however, no one could be elected to Parliament unless he owned real estate or personal property to the value of £600 a year as a county member or £300 as a member for a borough. Even more deep-seated than the equation of property with political responsibility was the tendency of landowners and industrialists to look upon their workers as chattels; they treated them often with a proprietary air that would have been more suitable under feudalistic conditions than in the shadow of factory chimneys. Legislation and court decisions tended also to favor property rights over human ones. The history of social reform in the period might well be written in terms of the conflict between the two. When, in a confrontation in Parliament or the law courts, human rights triumphed, it was often counted a famous victory.

Amplify "human rights" to "human dignity" and one arrives at the heart of the case the Victorians, workingmen and men of letters alike, made against the Utilitarian spirit. It was not a new case; the great romantics, especially Wordsworth and Shelley, had had hard words to utter about "utility" as the ruling criterion of worth. But the protest they initiated swelled only in the new generation, faced with the political economists—"the feeloosophers," as Cobbett called them in derisive allusion to the fact that many of them spoke in the accents of their native Scotland—and their glib rationalizations of the factory system and social laissez faire.

The most numerous protesters were the workingmen themselves. They may not have appreciated the serene logic of political economy; they may not, indeed, have known what political economy was or the names of its leading apologists. But they knew all too well that they were ill-fed, ill-housed, and ill-clothed, not to say recurrently out of work—and they were persuaded that they knew who was to blame. It was, to use a modern term Cobbett himself employed, "the System". That is, most immediately the employers who clothed their abdication from social responsibility in platitudes drawn from the speeches and treatises of the political economists; but also the other components of what they chose to regard as the power structure—the politicians, Parliament, the government bureaucracy, the Church.

But some notable elements in that structure actually shared the workers' enmity toward these brash, overbearing newcomers to English life. Many Tory landowners, aristocracy and gentry alike, correctly recognized in the manufacturing class, with its political economy doctrines, a threat to their long-standing political and social supremacy. The parvenus were also vulgar, in the way of parvenus; they made no secret of their animosity toward their social superiors; indeed, it was a blatant part of their creed. They were behind the various liberal moves to curtail the prerogatives and privileges the upper classes had acquired over the centuries from complaisant monarchs and Parliaments. Furthermore, the landowners, whose prosperity depended on protectionism (or so they insisted until the catastrophe confidently expected after 1846 refused to materialize), were more than eager to get their licks in against the political economists who made a fetish of free trade.

Allied with the landed interest, once more, was the Church, whose response was not, in this case, the mere sympathetic reflex it often was when Tory interests were imperiled; it had very good grounds for hostility on its own account. In its pure form Utilitarianism was, like some forms of the eighteenth-century rationalism from which it descended, aggressively anti-religious. It regarded religion as a curse of civilization, an affront to reasoning man, a fount of superstition and reactionarism, and in its Christian (or Protestant) garb a sheer perversion of Utilitarian values, for it exalted self-denial over self-interest, sacrifice over pleasure, and so contravened the assumptions of the moral arithmetic. By importing this anti-religious position into the Victorian age, the Utilitarians made an important contribution to the growing climate of secularism. The Church correctly identified the Philosophic Radicals as liberals who were striving, whether consciously or unwittingly, to destroy it as a force in the state and in society. They had led the outcry against the Church's excessive revenues and the corruption of its prelates which had resulted in the appointment of the Ecclesiastical Commission in 1835. They had also, as we shall see in Chapter VI, attacked the Church's prerogatives in Ireland. No wonder that the Oxford Movement, spearhead of a revitalized Anglicanism, was directed against the Benthamite-inspired liberals.

Opposed to the Utilitarians, also, were the Evangelical humanitarians (as distinct from the industrialists belonging to the same communion: their interests naturally were different). The humanitarians, led by Lord Ashley, supplied the social conscience requisite to promoting legislation that would in some degree protect workers from the indifference or rapacity of their employers.

And so, both on philosophical grounds and on the score of endangered or actually extinguished vested interests, the

Utilitarians accumulated a daunting array of enemies. Nevertheless, there was a piquant ambiguity in the conventional Englishman's response to this new species of public men, so outspoken in their assault on traditional values and institutions. Notwithstanding their radicalism, the political economists were, as a group, well-to-do, and they were also intellectuals with the gift of plausibility. They therefore had to be respected, in spite of everything. Radicalism and respectability were a combination with which experience had not prepared the early Victorian mind to deal, and in contemporary criticism of the political economists we find an amusing attitude of wariness, of uncertainty as to just how polite one had to be to these overweeningly confident self-appointed builders of a better society.

This was not true, however, of the most eloquent and implacable literary foes of Utilitarianism, Carlyle, Ruskin, and Dickens, who knew precisely where they stood and poured out their denunciation, two of them in accents reminiscent of Old Testament prophets, the third in scorching satire. To them, as to their romantic predecessors, a man was a rich and potentially noble amalgam of senses, feelings, imagination, and intellect; to the political economists he was nothing more than an economic unit, a contributory digit to a statistical total. If the romantic view was unrealistically broad, the Utilitarian one was unrealistically narrow. It suffered from moral myopia; its approach to ethical and social problems was a repellently mechanical calculation; above all, it set itself stonily against any indulgence of the imagination and the emotions. It rested, therefore, on a fatally incomplete comprehension of the springs and shades of human behavior. Benthamism offended all decent sympathies, those springing from Christian morality and, more immediately, from the romantic spirit which extolled the nobility of the individual person.

In Victorian fiction the Benthamite type appears most memorably as Gradgrind the Utilitarian theorist and Bounderby the rich factory owner, both in *Hard Times.* Between them, they embody most of the leading deficiencies Dickens or anybody else attributed to the breed. At least as significant as the characters who directly represent Utilitarian ideas and morality are the saved sinners and idealized specimens of a social group which, according to some Victorian social critics, was not beyond redemption. The elder Carson, in *Mary Barton,* has his weaknesses, and no doubt his mill hands had good reason for their enmity, but Mrs. Gaskell is at pains to depict him as a well-meaning person. Carlyle's archetypal "captain of industry," Plugson of Undershot in *Past and Present,* though he is an as yet unregenerate "bucanier," has potentialities; it is his kind of aristocracy—the aristocracy of the sweaty brow and solicitous heart—who will save English society if anyone will. Disraeli's Millbank in *Coningsby,* published just a year after *Past and Present,* shows the captain of industry at his most enlightened, a rich man who, like the famous cotton manufacturer Robert Owen of New Lanark, provides his workers with all the amenities (model village, church, library, garden allotments, singing classes) and, most modern touch of all, sees to it that his factory chimneys consume their own smoke.

Utilitarianism itself lost some of its rigor in the course of the years. The "mental crisis" of John Stuart Mill, who had been reared in accordance with the most stringent Benthamite principles of education, dramatically anticipated this development. As he recounts his experience in his *Autobiography,* when he was in his early twenties (1826–28) he suddenly realized that, as a walking exemplar of Benthamism, he completely lacked what he now considered to be an indispensable prerequisite of contentment—imagination and the ability to feel. His upbringing had sharpened his analytic mind, making it a superb instrument, but it had done nothing to release his emotions or awaken his aesthetic perceptions. Mill's salvation came through his fortunate discovery of Wordsworth and of Wordsworth's nature: a perfect symbol of the confrontation of polar opposites, Utilitarianism and romanticism, now proved moderately reconcilable. By 1840 Mill was identifying Coleridge and Bentham as "the two great seminal minds" of the time and treating the former more sympathetically than the latter; and in his classic work, *Utilitarianism* (1863), he signally modified the Benthamite account of man by allowing for quality in the pleasures to be weighed in the felicific calculus and recognized "the social feelings" rather than narrow self-satisfaction as the ultimate criterion of happiness and morality. Thus Mill softened Utilitarianism, and in effect filled in its most deplorable deficiency with humanistic values drawn from romanticism and, to a degree, from the Evangelical religion, which had affinities with romanticism.

4. The Benthamite Legacy

What, apart from rationalizing the spirit of competitive capitalism, were the chief results of Benthamism? For one thing, the Utilitarians instigated many legislative and legal reforms. Jeremy Bentham's lifelong ambition had been the complete overhaul of English law and administration, and although his grandiose program was never realized in its entirety, his fellow law-reformer Sir Samuel Romilly instituted, even before the year of Waterloo, a campaign which, with Benthamite support, eventually bore fruit in a series of acts eliminating many medieval and Tudor anachronisms. The fire that destroyed the old Houses of Parliament in 1834, two years after Bentham's death, might have been interpreted as a tribute to his success in modernizing the processes of government and law. It reportedly originated in a flue overheated by the burning of large quantities of wooden tallies, the means by which Exchequer accounts had been kept since some date before 1179. They were burned now only because the Exchequer had been abolished as a financial department the preceding year. Until its very last day, it had clung with similar tenacity to the use of Roman figures. Outworn custom died hard in England, and Jeremy Bentham had been its most implacable enemy.

Bentham's true monument is the whole of British (and to a great extent American) executive government, both central and local. He was a founder of the science of public administration, in which non-partisan, tenured professionals put legislation into action and constantly supervise the results. By centralizing in London governmental functions which had hitherto been performed, if at all, by local authorities—the new Poor Law administration was an initial case in point—the Benthamites achieved uniform standards and relatively efficient operation, insured by inspection.* In the offices created by Benthamite enactments across the early Victorian years, to be sure, dawdled the bureaucracy which Dickens satirized in *Little Dorrit*'s cataleptic Circumlocution Office, where the only alternative to doing things wrongly was not doing them at all. But it was also the Benthamite insistence upon expertise and opening careers to all talents which put an end to the civil service's being used, as it had been for many years, to provide job security for incompetents with good connections. The lethargic tribe of Tite Barnacles, who owned their sinecures to aristocratic influence, were replaced in the mid-Victorian era by civil servants selected by open competitive examinations.

An equally important Benthamite reform, accomplished in close cooperation with the Evangelical humanitarians,

* The Benthamites' emphasis on centralized government was one of the main reasons for the opposition to their reforms. Ever since the Glorious Revolution of 1688 had reduced the power of the Crown and vested it instead in the people (i.e., the upper and upper-middle classes), the diffusion of authority and responsibility throughout the country rather than its concentration in London had been looked upon as a fundamental safeguard of liberty. Conservative Victorians therefore interpreted every transfer of governmental function from county and borough to Whitehall, whether achieved or merely advocated, as a retrogressive step in the general direction of autocracy. Once more, however speciously, the analogy with France was invoked.

was the revision of the penal code. In the third decade of the century, somewhere between 200 and 223 offenses were punishable by death. (The authorities differed on the exact number, as well they might, given the chaos of the statutes.) Although it is true that in such circumstances some juries were reluctant to convict and some judges reluctant to impose the full penalty—only one out of every seven offenders convicted on a capital charge was sentenced to hang, and only one out of every six capital sentences was carried out—the possibility of being hanged for a petty crime was very real. Romilly had begun the slow work of prodding Parliament to trim the list as early as 1808, but his only immediate successes were in respect to pocket-picking (reduced to an offense punishable by transportation for life) and stealing cloth worth more than five shillings from a bleaching ground. After 1825, however, the rate picked up as a direct consequence of the Benthamites' growing influence, and the death penalty ceased to be attached to such crimes as forgery, housebreaking, stealing more than five shillings' worth of goods from a shop, sheep-stealing, damaging Westminster Bridge, and impersonating an inmate of the Chelsea Hospital for old and disabled soldiers. When Victoria became queen in 1837, only about ten capital crimes remained on the books.

But the most important Utilitarian legacy, and the most ironic in view of the popular identification of Benthamism with laissez faire, was the later Victorian trend toward state action. After the Manchester School and their intellectual mentors, the political economists, became a spent force, that side of the Benthamite creed which inclined toward enlarging the functions of government carried the day. Beginning with laws which were essentially protective (factory and public health acts, for example), the Benthamite spirit impelled successive Parliaments to move government into the additional role of provider. The state became responsible for the care of paupers, the destitute sick, lunatics; it set up schools where they were lacking and more closely supervised those that religious groups had established; it allowed local authorities to assess levies for public library buildings.

5. Socialism

In thus laying the legislative groundwork for the extensive system of social services to be provided by the twentieth-century welfare state, latter-day descendants of the two early Victorian radical movements, philosophic and popular, joined. The moderate philosophy of state intervention which John Stuart Mill came to advocate had its roots not only in Benthamite theory but in the sporadic socialist movement that began in the century's first decades, when Robert Owen proved at his planned factory community in Scotland that the industrial system and humanity could coexist if the employer had enough good will and resourcefulness. Owenite Socialism, advocating that the means of production be communally owned and the proceeds of labor equally shared, was one of the components of pre-Reform Bill radicalism and later added a contingent to the Chartist procession. Split into small groups, the Owenites were prominent in the abortive early trade union and cooperative movements.

After the collapse of Chartism in 1848 some of its causes were taken up by the Christian Socialist movement, led by a group of Broad Churchmen (see below, pp. 207–208), notably Charles Kingsley and Thomas Hughes, author of *Tom Brown's School Days*. Like their inspirer, Coleridge, they were convinced that the Church had an obligation to initiate and guide social action and seek social justice, even so far as to defend the workers against capitalistic exploitation. In his own series of "tracts for the times," *Politics for the People,* Kingsley wrote: "We have used the Bible as if it was a mere special constable's handbook—an opium dose for keeping beasts of burden patient while they were being overloaded—a mere book to keep the poor in order. . . . Instead of being a book to keep the poor in order, it is a book, from beginning to end, written *to keep the rich in order*."

Coming as they did from a well-known parson, these were strong, indeed radically subversive, sentiments. But for a few years, despite the scandal it caused in more conservative Church circles, Christian Socialism effectively showed ways in which the Church's social mission could work. It established settlement houses in the slums and supported the cooperative movement. At its night school, the Working Men's College, taught Ruskin and the Pre-Raphaelite artists Rossetti, Edward Burne-Jones, and Ford Madox Brown. And Christian Socialism transposed into a proletarian key the developing *mens sana in corpore sano* ideal which, thanks to Thomas Arnold, headmaster of Rugby in 1827–42, had become a dominant element in public school education. Team athletics and the spirit of "manliness," it was thought, would combine to produce Christian gentlemen in working clothes. Hence Hughes's being assigned to teach boxing, cricket, and rowing at the Working Men's College, and hence the derisive term "Muscular Christianity," which soon became a synonym for Christian Socialism. Hughes later wrote a book called *The Manliness of Christ;* it has been remarked that he conceived of Jesus as a model Muscular Christian.

After Christian Socialism faded, the cooperative movement kept one major socialistic activity alive and prospering. Beginning with a retail shop at Rochdale in 1844, it developed into a major working-class institution, the retail outlets being stocked in time from cooperative warehouses and these, in turn, from cooperative factories.

In 1881–84, the American single-tax advocate Henry George rekindled British socialism with a lecture tour and the publication of his *Progress and Poverty,* which became one of the greatest best-sellers of the day. The single-tax idea got nowhere in England, but George's campaign helped stimulate other economic reform movements. One was the

Social Democratic Federation, the first English Marxist organization of any consequence. Among its members was William Morris, but after a few years he broke with the S.D.F. and founded a dissident group, the Socialist League. At the same time also (1884), Beatrice and Sidney Webb organized the non-revolutionary Fabian Society, which sought and often achieved socialistic goals through such channels as the municipal ownership of public utilities, municipal slum clearance and public low-income housing, stronger trade unions, and more extensive state control of the conditions of labor. George Bernard Shaw and H. G. Wells were early members; Shaw stayed but Wells drifted away.

The early and mid-Victorian ascendancy of political economy as translated into governmental inaction by the Manchester School was responsible for the conditions which a combination of forces—neo-Benthamite mild collectivism, the vestiges of Evangelical humanitarianism, and popular radicalism in the form of various socialist organizations— had the job of remedying in the next generation. Whatever their individual tendencies, in the aggregate this oddly assorted confederation of reformers served their age well by publicizing social abuses, arousing the nation's conscience, and in the end obtaining the requisite governmental intervention. To the extent that it contributed to the slow improvement of life among the masses, Benthamism atoned for the gross negligence and rationalizing of inhumanity for which it had been held responsible during those worst decades of Britain's growth into an industrial power.

But from the point of view of literature, its principal significance lies not in its eventual contribution to the cause of collectivism but in what it stood for during the years of its greatest influence. Its sponsorship of the cult of material progress, its adamant refusal (before John Stuart Mill turned humanist) to admit to its structure of values such qualities as sentiment, compassion, beauty, poetry—its pedantry, its hard rationalism and dreary materialism—all these acted as marvelously irritant stimuli to Victorian thought. They led, as no other contemporary strain of thought did, to a thorough-going revaluation of the whole spectrum of human wishes. The reflections on individual and social values instituted by early nineteenth-century thinkers reacting to the concept of "utility" were carried on and amplified by scores of Victorian writers.

FORD MADOX BROWN's *Work* (1852). The full message of this celebrated example of Victorian allegorical painting is apparent only if, like Hogarth's *Industry and Idleness* (1747), it is systematically "read," inch by inch. It provides a moralized panorama of the English social structure at the beginning of the high Victorian era: the country gentry (center, background), the commercial middle class (left: the ladies' husbands and brothers, missing from the scene, presumably are busy at their offices), the intellectual middle class (right: the bearded figure is said to represent Carlyle), and the various ranks of the workers, from the dandified skilled artisan with the *Times* under his arm to the ragged street flower-seller. The tension between the leisured and the working classes is suggested by the mutual wariness of the blanketed whippet and the stalwart mongrel. The theme of the universal nobility of work is carried out not only by the several suggestions of unproductive idleness but by the fact that the laborers are repairing a sewer.

The exterior and interior of a typical Dorsetshire farm laborer's cottage, 1846.

A late-Victorian dinner party (1885).

THE TWO NATIONS. Young dandies, 1834: the men who supplied the metaphor for Carlyle's *Sartor Resartus*. Right, crossing sweepers: the homeless waifs typified by Jo in Dickens' *Bleak House*. It was at this time—the fifties and sixties—that outdoor photography began to be used to document social conditions.

152

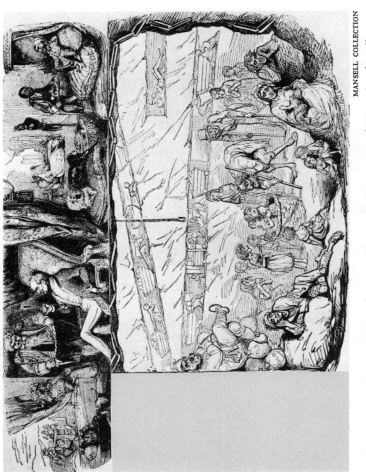

"CAPITAL AND LABOUR": *Punch*, 1843. In its earliest years *Punch*, though primarily a humorous weekly, manifested a strong social conscience. The cross-section of mine tunnels and the figures of crippled and starving workers were inspired by similar illustrations in the famous "blue book" of 1842, which resulted in immediate legislation regulating the labor of women and children in mines.

"LUDGATE HILL" (Gustave Doré, 1871). There is abundant contemporary evidence that the traffic jams in Fleet Street (foreground) were as fearsome then as they are in the London of a century later.

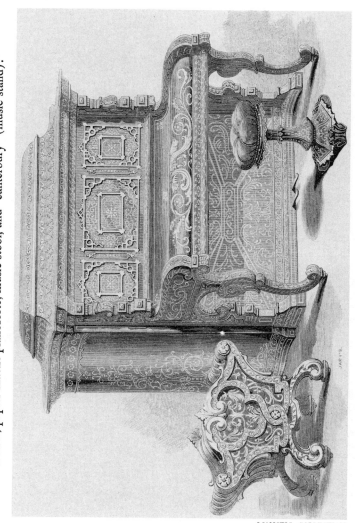

building was 1848 feet long, 408 feet broad, and (at the transept) 108 feet high. It was built in three months, used 293,655 panes of glass, and during the 141-day season it was open it attracted just over six million visitors.

Below, papier-mâché pianoforte, music stool, and "canterbury" (music stand).

MANSELL COLLECTION

St. Pancras Station, London. Typical Victorian architecture: traditional design (the lancet windows and soaring arches of a cathedral) and modern materials (cast iron and glass).

"THE RAILWAY MANIA." Construction work on the Birmingham Railway at Camden Town (London), 1837–38: a scene described in Dickens' *Dombey and Son,* Chapter 6. Below, "The Railway Juggernaut of 1845": *Punch*'s comment on the wild and ultimately disastrous speculation in railway stock.

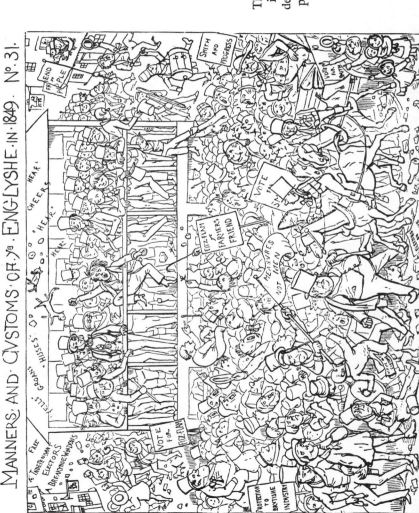

The cartoonist Dicky Doyle's impressions (in *Punch*) of democracy in action after the passage of the First Reform Bill.

159

PRE-KAPHAELITISM AND AESTHETICISM. Rossetti's *Ecce Ancilla Domini! (The Annunciation)*, 1850. Right, one of George DuMaurier's satires of the "Aesthetic" vogue (*Punch*, 1880).

TATE GALLERY

AN ÆSTHETIC MIDDAY MEAL.

At the Luncheon hour, Jellaby Postlethwaite enters a Pastrycook's and calls for a glass of Water, into which he puts a freshly-cut Lily, and loses himself in contemplation thereof.

Waiter. "SHALL I BRING YOU ANYTHING ELSE, SIR ?"

Jellaby Postlethwaite. "THANKS, NO ! I HAVE ALL I REQUIRE, AND SHALL SOON HAVE DONE !"

NEW YORK PUBLIC LIBRARY

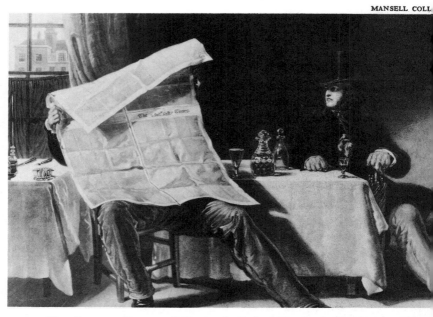

THE READING PUBLIC: I. Benjamin Robert Haydon's *Waiting for "The Times" the Morning After the Reform Debate* (1831). Below, a middle-class family gathered to hear the Bible read aloud (artist unknown).

THE READING PUBLIC: II.
R. B. Martineau's *The Last
Chapter*.
Below, the Great Hall
of Mudie's
Select Circulating Library.

COVER OF A PART ISSUE OF *Bleak House*. Like most of Dickens' novels, *Bleak House* was first published in monthly parts. The pictorial frame was intended to contain numerous allusions to the characters, episodes, scenes, themes, and symbols of the novel. To this end, the illustrator, in this case "Phiz" (Hablôt K. Browne), worked under Dickens' close supervision.

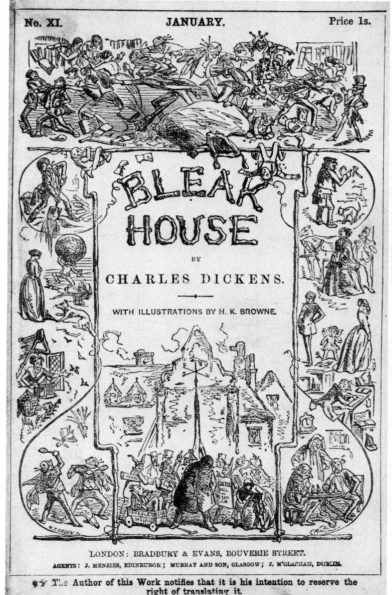

ELEMENTARY EDUCATION. A school run on the monitorial
system, 1839. Below, a village school, c. 1856.

W. P. Frith's *Ramsgate Sands.*

V

THE EVANGELICAL TEMPER

1. The Middle-Class Ethos

IF UTILITARIANISM AND EVANGELICALISM were conceived
of as two irregularly shaped designs and then superimposed,
one would be struck by the number of portions that merged
into a single image. The register would in no case be perfect, but the degree of overlapping is remarkable. As the
historian Élie Halévy observed, "The fundamental paradox
of English society [in the Victorian age] . . . is precisely
the partial junction and combination of these two forces
theoretically so hostile." [1] On the one hand, there were the
forces of cold analytical thought; on the other, those of
emotionalism (typically diluted to sentimentalism outside
the religious context). A quasi-fundamentalist brand of
Christianity was pitted against a vigorously skeptical, even
downright anti-religious secular movement. Yet, working
from sometimes antithetical premises, they joined to create
and rationalize what came to be known as middle-class
values.

A form of Protestant pietism, Evangelicalism was concerned less with doctrine and the forms of worship than
with the way men should live, and much less with life for its
own sake than as preparation for eternity. Salvation was
regarded as the goal of all earthly action, and divine grace
the means by which it could be earned. The Bible, inter-

preted with the utmost literalism, was the supreme guide to conduct. Burdened always with a deep conviction of man's sinfulness, the Evangelicals found hope in the doctrine of the Atonement: "Christ died for our sins." Sinful man could be saved—heedful of the original meaning of "evangelical," they conceived part of their mission to be to spread the joyful tidings, though often in the most gloomy terms—but salvation could be achieved only by conversion and submission to the will of God. The conduct of one's daily life was of utmost importance in qualifying the soul for eternity. Every act, no matter how trivial in earthly terms, would be of incalculable importance when the balance was struck at the gates of Heaven. Thus the Evangelical's anxious eye was forever fixed upon the "eternal microscope" which searched for every moral blemish and reported every motion of the soul: "diseased self-introspection," an unsympathetic Carlyle called it. Although, in contrast with proper Anglicanism, Evangelicalism tended to stress faith rather than works as the way to bring divine grace down upon the devout and pure in heart, in practice it was very active in Victorian philanthropic and humanitarian efforts.

The Evangelical movement began in the eighteenth-century Anglican Church as a reaction against the spiritual somnolence and emotional chill of a religion in the thrall of easygoing deism. The dominant party then was the Latitudinarian, which viewed faith as a matter of the head rather than the heart and refused to worry over doctrinal issues. The religious passion of the seventeenth century, reflected in the sermons and polemic writings of the great Caroline divines, had almost totally disappeared from the "high and dry" Church of England, which dismissed such fervor as indecorous "enthusiasm."

Beginning in the late 1730's, John and Charles Wesley kindled a revival, distinguished by unrestrained emotionalism and concentrating upon the welfare of the individual soul. The Wesleyans' appeal was largely to the working population, which went unserved by a Church traditionally allied with the upper classes, and although they remained nominally inside the Anglican communion, neither they nor most other Anglicans were happy about their presence there. In 1795, a few years after John Wesley's death, they formally seceded and thenceforth constituted the largest and most influential body of Dissenters, alongside whom were ranged such older denominations as the Presbyterians, Congregationalists, and Baptists.

Meanwhile, the Wesleyans' (or Methodists') ardor communicated itself to others within the Church, principally middle-class people who, while sharing their zeal for personal salvation, remained loyal to Anglican forms and doctrines. The Anglican Evangelical movement therefore was a continuation of the Methodist spirit within the old structure. Like "Utilitarian" and "Benthamite," the word "Evangelical" has two applications. The narrower designates only the Anglican, or Church, Evangelicals. The wider use embraces the whole spectrum of Protestantism from the Anglican Evangelical party (the "Low Church," as it came to be called in Victorian times, reviving a term previously applied to Latitudinarianism) to the variety of Dissenting sects presided over by the Wesleyans. In what follows, the word will be used in this inclusive sense except where explicitly qualified.

As a specifically religious influence, Evangelicalism was most important from the 1790's to the 1830's. Believing that the convulsion in France had stemmed from religious indifference, deistic rationalism, and outright atheism, many people renounced those formerly fashionable attitudes and fled back to something like fundamentalist religion. As a party in the Anglican Church, the Evangelicals kept a moderate amount of power throughout the first half of the century, raising their voices with especial shrillness against such developments as the Broad Church and Oxford Movements (Chapter VI). But Evangelicalism is chiefly important in the history of English culture for the moral tone it lent society down to the last quarter of the century. Some of its characteristic moral standards, tastes, and avoidances are current today, though with ever-diminishing strength, as vestiges of what is popularly called Victorianism. In many ways, our abandonment of moral restrictions in favor of extreme permissiveness is simply the final phase of the reaction against Evangelical concepts of morality and value that began about a century ago.

To the Utilitarian repertoire of political, social, and economic doctrine, then, Evangelicalism added the weight of a combined religion and moral ideology. The two forces often merged in the persons of individual men. It is a cliché of Victorian history that the weekday businessman was the Sunday Evangelical. The eye that was fixed on the profit-and-loss ledger six days a week shifted to a hopeful contemplation of the heavenly account on the seventh, and the teachings of the political economists which moralized his activity from Monday to Saturday gave way to Scripture on the Sabbath.

Evangelicalism, and especially Nonconformism, supplied much of the fierce energy with which middle-class businessmen pursued their secular vocation. The same strenuousness carried over into the buoyant national spirit. If it was possible for man to redeem his soul through his own exertions (namely, the exercise of faith), then what other goal could not be attained? The confidence the Victorians felt in their power to build an ever richer and more comfortable society undoubtedly owed much to the spiritual energy generated by Evangelical commitment, which spilled over into worldly affairs and prevented the age from sinking into the satiated lassitude portrayed in Browning's poem "Cleon."

Work, in a secular context, was the counterpart of faith in a religious one, and its efficacy too was regarded as infallible doctrine. "Industry" and "work" were holy words in the contemporary lexicon, and the moral imperative they embodied was identified with that of faith and elevated into a virtual eleventh commandment by Carlyle: "For there is a

perennial nobleness, and even sacredness, in Work. . . .
Work, never so Mammonish, mean, *is* in communication
with Nature; the real desire to get Work done will itself
lead one more and more to truth, to Nature's appointments
and regulations, which are truth. . . . The latest Gospel
in this world is, Know thy work and do it. . . . Admirable
was that of the old Monks, *'Laborare est Orare,* Work is
Worship.' " Utilitarians and Evangelicals alike subscribed to
the ethic of work as the prime means of fulfilling one's
earthly destiny and, in the case of the Evangelicals, qualifying oneself for heavenly reward as well. Although Utilitarianism was essentially hedonistic in its moral bias, it had
realism enough to understand that life as currently constituted could not provide instant happiness (defined primarily
in terms of physical comfort and material possessions: the
premise of an acquisitive society). Happiness could be
earned only through sustained labor and the sacrifice of
immediate pleasure. So also to the Evangelical: the attainment of Heaven was a long-term proposition. By diligent
application to one's earthly task, one accumulated money in
the spiritual bank which would pay off later—how much
later, only God could tell—in the accumulated capital, plus
compound interest, of divine grace.

"Produce! Produce!" cried Carlyle in *Sartor Resartus.*
"Were it but the pitifullest infinitesimal fraction of a Product, produce it, in God's name!" The exhortation was intended for the soul's benefit alone, but it inadvertently
provided a most acceptable link between the age's economic
ambitions and that part of its ethos which it had inherited
from the Puritans. The moral code of Protestantism, especially
that of Nonconformist Protestantism, put high value upon
such qualities as frugality, self-denial, dedication to one's
appointed occupation, constant awareness that the night
cometh when no man can work. The prudential virtues
which had energized the commerce of the Tudor and later
periods proved to be admirably adaptable to the conditions
of the new industrial society. And of these "huckstering

virtues," as Mill called them, the greatest was unremitting diligence.

The conviction that work conquers all supplied the escape clause in the seemingly tight determinism of political economy. It was true that Malthusian and Ricardian doctrine seemed to lock the individual into an economic system as pitiless as the mathematical laws that were supposed to underlie it. But, like a machine-age Prometheus, the employer or merchant could rend the chains which bound him by industry, ingenuity, and the practice of the appropriate virtues, such as abstinence and thrift.

The same code of prudential morality to which the employing class subscribed was enjoined upon the worker. By toiling harder than his fellows, he could produce more goods and thus earn more money; and by practicing continence, he could limit the numbers of those who, like himself, were to claim a portion of the restricted wage fund. By avoiding the public house and storing the money thus saved in a savings bank or "friendly society" (for insurance and burial expenses) he could improve his condition in life, the laws of political economy notwithstanding. Of all the maxims in the sententious Victorian vocabulary, "Heaven helps those who help themselves" was among the most ubiquitous.

Character-building, with this the presiding motto, was a joint Evangelical-Utilitarian enterprise. The profitable ethic of work, combined with cultivation of all the other relevant virtues, was recommended by innumerable writers in the popular media. The literature of How to Get Ahead, typified by Samuel Smiles's best-selling *Self-Help* (1859), had an incalculable effect on the ordinary Victorian's value system and moral orientation. Fictional self-made men like Dickens' ironmaster Rouncewell, Mrs. Gaskell's Mr. Thornton, and Charlotte Brontë's Mr. Oliver joined with Smiles's real-life heroes to inspire readers to emulate them; the prestige value of the myth of success against impossible odds is suggested by the trouble to which Bounderby in *Hard Times* went to invent the cock-and-bull story of his heroic triumph over his gutter origins.

Thus, reaffirming the ancient Hebrew morality of stern discipline and devotion to one's task, Evangelicalism provided a rationale which was especially valuable as it enabled men of affairs to face down those who expressed compassion for the unfortunate and destitute. To those who questioned whether Malthusianism and the stony philosophy of the new Poor Law were precisely in harmony with Christian charity, Evangelicalism replied that work, with its associated exercise of self-denial, was the universally available solution for personal distress. The disciplined worker was, in the long run, the successful worker; poverty was, almost by definition, the consequence of laziness and spendthrift habits. This, at least, was the middle-class credo, nowhere more forthrightly phrased than in the gospel according to Smiles: "National progress is the sum of individual industry, energy and uprightness as national decay is of individual idleness, selfishness and vice. What we are accustomed to decry as great social evils will, for the most part, be found to be but the outgrowth of man's own perverted life." But the dogma carried less persuasion to the masses of workers, whose economic fate, notwithstanding the cheery assumption that they could work out their own destiny with sufficient perseverance, was inexorably determined not by the laws of political economy but by the market's vicissitudes and the employer's self-interest. The recommendation of work as the panacea for social ills had a distinctly hollow ring when thousands of able-bodied men and their families found there was no work to be had.

In the implicit understanding between employers and workers which supposedly pointed both groups along the road to success, there was, however, one discriminatory clause. This was the important proviso that honesty, though its rules might sometimes be bent in a good cause (the employers'), was an inflexible requirement in the case of workers. There was nothing an occasionally unethical businessman loathed with greater self-righteousness, and cracked down harder upon, than dishonesty on the part of a subordinate. This moral differential did not escape the workers, because there was much evidence that men of determination and resourcefulness could also be men who, shrewdly and none too scrupulously operating in a value system tailored to their needs, interpreted their success as vindicating that system. The social historian G. D. H. Cole aptly summarizes the ambiguity involved:

To most of these men, and to most of their contemporaries, this rise seemed to have been due to certain personal qualities which they possessed above other people. Their admirers spoke of these qualities as "initiative, enterprise, personal driving force," and also as "abstinence, frugality, and a self-control which enabled them to brush aside pleasure and other distractions, and to concentrate their energies on doing with all their might the job they had marked out for themselves." Their detractors painted a different picture, in which initiative and enterprise were metamorphosed into greed and overreaching, personal driving force into lust for irresponsible power, abstinence and frugality into meanness, avarice and a will to impose privation upon others, and self-control into a soulless lack of cultural values which left the new capitalists with no other interest in life than the pursuit of wealth in this world and of salvation in a next world conceived in the image of their own spiritual poverty.[2]

Cole does not speak of outright dishonesty, but it is certainly implied. And, considering the encouragement the laissez-faire spirit gave to free-wheeling business practices, it was inevitable that the Victorian business world should have seen some pretty sharp dealing—not merely practices that could be rationalized, however fallaciously, by invoking the laws of political economy, but sheer chicanery that would be considered inadmissible by the standards of Ben Jonson's day as well as our own. The operations of the Anglo-Bengalee Disinterested Loan and Life Insurance Company in *Martin Chuzzlewit,* and other such enterprises, are faithful fictional representations of the not infrequent level of business probity in real life. The ultimately disastrous manipulations of George Hudson, "the railway king," at the height of the mania for capitalizing, if not actually building, railroads in the mid-forties were followed within a few years by the dramatic suicide on Hampstead Heath of the ruined financier John Sadleir, a headline event that Dickens promptly adapted in *Little Dorrit.* Trollope's *The Way We Live Now* offers a depressing view of high finance in 1874–75.

Legislation to curb shady practices and protect investors came only very slowly; the commercial world, understandably, had as deep a commitment to caveat emptor as to laissez faire. Only after such disastrous failures as Sadleir's, which, as Dickens shows in *Little Dorrit,* meant ruin for thousands of investors, was a Limited Liability Act passed by which each investor's responsibility in case of a business failure was restricted to the amount of his investment, instead of all his property being liable to seizure. Yet, despite the temptations the Victorian businessman faced, the overall standard of commercial morality was remarkably high. In the absence of legal restraints, Evangelical scruples served well. Overoptimism and recklessness proved the ruin of more entrepreneurs and investors than did overt intent to defraud.

In its own sphere, Evangelicalism complemented the individualism of laissez faire by stressing the importance of the private conscience instead of theological dogma. Despite the hierarchical tendencies of Methodism, it too was opposed to institutionalism as represented by a highly organized and authoritative church. It was essentially a religion of private initiative. In effect, Evangelicalism translated into religious terms the laissez-faire premise that every man was the best arbiter of his own conduct once he was illuminated by the Truth that was provided, in the one instance, by classical economics, and, in the other, by Scripture.

In the eighteenth century, Evangelical religion had a leveling influence in that it largely dispensed with the Calvinistic idea of the elect. As Browning had Pippa sing in *Pippa Passes,* "All service ranks the same with God." The very fact that the Wesleys found their main constituency among the poor gave their movement a certain democratic climate. But the shock of the French Revolution stifled whatever incipient democratic tendencies Evangelicalism possessed, and its preachers and tract writers, both Anglicans and Dissenters, were second to none in their devotion to the old system of fixed ranks. Their message to the poor was summed up in three words: Know Thy Place. As the Victorian hymn had it:

> *The rich man in his castle,*
> *The poor man at his gate,*
> *God made them, high or lowly,*
> *And ordered their estate.*

In this respect, then, Evangelicalism was leagues apart from Utilitarianism, which advocated political democracy in the form of universal suffrage. Its contribution to the democratizing of Victorian England was indirect, and social rather than political. As its spirit was generalized from a primarily religious one to one affecting personal and social morality, its effect spread from the middle and working classes to the higher social strata. Social communities which had no advantage to be gained from the sanctioning of individualistic economics and get-ahead business practices and were indifferent to its religious tenets adopted its moral standards. Thus the Evangelical ethos was diffused through most of society. In a nation riven by economic and social disparities, the widely accepted principles of moral Evangelicalism had a reconciling effect, bringing the classes together in what might be called an ethical democracy. Their often abrasive relations were eased by their possession of a common morality.

2. *Respectability and Other Virtues*

The essence of that morality is summed up in the single word "respectability." It was a "good" term, signifying social approval elicited by conduct that conformed to the Evangelical mode. Typically, whenever a newspaper had occasion to refer to a member of the lower classes for whom a certain amount of sympathy was bespoken, he was described as "respectable" or "respectably dressed." He therefore belonged to the in-group, regardless of his humble station.

Here, of course, individualism ceased. Respectability was not subject to private definition; its attributes represented a consensus. They included sobriety, thrift, cleanliness of person and tidiness of home, good manners, respect for the law, honesty in business affairs, and, it need hardly be added, chastity. Exercise of all these tended to content one's mind and, equally important, to invite the approbation of others. It was like living in a state of grace on earth.

Adding weight to these moral qualities was "seriousness," a bent of mind often designated by that word in Victorian fiction. To be serious was to cherish Evangelical religious views; more generally, a serious person was puritanically opposed to the vanities and frivolities of life, devoid of humor, and intolerant of others' frivolity and indulgences. Less dour in its implication but equally descriptive of the middle-class moral ideal was the epithet "earnest," which, while not excluding humor and innocent pleasure, alluded to the same zealousness and above all sincerity in the pursuit of presumably worthwhile personal and social goals. In the everyday Victorian vocabulary, "respectable" and "earnest" were nearly always terms of approbation; the intention behind "serious" varied with the user. Dickens, for example, paid his respects to the "seriousness" fetish in *Nicholas Nickleby,* in a dialogue between Tom, clerk in a London employment agency, and a fat lady looking for work:

" 'Mrs. Wrymug,' " said Tom, " 'Pleasant Place, Finsbury. Wages, twelve guineas. No tea, no sugar. Serious family—' "

"Ah! You needn't mind reading that," interrupted the client.

" 'Three serious footmen,' " said Tom, impressively.

"Three? did you say?" asked the client in an altered tone.

" 'Three serious footmen,' " replied Tom. " 'Cook, house-maid, and nursemaid; each female servant required to join the Little Bethel Congregation three times every Sunday—with a serious footman. If the cook is more serious than the footman, she will be expected to improve the footman; if the footman is more serious than the cook, he will be expected to improve the cook.' "

On the whole, most of the personal qualities included in the code of respectability were solid and incontrovertible. Of themselves, sobriety, thrift, industriousness, and the rest are admirable. But as a group they had several deficiencies which rendered them vulnerable to criticism then and even more so today. One was that many of these values contained the seeds of their own negation: carried too far, a virtue could easily become a vice. Chastity, or, more generally, strict notions of sexual behavior, could, and notoriously did, turn into prudery; insistence upon unremitting diligence became an unwholesome obsession with work for its own sake; "seriousness" became pompous solemnity and bigotry; "earnestness" and "manliness" became priggishness.

Many of these ideals were based on materialistic or self-serving assumptions. The goals toward which they led were those of wealth, physical comfort, the approbation (or envy?) of one's neighbors, the smug satisfaction that comes from an awareness of success virtuously arrived at. At mid-century Arthur Hugh Clough wrote an excoriating interpretation of this advantageous creed as "The Latest Decalogue":

> *Thou shalt have one God only; who*
> *Would be at the expense of two?*
> *No graven images may be*
> *Worshipped, except the currency:*
> *Swear not at all; for for thy curse*
> *Thine enemy is none the worse:*
> *At church on Sunday to attend*
> *Will serve to keep the world thy friend:*
> *Honour thy parents; that is, all*
> *From whom advancement may befall:*
> *Thou shalt not kill; but needst not strive*

Officiously to keep alive:
Do not adultery commit;
Advantage rarely comes of it:
Thou shalt not steal; an empty feat,
When it's so lucrative to cheat:
Bear not false witness; let the lie
Have time on its own wings to fly:
Thou shalt not covet; but tradition
Approves all forms of competition.

Moreover, this moral code, derived from an essentially gloomy theology preoccupied with man's sinful nature, was one of avoidances and denials rather than of judicious selection among positive pleasures. Evangelical middle-class morality strikes us as being bleak, austere, perversely self-denying at the same time it was self-satisfying. And so it was, at least in its extreme manifestations. Ruskin's account in *Praeterita* of his toyless early childhood in the home of well-to-do Evangelicals is as classic a description of one kind of fanatically doctrinaire upbringing as John Stuart Mill's, in his *Autobiography*, is of another.

Neither the elder Ruskins nor James Mill can be accused of the slightest hypocrisy—on the contrary, it was the very integrity of their principles which was so formidable and psychically devastating to the victim. But in households dominated by lesser minds there is no question that the taboos and inhibitions often were enforced *pro forma,* and that behind the manifestations of piety and righteousness lurked less attractive qualities. The malevolent glee with which early twentieth-century critics of Victorianism, presided over by Lytton Strachey, portrayed the two-facedness of some eminent representatives of their age was not without justification. For the truth was that, just as Utilitarianism failed to take account of the realities of human nature, so did the Evangelical ethic. Praiseworthy as many of its tenets were, they overlooked the presence of the Old Adam, who continued to seek delight in indulgences sanctioned neither by the greatest-happiness principle nor by the decalogue of respectability. It was in the nature of things that the Victorians should sometimes have been guilty of hypocrisy; they would not otherwise have been human.

One must not assume, however, that the Evangelical code was universally or uniformly applied. As in all large social groups, there were liberals as well as strict constructionists. Every Evangelical community whose members made sanctimonious fools of themselves (from a Stracheyan viewpoint) was matched by another whose temperate and humane interpretation of the rules strikes us as reasonable and possibly even engaging. There were plenty of Evangelical families who laughed and played. Not all households sought to euphemize or suppress the notion of sex functions out of existence; not all kept the Sabbath holy, as the Ruskins did, by turning pictures to the wall, eating only cold meals (so that the servants would not have to desecrate the day by working), and devoting the long hours of enforced inactivity between church services to reading the Bible or religious papers. Because fanaticism and absurdity always make good copy, they have figured in popular histories of Victorian manners somewhat more prominently than their actual incidence warrants. In addition, widely adopted though the code was, it never touched most of the industrial and urban proletariat, except insofar as their lives were made the more confined by Evangelically sponsored laws affecting public amusements and such related matters as the hours during which taverns could be open. In any event, the severity of the code, like the Benthamites' iron rationalism, moderated with the passage of time. Evangelical repression reached its apogee in the first half of the Queen's reign, after which there was a gradual liberalization of manners.

Nor must it be assumed that the Victorian spirit was devoid of humor. Although there was little literary satire of the quality of, say, Byron's *Don Juan,* in other genres—humorous periodicals like *Punch,* stage productions like the Gilbert and Sullivan operettas—satire flourished. Despite the fierce denunciatory tone of much of his writing, Carlyle's loud, derisive laugh, in person as well as in print, was legendary in his own time; the strong comic element in his makeup is perhaps too little regarded today. Dickens and Thackeray, in addition to their other gifts, were two of the greatest humorists England has produced. Indeed, everywhere one turned, the seriousness and earnestness of Victorian life were balanced by the comic impulse, expressing itself in ways as various as the nonsense verse of Edward Lear, the parodies of Thackeray, Richard H. Barham, and C. S. Calverley, the surrealistic humor of *Alice in Wonderland,* and the puns and riddles for which the Victorians had an apparently insatiable appetite and an inexhaustible tolerance.

3. Humanitarianism and the Reformation of Manners

From the wealth of energy spoken of earlier in this chapter the Evangelicals had enough left over after business had claimed its due to drive their numerous humanitarian causes as well as their less pleasing crusade for the "reformation of manners." It was Evangelical compassion which kept the spirit of social reform alive in the decades when political economists rejected it on the ground that suffering was a divine arrangement for keeping the numbers of the poor in check. Galvanized to action as they were by man's inhumanity to man, they had to their credit a number of reforms, most achieved before the Victorian age began, which mitigated the brutality of law and social custom inherited from the eighteenth century. Lord Ashley, the most tireless of Victorian social reformers, became an Evangelical in his thirties; Edwin Chadwick, whose specialty was public health, combined Evangelical reformist ardor with a Benthamite passion for fact-finding, law-making, and efficient administration.

Most conspicuous among the early Evangelical defenders of the oppressed and rescuers of the unfortunate were a coterie of wealthy Church of England businessmen and their families, known familiarly as the Clapham Sect (from the London suburb where they lived) and irreverently as "the Saints." To them belonged William Wilberforce, who after a campaign lasting many years finally accomplished the abolition of the slave trade (1807) and then of slavery itself in the British colonies (1833). The Claphamites' influence on English culture survived the decline of Evangelicalism by many years, even though its latter-day effects could hardly have been predicted. The Bloomsbury group of the twentieth century's first decades descended from the distinguished Stephen family in the persons of Virginia Woolf and her sister Vanessa Bell, and from the Thorntons in that of E. M. Forster. The Macaulays also were prominent members of the Clapham Sect.

The Evangelicals were largely responsible for the abolition of flogging in the army and navy and for the amelioration of some of the worst conditions in the nation's prisons, although in the latter case much more remained to be done. The whole issue of penal philosophy and management continued to be controversial. Dickens, for one, took an almost professional interest in the rival "separate" and "silent" systems, the former requiring continuous confinement in separate cells, the latter permitting communal living and working but with all forms of communication among the prisoners strictly forbidden. Neither system, of course, was concerned with their rehabilitation.

The Evangelicals' far-flung humanitarian concerns prompted them to found literally hundreds of philanthropic and missionary organizations, some with dense networks of local branches and committees reaching across the country. The diversity of these causes, as well as their individual limitations, may be inferred from this small selection of late eighteenth- and early nineteenth-century societies, some of whose titles are almost as long as their constitutions: the Ladies' Association for the Benefit of Gentlewomen of Good Family, Reduced in Fortune Below the State of Comfort

To Which They Have Been Accustomed; the Friendly Female Society, for the Relief of Poor, Infirm, Aged Widows, and Single Women, of Good Character, Who Have Seen Better Days; the Guardian Society, for the Preservation of Public Morals by Providing Temporary Asylums for Prostitutes; the London Orphan Asylum, for the Reception and Education of Destitute Orphans, Particularly Those Descended from Respectable Parents; the National Truss Society for the Relief of the Ruptured Poor; the Society for Returning Young Women to their Friends in the Country; and the Royal Humane Society (to restore "persons in a state of suspended animation"). Seemingly, the Evangelicals had a society to cover every contingency.

As is implied by the wording of several of these titles, and by such an additional one as the Society for Promoting the External Observance of the Lord's Day and for the Suppression of Public Lewdness, the Evangelicals externalized their religion not only in philanthropic exertions but in the form of a preferred system of social morality. Here again the Victorian middle-class temper resembled that of the Evangelicals' spiritual ancestors, the Puritans of the late sixteenth and seventeenth centuries, with (once more) a fortuitous assist from the Benthamites. They believed that public morality depended upon private virtue. The well-being of society was derived from the spiritual health of its individual members (the Utilitarians' "happiness," the Evangelicals' "state of grace"). While the Benthamites sought to cultivate the individual's intelligence as the necessary preliminary to his attainment of "rational" happiness, the Evangelicals concentrated on purifying his soul and leading his steps along the path of righteousness. Not only did they make their moral convictions available for the guidance of the unenlightened: they worked to make them prevail. In their zeal to save souls, they sought to impose their standards of right living (of whose absolute authority, residing in divine inspiration, they had no doubt) upon society as a whole.

The Victorians witnessed the climax of a campaign which had been mounting for several decades. The movement to purify the moral climate of England, toward which the Church as a whole had adopted a laissez-faire attitude, had begun in the 1780's under the auspices of a group of Evangelical clergymen within the Church. It was responsible for George III's Proclamation for the Encouragement of Piety and Virtue, and for the Preventing and Punishing of Vice, Profaneness, and Immorality (1787) and its oldest instrumentality was the aptly named Society to Effect the Enforcement of His Majesty's Proclamation Against Vice and Immorality (soon understandably abbreviated to "the Proclamation Society"). This organization was the prototype of all subsequent English and American organizations dedicated to the enforcement of public morality by suasion or statute. The crusade was intensified in the wartime conditions of the ensuing decades, when "immorality" was almost equated with treason, for it was thought to be sapping the strength of a beleaguered nation. As a result, the Evangelicals undertook to reform the whole of the middle class to which they belonged; the working class, over whose morals they felt impelled to exercise a special guardianship; and, not least, the aristocracy, which, as typified say by Horace Walpole, was worldly and cynical, if not immoral. The drive for souls was successful enough in the 1790's to produce the spectacle of high society taking up religion as a fascinating new diversion and an example to the lower classes. Lines of carriages bearing noble crests were seen on Sunday mornings in front of churches which hitherto had attracted but a handful of worshipers. "This novel appearance," reported an observer, "prompted the simple country people to enquire what was the matter."

The flagrant immorality practiced in certain sectors of fashionable society during the Regency attests to the presence, if not of backsliders, then of groups who never went in for church attendance or tract distribution in the first place. Nor did the libertinism and extravagance traditionally attributed to aristocratic life wholly disappear in the Victorian period. There were still fast-living men (and not a few women) in the upper reaches of society. But it is significant that they never enjoyed the approval of the Queen, whose court, before the death of the Prince Consort in 1861 and her retreat into protracted mourning, was heavy with conventionality. Thanks to the Evangelicals' reformation-of-manners campaign, a social class which in the eighteenth century had been distinguished by amoral worldliness now minded its manners and became, for the most part, even "respectable."

The oldest and most enduring of the Evangelicals' many causes was Sabbatarianism. To keep the Lord's Day devoid of pleasure, they pressed for the strict enforcement of existing laws, some of which had been placed on the books as early as the seventeenth century, and the passage of new ones to extend the coverage. They fought to prevent public houses, theaters, and all other places of amusement from opening on Sunday, and successfully opposed military band concerts in the London parks. To keep the Sabbath equally devoid of labor, they backed laws to ban retail sales, to suspend the operations of the Post Office, and even to forbid trains from running. Although they were not uniformly successful—working-class sentiment, expressed in no uncertain terms, kept the public houses open, and businessmen saw to it the mails were kept moving—they did triumph to the extent of making the *dimanche anglais* a phenomenon at which visitors from the irreligious Continent never ceased to wonder and shudder. The stupor of the English Sunday, whose stillness was broken only by the incessant jangling of bells calling the population to worship, evoked Dickens' repeated complaint, most notably in *Little Dorrit*. Not until late in the century could museums and art galleries, for example, be opened on Sunday afternoons.

Strict Evangelicals—emphasis must be laid on the "strict," because here as elsewhere not all shared their bias —did not limit their opposition to frivolity to a single day in the week. They categorically disapproved of private and semi-private amusements such as dancing and card-playing (synonymous with gambling), and of all but the most innocuous kinds of public entertainment. Unlike their Puritan forebears, they did not seriously try to shut down the playhouses, but they contributed nothing to their prosperity. If the theater, as distinct from the literary art of the drama, flourished in Victorian England, as it did in respect to virtuoso acting and spectacular staging, no thanks were due to the many thousands of serious families who were convinced that the playhouse was the favorite resort of the devil. It was the Evangelicals' compassion rather than their scruples, however, which had the salutary effect of driving from the Victorian scene the grosser kinds of spectator sports, such as cockfighting, bullbaiting, and bearbaiting, which had survived from the Regency. Prizefighting, which in Hazlitt's day and for many years thereafter involved bloody, barefisted encounters lasting as many as seventy-five rounds, held in outdoor locations hopefully beyond the authorities' ken, acquired a measure of acceptance although not of respectability in 1866 through the adoption of the Marquis of Queensberry's rules.

Then there was the liquor problem—a genuinely urgent one in the period, not merely an obsession of narrow minds. From the Hogarthian eighteenth century the nineteenth had inherited the cheap gin whose potency earned it the reputation among the laboring class of being "the quickest way out of Manchester." When less injurious recreations were unavailable in the city slums and the factory towns—and in the worst decades of the era there was little alternative—working men and women found their only solace in getting dead drunk. The crime reports are replete with all too authentic instances of the brutality, extending to mayhem and outright murder, which resulted from excessive drinking. Apart from its vicious effects, it reduced the workers' productivity and increased absenteeism. For a combination of moral and pragmatic reasons, therefore, the religious groups supported an endless series of teetotal campaigns, complete with magazines, lectures, and mass pledges. They probably kept the drink habit from spreading, and in the long run it seems that they actually managed to reduce consumption. At least, the nation never again drank as much as it did in 1875, the most bibulous year on record, when the annual per capita consumption of spirits was 1.3 gallons, and of beer 34.4 gallons. But public drunkenness continued to be a common sight.

4. Conformity and Insularity

Irrespective of the worthiness of their various causes, the Evangelicals often succumbed to intolerance and sheer bigotry, a risk taken by all crusaders who know that God is on their side. It will not do to minimize the lengths to which the more zealous members of the middle class, scorning any policy of live and let live, went in their effort to transform the whole of Victorian society into their image. Theirs was a noble impulse—to share with all the bliss of salvation which they were persuaded they had themselves earned, or would have earned when their missionary goal was accomplished—but it had distinctly unpleasant effects, for it was they who perfected the weapon of social disapproval. In an age when respectability was a goal to which most people aspired, meaning above all the approval of one's peers, the pressures for conformity were stronger than they had perhaps ever been. It was not merely a matter of satisfying the pedantic moralists who fussed about trivial details of language and behavior: one felt, however subconsciously, the weight of a whole society's ethos, its criteria of decorum, which rested, ultimately, on religious grounds. This, as John Stuart Mill in particular was aware, is the hardest kind of censorship to define and combat, just because it is so intangible and elusive. Hence the urgency of his defense of non-conformity—sturdy independence of conduct as well as of ideas—in *On Liberty*. In this great essay, applying the principle of laissez faire to the realm of the intellect and the will, Mill expressed his alarm over the part the Evangelicals and others of like mind played in what he rightly deemed the intolerable imposition of orthodox opinion and rules of respectable behavior upon all.

Yet those pressures were not all-pervasive; or at least there were numerous people strong enough to withstand them. Dickens' numerous eccentrics, amiable like Mr. Dick, grotesque like Miss Havisham, reflected the presence of many such characters in real life, men and women who, for various obscure or manifest reasons, defied the tyranny of convention. The elderly Charles Waterton, a widely traveled naturalist of great accomplishment, would climb trees like an "adolescent gorilla" and scratch the back of his head with the big toe of his right foot. He entertained the inmates of the local madhouse at parties on his lawn; and when he had sane guests to dinner, he threatened their mental balance by disappearing under the table on all fours and growling and nipping their legs. Lytton Strachey's eldest uncle, who had spent five years of his youth in India, lived his remaining fifty-six years in England with his watch set to Calcutta time. As a consequence, he was a thoroughly nocturnal creature, beginning his candle-lit day by taking breakfast when more custom-bound people were having their afternoon tea. He always wore galoshes, regardless of the season, and left his nephew, as Lytton's sole legacy, a generous supply of unworn colored underwear.

There were Victorian monomaniacs, too, like Sir Thomas Phillipps, crusty, violent-tempered, bigoted, litigious, and sadistically cruel to his family—an obsessed man who for fifty years collected every scrap of printed and manuscript matter he could lay his hands on, because, as he said, "I wish to have *one copy of every Book in the World.*" He crammed 100,000 volumes, including many manuscripts of superlative value, into packing-case shelves that occupied every square foot of space in his tindery Gloucestershire country house, whose windows were never opened and whose furniture and wallpaper were in such decay that visitors were tempted to conclude that nobody had lived there for a century. He and Miss Havisham would have made a congenial pair.

Phillipps' debts to booksellers forever outran his income; an aristocratic contemporary of his could afford to pay as he went when indulging his whim. The fifth Duke of Portland, desiring seclusion, built a great underground hall at his seat, Welbeck Abbey; a thousand-yard tunnel from the house to a vast enclosed riding rink; and, most spectacularly, a tunnel one and one half miles long and broad enough to accommodate two carriages abreast. This led from his house to the town of Worksop, where his curtained carriage, with him inside, was lifted onto a railway car for transportation to London. The garden adjoining his town mansion was surrounded by an eighty-foot-high screen of ground glass and cast iron. The Duke's handkerchiefs were a yard square, he wore three pairs of socks with his cork-soled boots, his kitchen garden occupied twenty-five acres, and a chicken was always turning on the spit in case His Grace developed an untimely fancy for a snack.

The universities, needless to say, had more than their share of odd characters. One reads, for example, of a certain aged Cambridge fellow who had lived in a set of rooms since earliest manhood, but who never emerged from them except at twilight. He would then shuffle out into the quad and poke with his thick stick at the worms in the grass, muttering, "Ah, damn ye; ye haven't got me yet!"

That men and women of magnificently independent impulses continued to thrive unmolested was witness to the fact that English toleration of eccentricity was stronger even than the pervasive pressure toward conformity—which is saying a good deal. Simultaneously, another star shone in the nation's crown, the hospitality it gave to the many political refugees who fled the Continent in a century of constant struggle between liberalism and reactionary despotism.

It was a source of national pride that no exile, whatever his political sympathies, was denied asylum. Dante Gabriel Rossetti's father was such a refugee. Among many others were the considerably better known Italian patriot Giuseppe Mazzini; the Hungarian Louis Kossuth; Karl Marx, who wrote *Das Kapital* in the reading room of the British Museum; the French king Louis Philippe and his successor Louis Napoleon (later Napoleon III), who had served as a special constable in London during the 1848 Chartist scare, eight months before being elected president of the Second Republic, and who spent his last years in England after losing the Franco-Prussian War.

This exemplary open-door policy was in singular contrast to the nation's attitude toward another kind of importation, that of contemporary art and ideas. Here, under the domination of the Evangelical temper, insularity carried the day, on occasion rising to the stridency of outright xenophobia. Partly because Evangelicalism had begun to flourish as a social force, with particular emphasis on the danger of "foreign" (i.e., radical, irreligious) ideas, in a time when England was cut off from the Continent by the exigencies of war, it associated true morality with true Englishness, and thus intensified the insularity which persisted for several decades after normal intercourse with the Continent was resumed. No longer was the culture of western Europe the inspiration and measure of contemporary English culture, as it had been in the bountiful eighteenth century. Instead, for the greater part of the Victorian period England, basking in its knowledge that it was the world's supreme economic and naval power, chose to regard itself as the world's first moral and cultural power as well. Mr. Podsnap, in *Our Mutual Friend,* "considered other countries a mistake, and of their manners and customs would conclusively observe 'Not English!', and presto they would be swept away." He had to acknowledge the regrettable fact that foreign nations "do—I am sorry to be obliged to say—as they do." A dozen years later, the H.M.S. *Pinafore*'s crew sang their lusty anthem in praise of Ralph Rackstraw, able seaman, who

> *might have been a Roosian,*
> *A French, or Turk, or Proosian,*
> *Or perhaps Itali-an!*
> *But in spite of all temptations*
> *To belong to other nations,*
> *He remains an Englishman!*

Well-to-do families traveled at a leisurely rate from country to country, drinking the spa waters in Germany, admiring the Alps, and inspecting the ruins in Italy, but it was notorious how much of England they carried about with them and how little of the spirit of the place rubbed off on them. (The rubbing went in the other direction: the natives resented the touring Britons' contempt, arrogance, and bad manners.) The blandishments of France and Italy were resisted the more resolutely because these were Catholic countries, and one of the deepest prejudices of the Evangelical mind was its anti-Romanism.

As a result, English thought and literature were affected less by developments in Europe than in any preceding epoch. Carlyle, it is true, was steeped in German philosophy, but he had acquired his transcendentalism under the auspices of the romantic age, and two of his generation's keenest intellects, Newman and Mill, knew little of contemporary German idealistic thought. The traffic, again, was the other way: Dickens' novels made a deep impression on Dostoevski, and Ruskin's writings on Tolstoy and Proust. As to the results of this intellectual and artistic parochialism, one need but consult Matthew Arnold's essays. It was only in the sixties that contemporary French poetry began to have an impact on advanced English spirits like Swinburne, and only in the eighties and nineties that French naturalistic fiction affected the aims of novelists like George Moore and George Gissing.

This insularity was simply part of the Evangelicals'

unintellectual temper. It is generally agreed that neither Evangelical Anglicanism nor Dissent contributed much to the sum of theological ideas; their clergymen were more interested in saving souls than in deep thought. Like shepherd, like flock: the rank and file of Evangelicals were indifferent to the things of the mind and the secular imagination. As the criticism of men like Mill and Arnold makes plain, their presence inhibited the free development of the Victorian intellect, opposing reason and the analytical habit with an uncritical congeries of simplistic truths derived from Scripture and the pieties of Christian moralists. They were suspicious of abstract thought, if not actually hostile to it; in many instances they seem to have been incapable of it.

It is true that a number of men and women with great intellectual gifts came from Evangelical homes or were otherwise exposed to Evangelical influence in their formative years: the Brontë sisters, Ruskin, George Eliot, Macaulay, Kingsley, Samuel Butler, Gladstone, Henry Edward Manning, and Newman, to cite only those who are best remembered today. But it is also true that most of them reached full stature of mind only under later, more liberating circumstances. The best measure of their reaction against the Evangelicalism of their youth is offered by the fact that two of them ended as Roman Catholic cardinals and a third—George Eliot—as a leading exponent of an ethical religion devoid of supernaturalism and dogma.

5. Literature and "Circulating Library Morality"

During the decades early in the century when Evangelicalism was most resolute in its avoidances, fiction was at the top of its literary Index Expurgatorius. Religious magazines echoed with denunciations of the novel, which was believed to stimulate the imagination to a false perception of reality. "Instead of embellishing life, as it is falsely represented to do," asserted one writer, "it heightens only imaginary and unattainable enjoyments, and transforms life itself into a dream, the realities of which are all made painful and disgusting, from our false expectations and erroneous notions of happiness." For this and other reasons, fiction was barred from countless serious households. By the thirties, however, Scott's fame had induced many who had formerly averted their eyes from fiction to inspect his novels, and what they found there was unexceptionable. When Dickens burst upon the scene at the same time, it took an extraordinarily scrupulous reader (there were some) to find any offense in *Pickwick Papers*. Thanks mainly to these two novelists, the Evangelical stand against secular fiction was modified, and although, as we shall see in a moment, severe canons of propriety were maintained through the era, fiction ceased being a pariah among the literary genres except in the view of the most austere religious groups. But the obloquy that had been attached to it during the first third of the century had much to do with delaying its claim to critical attention.

Most of what the stricter Evangelicals read lay beyond the borders of literary art. Their ordinary appetites ran strongly toward didactic and inspirational reading matter, as platitude-laden as it was cliché-bound. But they read a great deal, and in various ways they did much to widen the reading public. Theirs was a veritable religion of print, resting as it did upon the Bible as the inerrant word of God. Daily communion with the Bible was necessary for salvation, for without its inspiration one could not achieve the faith requisite for divine grace. The ability to read therefore was highly prized, and the Evangelicals nurtured it in their educational activities. The large market they formed for improving literature encouraged the development of the cheap production and distribution techniques that revolutionized the Victorian book trade.

Even more important, the Evangelicals' bibliolatry profoundly influenced the quality of Victorian prose. Not only was Biblical language encountered every day at home (family prayers and reading the Bible aloud were the Evangelicals' main contribution to Victorian domestic routine): quotations from the Bible threaded through the sermons at church and chapel, the lessons at Sunday School, the services at weekday prayer and revival meetings. The language of religion also colored the discourse in schools, for most Victorian popular education was conducted by religious groups, both Dissent and Church, and most of the schools catering to the middle class and gentry were likewise under the influence of religion in that their teachers were clergymen.

From earliest childhood, consequently, on all levels of society, both at home and at school, the Victorians were accustomed to Biblical language and story to an extent almost inconceivable today. This meant that writers, if they chose—and they often did choose, for the sake of maximum effect—could employ a prose redolent with Biblical style and dense with Biblical allusion. Such was the case with secular prophets like Carlyle and Ruskin, and with the innumerable popular propagandists for economic and political causes. Rhetoric and rhythms drawn from Scripture were as basic to much Victorian argumentative prose as classical devices were to the literary art of the eighteenth century. They enabled Victorian writers to communicate, in readily understandable and persuasive terms, with a susceptible audience many times larger than the select Augustan one which could alone have responded to discourse framed in neo-classic terms.

Because their scruples prevented many Evangelicals from attending public entertainments and even from participating in such household recreations as card games, they occupied their free time in reading. This was as true of middle-class Victorians in general, most of whom enjoyed a wider choice of recreations, as it was of the Evangelicals in particular. The fireside was the center of family life, and the products of the press were as indispensable to household custom as tableware and furniture. In addition to private reading, there was that familiar institution of the middle-class Victorian household, the reading circle, in which most members of the family, children and adults alike, joined to hear one of their number, usually the father, read aloud from a book or magazine.

The popularity of the reading circle had a momentous effect upon the content of Victorian literature. The Evangelicals suffered from an often neurotic anxiety lest the impressionable mind be sullied by impure thoughts. It was requisite, therefore, that all the reading matter their hands took up, and paramountly that which was to be read aloud in a group including women and children, be devoid of the faintest impropriety of language or thought. The pale cheek of the archetypal "Young Person," Georgiana Podsnap, whose parents were obsessively concerned lest any remotely disturbing suggestion or indelicate word imperil her innocence, served as a moral litmus paper, a norm to whose supposed sensibilities editors and publishers ceaselessly deferred.

This is what was meant by the Victorians' notorious prudery, which extended, of course, to all language—ordinary speech as well as print—and to pictures and sculpture revealing more of the human body than many people were prepared to admit existed. Indelicacy was almost as much to be deplored as blasphemy.

The most celebrated instance of expurgated literature in the century was the Reverend Thomas Bowdler's significantly named *Family Shakspeare* (1818, and therefore pre-Victorian), in which every phrase that Bowdler thought would offend an innocent mind was deleted or replaced by a pale (and often misleading) substitute. As a contemporary reviewer observed, "the editor has sometimes shewn the truth of the old saw, that the *nicest* person has the *nastiest* ideas, and has omitted many phrases as containing indelicacies which we cannot see, and of the guilt of which our bard, we think, is entirely innocent." Bowdler's nose was super-sensitive but not always dependable, and the comprehensiveness of his expurgation policy was matched only by the inconsistency with which he applied it. He totally eliminated Doll Tearsheet from the second part of *Henry IV*, cut three-fourths of the drunken porter's speech in *Macbeth*, and deleted the English-lesson scene between the French princess and her serving woman in *Henry V* (III. iv).

While he euphemized Falstaff's "belly" into "body," in such plays as *Romeo and Juliet* and *Othello* Bowdler deemed "body" too offensive even when it occurred in perfectly inoffensive passages. His treatment of *Othello* was especially unpredictable; while cutting or obfuscating some of the most explicit sexual references, he let others stand. Sometimes he converted a line to utter nonsense (as in substituting "bonds" for "bawds" in Polonius' line to Ophelia, "Breathing like sanctified and pious bawds"); at other times the correction involved a distinction without a difference (in *Measure for Measure*, Lucio's "He hath got his friend with child" was inexplicably "purified" to read "His friend's with child by him"). Yet, while he sniffed out and expunged many expressions of unexceptionable innocuousness, Bowdler failed to detect many genuine ribaldries of which we, with our more sophisticated knowledge of Elizabethan English, are unperturbedly aware. He later applied himself to a similar purifying of Gibbon's *Decline and Fall of the Roman Empire*, and his successors throughout the Victorian era took similar care of numerous other classics of English literature, including Chaucer.

Bowdlerization was among the least praiseworthy contributions the Evangelicals made to Victorian literary culture. The same opposition to plain speaking severely limited contemporary authors, who had to abide by the same mush-mouthed conventions that governed "genteel" speech in everyday life. Dickens' opinion of such taboos was made sufficiently plain in *Oliver Twist:*

> "I tossed off the clothes," said Giles, throwing away the tablecloth, and looking very hard at the cook and housemaid, "got softly out of bed; drew on a pair of—"
> "Ladies present, Mr. Giles," murmured the tinker.

"—Of *shoes,* sir," said Giles, turning upon him, and laying great emphasis on the word . . .

Editorial squeamishness (which the editors themselves disclaimed, asserting that they were merely acting on behalf of the readers who called the tune) seems to have reached its peak in the sixties and seventies. George Eliot was one sufferer. Before *The Mill on the Floss* appeared in 1860, her publisher was bothered by her description of Mrs. Moss as "a patient, loosely-hung, child-producing woman." She obliged by changing Mrs. Moss into "a patient, prolific, loving-hearted woman." But the chief victim was Thomas Hardy. Novel after novel had to submit to either rejection or blue-penciling at the hands of nervous editors. In *The Hand of Ethelberta* he had to substitute "sentimental" for "amorous"; in *Far from the Madding Crowd,* "lewd," "loose," and "bawdy" became "gross," "wicked," and "sinful." In *Tess of the d'Urbervilles,* which no magazine would take in its unexpurgated form, the editor of the *Graphic* required that the seduction scene be omitted and a mock marriage substituted; and Angel Clare had to convey the milkmaid across the flooded stream in a wheelbarrow, not in his arms. It was only with difficulty that Hardy persuaded the publishers of his novels in book form to restore what finicky magazine editors had forced him to tone down or eliminate.

It was not only "advanced" authors like Hardy who sometimes grew restive under such restraints. Thackeray, for instance, complained in the preface to *Pendennis,* written when Hardy was a boy of ten, that "Since the author of Tom Jones was buried, no writer of fiction among us has been permitted to depict to his utmost power a MAN. We must drape him, and give him a certain conventional simper. Society will not tolerate the Natural in our Art." Aspirations toward realism in fiction were constantly defeated by this informal censorship, which was more effective than any legal measures could have been. The censors comprised a symbolic group: the legendary Mrs. Grundy, Bowdler's ghost, the excessively virginal Miss Podsnap's anxious Mama and Papa, and Charles Edward Mudie, the proprietor of the famous "Select Circulating Library" (note the reassuring "Select") to which scores of thousands of families in London and the country subscribed. Mudie, a man of strong Evangelical views, could make or break an author's career by his acceptance or rejection of a new book. His favor could mean the sale of several hundred copies, a substantial part of an edition, to him alone; added to this would be a boost in retail sales if the size of Mudie's purchase were well publicized. Mudie stocked 2,400 copies of the third and fourth volumes of Macaulay's *History of England,* 1,000 of *Adam Bede,* 2,000 of *The Mill on the Floss,* 3,100 of *Silas Marner,* and 2,500 of Tennyson's *Enoch Arden.* On the other hand, after receiving complaints from a number of subscribers, he withdrew from circulation the few copies he had bought of Meredith's *The Ordeal of Richard Feverel,* and later he banned George Moore's realistic *A Modern Lover* and *A Mummer's Wife* from his shelves.

There evidently is no record of the number of books Mudie did not buy in the first place because of his—or his readers'—scruples, but it is easy to understand why no publisher, debating whether or not to publish a proffered manuscript, could afford to forget Mudie's presence in the background. Not until the last two decades of the century did the long-smoldering resentment of Mudie's tyranny turn into a frontal attack as Hardy, Henry James, and George Moore (the last-named in a pamphlet called *Literature at Nurse, or Circulating Morals*) sharpened their polemic pens. They succeeded in sapping the circulating libraries' power, which had been waning for some time anyway, and won their profession a slightly increased independence. But as the twentieth century began it was still impossible, in books and periodicals intended for the general reader, to use language and discuss certain topics which we today regard as totally inoffensive.

Mudie was only the most famous of those who guarded

library subscribers' morals. His competitors often followed his lead in rejecting books about which the slightest question could be raised, and certainly they responded to the same pressures. After a bishop announced he had burned his copy of *Jude the Obscure,* the powerful firm of W. H. Smith and Son, who had a virtual monopoly on the nation's railroad-station bookstalls, withdrew the book from circulation—and ended Hardy's career as a novelist. Beyond the commercial libraries, there were the people who sponsored and managed the mechanics' institute libraries, the schools for middle- and lower-class children, and free libraries. They scrutinized every purchase for lurking mischief, and, while the censorial impulse varied widely from place to place, the net result was to deprive potential readers of access to books from which they would have drawn much enjoyment and enlightenment. The watch-and-ward mentality which quarantined adults and children alike against the supposed infections of print is one of the heaviest charges to be alleged against the Evangelicals, not least because it originated as early as the 1780's and thus cast its shadow across a whole century.

Although fiction was the most frequent scene of censorship, poets too had sometimes to be reminded of Mrs. Grundy's formidable presence, as three episodes from the 1860's illustrate. Shortly before her death in 1861, Elizabeth Barrett Browning, responding to Thackeray's request that she contribute to the *Cornhill Magazine,* sent, among other poems, one called "Lord Walter's Wife." Thackeray, in a letter which he said he found most difficult to write, had to decline it. "In your poem, you know, there is an account of unlawful passion, felt by a man for a woman, and though you write pure doctrine, and real modesty, and pure ethics, I am sure our readers would make an outcry, and so I have not published the poem." Five years later, Swinburne offered his collection of *Poems and Ballads,* which included some feverishly erotic specimens, to Byron's publisher, the ultrarespectable firm of Murray. Murray declined the volume with alacrity. It was then accepted by the liberal and respected firm of Moxon, which, though its former proprietor had been successfully prosecuted for reprinting Shelley's *Queen Mab* twenty-five years earlier, was willing to take a chance. But the outcry upon publication was frightening; one critic denounced the poet as "an unclean fiery imp from the pit" and "the libidinous laureate of a pack of satyrs." The volume, he said, was "crammed with pieces which many a professional vendor of filthy prints might blush to sell if he only knew what they meant." The Moxon firm, fearing that a police case was in the making, suppressed the book, and Swinburne thereupon transferred it to the sort of vendor his critic had recommended—a house which specialized in under-the-counter literature.

Two years later Tennyson wrote for *Macmillan's Magazine,* the *Cornhill's* rival, one of his finest poems, "Lucretius." It included the lines

> *And here an Oread—how the sun delights*
> *To glance and shift about her slippery sides,*
> *And rosy knees and supple roundedness,*
> *And budded bosom-peaks—who this way runs*
> *Before the rest . . .*

But when the poem appeared in *Macmillan's,* the passage was condensed to

> *And here an Oread—and this way she runs*
> *Before the rest . . .*

Notified of the deletion before the issue was printed, Tennyson wrote to the editor, ". . . please yourself, but send the full passage to America. They are not so squeamish as we are."

Although legal censorship did exist, it applied only to obscene publications (a term which, as in a famous case in the 1870's, was taken to extend to books containing pages on birth control). After the several waves of prosecutions against authors, printers, and sellers of radical political and "atheistic" books and papers between the 1790's and the mid-1830's, the right to express unorthodox opinion went unabridged as far as the government was concerned. Juries, always reluctant to convict, were growing more and more sympathetic to the defendants; and, perhaps more important, the Benthamites' unswerving dedication to the principle of free speech and print had its effect. Nonetheless—and here the Evangelicals must be exonerated of specific blame; the pressure came from a much broader segment of the population—informal censorship still operated in the world of ideas. Carlyle's *Chartism* (1840) was too hot for any respectable periodical to touch, and it had to be published separately. The *Fraser's Magazine* serialization of Kingsley's *Yeast,* on conditions of life among the agricultural workers, had to be speeded to its end because many readers complained and threatened to cancel their subscriptions. Ruskin's "Essays on the Elements of Political Economy" suffered a similar fate: *"Unto This Last"* was cut off after three installments in the *Cornhill,* and its continuation, *Munera Pulveris,* soon came to an equally premature end in *Fraser's.*

In these cases, of course, only temporary suppression was involved, not definitive censorship. The authors were understandably angered, but their work soon reached the public in the complete form they intended. Nor was effective suppression sought in the several famous cases of heterodox books which raised the temperature of the mid-Victorian Church. *The Nemesis of Faith,* in which Carlyle's future biographer James Anthony Froude described in thin fictional disguise his odyssey into doubt, was publicly burned in the hall of his Oxford college. A stubbornly unconvinced scientist-theologian, Dr. William Whewell, refused to admit *The Origin of Species* to the library of Trinity College, Cambridge, and did everything he could to prevent its otherwise falling into the hands of students. John William Colenso was relieved of his bishopric of Natal and excommunicated (both temporarily) for writing *The Pentateuch and Book of Joshua Critically Examined,* which denied the authenticity of the Mosaic books. Two of the seven distinguished authors

("Septem contra Christum," as their opponents called them) who contributed to a moderately liberal symposium on current theological issues, *Essays and Reviews,* were condemned for heresy by the Ecclesiastical Court, but the decision was reversed on appeal to the Privy Council. Such episodes merely meant that the Church was bent on disciplining its more adventuresome clerics; no official attempt was made to prevent the dissemination of their views.

With their sophisticated view of humanity, leading Victorian novelists found Evangelicals irresistible subjects for caricature or for realistic portraiture which ranged from the sympathetic to the scathing. The free-lance and free-loading preachers Stiggins (*Pickwick Papers*) and Chadband (*Bleak House*)—Dickens dispenses with their given names—and Melchisedech Howler (*Dombey and Son*) are among Dickens' most hilarious comic characters; the sting that went into the descriptions is unmistakable. The Reverend Obadiah Slope (*Barchester Towers*) is the unctuous Evangelical clergyman seen in the milieu of a cathedral chapter. But perhaps the most acidulous portrait of the type in Victorian fiction is Robert Brocklehurst in *Jane Eyre,* the sponsor of "Lowood Institution" (actually the Cowan Bridge School for Clergymen's Daughters, where two of Charlotte Brontë's sisters contracted fatal illnesses). Whereas Dickens' and Trollope's Evangelical clergymen were imaginary, Brocklehurst was drawn from life. His original was William Carus Wilson, a nationally known Low Churchman.

A more sympathetically drawn clergyman in *Jane Eyre* is St. John Rivers, who dies during his mission to convert the heathen. In *Bleak House,* by contrast, the victims of missionary zeal are the husband and children of busy Mrs. Jellyby, whose exertions in behalf of the natives of Borrioboola-Gha leave her no time to care for the charity cases in her own disheveled home. She shares Dickens' dubious honors with Mrs. Pardiggle, the model of the peripatetic Bible saleswoman and all-around busybody. Wilkie Collins' contribution to the gallery of officious Victorian religious females is Miss Drusilla Clack (*The Moonstone*), who leaves behind her a spoor of tracts intended to convert both her hosts and their servants from their sinful ways. Of all fictional Evangelicals, however, George Eliot's are probably the most diversified both in character and in their creator's view of them: Dinah Morris, the female Wesleyan preacher in *Adam Bede;* Amos Barton, the mediocre curate in *Scenes of Clerical Life;* and Bulstrode, the fraudulent banker in *Middlemarch.*

Much of the great Victorian critical prose which retains its timeliness in our own day is, in one way or another, a protest against the stifling effects of the Evangelical code upon the intellectual life and the comeliness of personal and social existence. In one of his ironical observations, G. M. Young comments that "On one of its sides, Victorian history is the story of the English mind employing the energy imparted by Evangelical conviction to rid itself of the restraints which Evangelicalism had laid on the senses and the intellect; on amusement, enjoyment, art; on curiosity, on criticism, on science." [3] The English mind so employed is seen best in the literature left by the opinion-molding writers, who mounted continual protests against the parochialism, the strait-laced morality, the neglect of the mind and of the sense of beauty which characterized the Evangelical temperament in its more rigorous, and unfortunately most influential, manifestations. "Sourness of spirit" we can perhaps call it: the antithesis, at any rate, of the humanist's broad and luminous ideal.

But the ledger has another page. The Evangelical moral code involved certain ideals of conduct which, to most modern observers, were positively healthy. Prominent among these were deeply felt familial affections and an equally profound sense of social obligation which found expression in deeds of compassion and charity. The Evangelicals' sense of moral responsibility was one thing, sometimes the only thing, which most Victorian agnostics salvaged from the wreckage of a faith they could no longer accept. The very loss of that faith in many cases intensified the promptings of the conscience. To their Evangelical heritage is due the impression we have of the Victorians at their best as being dedicated to stout, upright, even defiant morality. If the seriousness with which they regarded their principles too often stiffened into an unbecoming solemnity, the fact remains that they were people of high integrity, motivated by an abiding sense of responsibility.

VI

RELIGIOUS MOVEMENTS

AND CRISES

1. High Church, Low Church, Broad Church

IT HAS BEEN SAID of the nineteenth century in England that "probably in no other century, except the seventeenth and perhaps the twelfth, did the claims of religion occupy so large a part in the nation's life, or did men speaking in the name of religion contrive to exercise so much power." [1] The chief religious events to be touched upon in this chapter were in no way removed from the broad intellectual current of the age, as similar events usually have been in more recent times. On the contrary, they were an inextricable part of the cultural fabric; they engaged the attention of the general educated public, to whom they were issues of great moment; and they involved principles for which men of commitment willingly sacrificed careers and endured vilification.

The ordinary Victorian had been reared in a culture circumscribed by Christian teaching. In addition to a common literary and argumentative vocabulary, the Bible provided the accepted cosmogony, a considerable part of ancient history as it was then known, and above all the foundations of his morality. Religion had determined his whole outlook upon life, his assessment of its nature and purpose; and when what he had been taught to believe were its eternal verities were cast into question, he suffered accordingly. Reverberations of the intensifying assault upon received Christianity are found widespread in the age's literature. Some Victorian voices speak with assurance, but others with poignant doubt. Taken all together, their response to the growing anti-religious forces constitutes a high, sometimes tragic drama of the national soul.

Although in retrospect the decline of religious authority was the most consequential as well as the most dramatic spiritual development of the time, it was not the whole story. The Church also was the site of constructive movements which strengthened it for the time being and brought it in close touch with secular tendencies. Each nurtured and influenced the other.

The Church of England's condition in the immediate pre-Victorian era did not encourage confidence in its future. Already it was under attack because of its internal corruption and failure to serve a changing society; if the coming series of crises involving the very credibility of religion could have been foreseen, its intellectual torpor would have caused equal concern. Except for the discomfiting presence of the Evangelical party, the Church remained as it had been in the eighteenth century, observing empty forms and trailing clouds of deism. The Latitudinarian party was in control, its unruffled rationalism discountenancing any expression of emotion. Anglicanism was a gentleman's religion, administered by clergy of worldly tastes and ambitions largely unaffected by the spirit of Christianity. The bishops, nearly all of whom were connected with the aristocracy by blood, marriage, or patronage—several had tutored their noble patrons in their youth—functioned mainly as a powerful bloc in the House of Lords. In such time as they could spare from their wheeling and dealing in the rich emoluments of clerical life, they supported Tory policies down the line. The Lords Spiritual, indeed, were known to the irreverent as the Tory party at prayer.

Meanwhile, few of the parsons under their governance bothered with parish duties; more than a few were of the kind who turned up in the pulpit, on obligatory occasions, dressed for foxhunting. They were spiritual descendants (if the adjective is not misapplied in this context) of the unintellectual, easygoing clergymen who ride, drink, and lounge in the pages of Fielding, and of the Reverend Laurence Sterne, whose pen enabled him to flee from a parish in rural Yorkshire to the worldly, even rakish ambience of London society. Often they sat with or in place of the local squire on the magistrate's bench, a role that did not always endear them to the rustics who were haled before them. Their comfortable philosophy of social relations was well summarized in a sermon preached by Parson Dale in Edward Bulwer-Lytton's *"My Novel!"*: "If there were no penury and no pain, what would become of fortitude?—what of patience?—what of resignation? If there were no greatness and no wealth, what would become of benevolence, of charity, of the blessed human pity, of temperance in the midst of luxury, of justice in the exercise of power?" As regarded the last item, the offender who received a stiff sentence for some misdemeanor might have reflected, "What indeed?" At all events, in its rocky conservatism and isolation from evolving human needs the informal league of Tory landowner–Tory parson–Tory bishop constituted the most redoubtable single obstacle to political and social reform.

In the superheated climate between Waterloo and the First Reform Bill, the Church was as vulnerable as the government to Benthamite and working-class radical attack. The anti-clericalism which had helped ignite the French Revolution now was becoming equally combustible on English soil. Liberals of any stripe could not easily overlook the fact that in the first test of the Reform Bill in the House of Lords, the bishops had voted against it twenty-one to two, with seven abstentions; if the twenty-one had voted the other way, the bill would have passed the Lords by one vote.

The Church's spiritual lethargy and political reactionarism were complemented by its corruption. Pluralism and absenteeism were rampant. The Bishop of Llandaff, for example, enjoyed the income of sixteen livings (endowed church offices such as rectories), fifty-nine lesser clerics held five or more, while 3,747 held from two to four each. Llandaff visited his see only once in thirty-four years, and few of his colleagues turned up in their own dioceses more than once a year or so. (It was remarkable how many doctors were ready to certify that their episcopal patients required a healthier air than that breathed in their cathedral towns.) The Archbishop of Canterbury appointed his twelve-year-old grandson to a sinecure worth £900 to £1200 a year. The Bishop of Ely shared with his son and son-in-law over £30,000 a year in church revenues, and the Bishop of Norwich's son-in-law, among other beneficiaries by blood or marriage, enjoyed the income from seven ecclesiastical offices, amounting in all to £10,000. In one case, which must not have been unique, a clergyman was paid for fifty years to minister to a non-existent parish, St. Edmunds, North Lynn, which had been washed into the sea in the sixteenth century. Even the Church had its rotten boroughs.

Bishops and archbishops lived in almost regal splendor, and they obviously could afford to do so. Meanwhile, numbers of ordinary clergymen were on the edge of starvation. The year after the First Reform Bill was passed, out of almost 12,000 incumbents and curates in the Church, 4,361 received less than £150 a year, and half of the curates, who were the ones that attended to the Lord's work insofar as it was attended to at all, earned less than the legal minimum of £80. Almost 5,000 livings did not even have habitable houses. Although some of these inequities were smoothed out in the Whig-Peelite wave of ecclesiastical reform in the mid-thirties, enough remained to lend credibility to such characters as the philoprogenitive Mr. Quiverful in Trollope's *Barchester Towers* (1857), whose meager salary, in fulfilment of Malthusian prophecy, never was enough to feed his relentlessly increasing family.

These were the men who ruled and served the Church. How well prepared were they to meet the intellectual troubles ahead, which would provide a sterner test than any radical assault upon their vested interests? It depended upon which party they belonged to. First, there were the Evangelicals, whose minds, as Matthew Arnold pointed out (presumably alluding to both Anglicans and Dissenters), typically were both narrow and inflexible, not instruments which could successfully cope with the shocks to come. Resting their faith as they did upon the entire and exclusive Word of God, they were peculiarly vulnerable when confronted with the higher criticism of the Bible, which denied their major premises that Jesus was the son of God and that both testaments were literally true in every detail. But they were no better equipped to face the anti-religious implications of the new science, which undermined the historicity of Genesis. Conceiving of Bible-based Christian faith as a perfect, self-contained entity not subject to piecemeal amendment or selective acceptance, and wedded to simple, emotionally directed habits of mind which put them at a disadvantage in an intellectual arena dominated by the language of scientific thought, they were forced to retreat into profitless polemic.

As it turned out, there was more hope in the Broad Church movement, the nineteenth-century heir of the Latitudinarian tradition, with its moderate skepticism and indifference to sharply defined dogma and prescribed forms. (In the Victorian period "Latitudinarian" was used synonymously with "Broad Church," and in most people's usage the more general word "liberal," in a religious context, meant "Broad Church" also.) This group—unlike the Evangelicals it never attained the strength of a full-fledged party —constituted a kind of rudimentary ecumenical movement, seeking to bring various Christian denominations together on common grounds of belief.

The Latitudinarians were somewhat better prepared

than other religious groups to withstand the assaults to which Victorian Christianity was subjected. Imbued with the spirit of free inquiry, they kept an open mind toward science. Certain Broad Churchmen, notably Charles Kingsley, were conspicuous among the few Anglican clergymen who refused to be disturbed by Darwinism; they took it in stride and suggested ways in which, as things turned out, Christianity did in fact find it possible to come to terms with the implications of biological evolution. The Latitudinarians were similarly forearmed against the explosive arguments of the Biblical critics. Coleridge, as an expositor of Christian belief, had laid an emphasis unusual for his time (outside Evangelical quarters) upon the spirituality, the non-rationalism, of religion. Faith rested not upon the literal and historical accuracy of the Bible but upon the spiritual truths, independent of supernatural or natural "evidences," which Revelation contained. This interpretation of the Bible enabled Latitudinarians to remain relatively serene at a time when others were being driven into unhappy doubt or, like the Evangelicals, were taking refuge in obscurantism. In such respects the Broad Church was the most fortunate of the principal Victorian religious movements.

In its time, however, Latitudinarianism was regarded with suspicion and alarm by the more orthodox. Its advocacy of open-minded criticism and toleration of mildly heterodox dogma would, it was feared, lead ultimately to the complete rejection of Christian belief. Yield liberalism an inch, and it would take an ell. Newman said it was the halfway house to atheism.

2. The Oxford Movement

On the other hand, the Oxford Movement, as events proved in the first decade of Victoria's reign, was the halfway house to Romanism; and between Romanism and atheism, in many Englishmen's horrified estimation, there was little to choose.

As the name implies, this was a movement originating among, and carried on by, academic clergymen who were members of Oxford University, a stronghold of Toryism and tradition. (Cambridge, meanwhile, was the headquarters of the Evangelicals, whose political orientation was for the most part Whiggish.) The movement is also called "Tractarianism," in allusion to the series of ninety position papers, entitled *Tracts for the Times,* which various leaders of the group published between 1833 and 1841. A third name, "Puseyism," customarily used with disrespectful or even worse intention—it often appears in Victorian fiction—refers to one of the central personalities in the movement, Edward B. Pusey. The reason for still another approximate synonym, "Anglo-Catholicism," will shortly become apparent.

The Oxford Movement began as a protest against political events and tendencies which men like Pusey, John Keble, and John Henry Newman interpreted as foreshadowing the complete subservience of the Church to the temporal power ("Erastianism"). The composition of the reformed Parliament of 1833 convinced the Oxford men that the political deck was triply stacked against the Church. For one thing, there was a strong bloc of Dissenters and Roman Catholics, reflecting the full impact of the recent repeal of the Test and Corporation Acts, followed closely by Catholic Emancipation, which had made it legal for non-Anglicans to sit in Parliament for the first time since the seventeenth century. For another, Parliament was now controlled by the Whigs, historically the party which opposed the Tories' close and mutually profitable ties with the Church. And, even worse, behind the Whigs stood their new allies, the Benthamites, whose hostility to organized religion in general, and to the Anglican Church in particular, was notorious.

The Whigs lost no time in proposing to abolish ten of

the twenty-two Irish bishoprics, a reasonable measure in light of the fact that the 6,400,000 Roman Catholics in Ireland were required to pay tithes to support an Irish (Anglican) Church which numbered but 850,000. The Oxford men regarded the proposal as motivated by political expediency, its first object being to placate the perennially restive Irish, who could air their grievances through the Roman Catholic representatives they were now able to send to Parliament, and its final purpose being the diminution or even the destruction of the Church's power in secular affairs. They refused to recognize that behind the Whigs' moves, whatever their immediate occasion, lay the resentment the Church had accumulated through its long-standing and by now well publicized corruption and its stiff-necked insistence upon its many privileges and prerogatives as the Established Church. If the Irish had grievances, so did multitudes of English Dissenters, for the same reason among others. While supporting their own houses of worship, they had also to pay rates for the upkeep of a parish church belonging to a religion of whose tenets they disapproved but in which they had to be married if the union were to be legal, in which their children had to be baptized if their birth were to be registered, and in whose graveyard they could be buried only in silence or with the Anglican rite.*

The Oxford Movement dated from July, 1833, when Keble preached at Oxford what came to be known as his "National Apostasy" sermon. His theme was "Save the Church!": that is, put a halt to Parliament's interference in its affairs. To relieve the Irish of their legal obligation to pay tithes to the religion officially established in their country, even if it was not their religion, was apostasy—an act of

* All these grievances were remedied sooner or later. From 1837, legal marriages could be performed in non-Anglican places of worship as well as by the civil authorities; at the same time, the civil registration of births, marriages, and deaths, hitherto recorded in the parish registers, was instituted. Compulsory church rates were abolished in 1868, and in 1880 the reading of Dissenting burial services in Anglican churchyards was legalized.

betrayal. What exercised Keble was not the immediate political expedient of Irish disestablishment but the principle it violated, that of the Church's superiority to, and independence of, the temporal power.

From this beginning, the movement developed during the 1830's into a campaign against what its sponsors looked upon as several interrelated evils. It was, like the Whigs', a reform movement, but the similarity ended with the word. Church reform to the Tractarians had nothing to do with church rates, nepotism, pluralism, absenteeism, sinecures, or simony (the Whigs were taking care of these, meanwhile, through the Ecclesiastical Commission). The Oxford Movement was anti-rational, because it concentrated upon the long-neglected spirituality of religion. Not the least of the ironies of Victorian history is the fact that some of the leading Tractarians had come from Evangelical families or, like Newman, had acquired Evangelical leanings from other associations; their religious temper was as much emotional as intellectual. The movement was also anti-liberal, the term "liberal" in this case referring both to the Broad Church's relaxed attitude toward doctrine and to the Benthamite Whigs' Erastianism and their determination to trim down the Church's privileges. It was anti-individualistic, also in two respects. One was that it opposed the congregational emphasis of Dissent and sought to restore the former authority of the bishops, who in the eighteenth century had let it go by default in favor of the more lucrative and ego-satisfying game of ecclesiastical politics. The other was that it asserted the Church's authority in matters of faith, as contrasted with the Puritan-Evangelical stress on the Bible as illuminated by the inner light of the individual. Against individual liberty of interpretation, therefore, it posed an authoritarianism whereby decisions of bishops were binding and assent to the Church's dogma obligatory. The Oxford Movement, finally, was anti-relativistic, because it stressed absolutes such as the ultimate reality of the truth of which the Church was the consecrated receptacle and expositor.

The Tractarians' argumentative strategy consisted of an appeal to history. Their conception of the Church was analogous to Burke's conception of the state. Far from being finished institutions, both were growing organisms, the products of long centuries of development and possessing still undiminished vitality. Newman, the best scholar in the group, delved into the early history of Christianity in an effort to remind the Church of the unbroken continuity between its glorious past and its imperiled present and of the foundations upon which rested its claim to supremacy over all temporal power. Its origins lay in the first five centuries of the Christian era, before the schisms began—"when the apologists had defended the Church against the pagans by out-thinking them and the martyrs had witnessed to the power of the Resurrection by out-dying their opponents . . . when, although the Roman Empire fell into decay, the *imperium in imperio,* the Christian society, triumphed over its grave." [2]

By tracing how authority was transmitted in those early centuries Newman sought to show that the Church of England was actually "the Catholic Church in England," the true church, in direct line of descent from St. Peter. He thus reaffirmed the doctrine of apostolic succession, which held that the power of the sacraments, the very heart of the Church's ministry, lay in the fact that they were administered by bishops and clergy whose own powers derived eventually from Christ. (This came as something of a surprise to the bishops of Newman's time, whose strong suit seldom was theology.) The Church therefore was a corporate means of grace, the ordained mediator between God and man. Given this sacramental mission, it followed that the Church should be wholly exempt from state control. The voice to be heeded was St. Peter's, not that of the Whig politicians.

Newman applied to doctrine the same concept of development that directed his interpretation of the Church as an institution. The terms of belief had not remained static;

they too were an organism that grew and changed. In the case of Catholic doctrine, the normal course of development had been diverted by historical accident. On the basis of researches into the historical circumstances attending the sixteenth-century English Church's break from Rome, Newman argued that no actual schism had occurred. In *Tract 90* (1841), last of the long series, which also ended his acceptability to the Church of England, he attempted to demonstrate that the Thirty-Nine Articles, the doctrinal basis of the distinction between the Anglican and Roman churches, had been designed to meet an immediate strategic need and were framed, therefore, with intentional ambiguity. Read in the way Newman argued they could be read, they did not conflict, as had been assumed, with Roman Catholic doctrine. In thus analyzing the historical occasion and language of the Thirty-Nine Articles, Newman's method was analogous to that by which modern literary scholars seek to reconstruct what a given poem or play meant to its author and what he intended it to mean to the people of his time.

The result of all this study of ecclesiastical history was, in essence, to nullify the Protestant Reformation. As Hurrell Froude, a brilliant young charter member of the movement who died at thirty-four, remarked: "We are Catholics without the Popery, and Church-of-England men without the Protestantism." Slowly but inescapably Newman came to realize that "the Church of Rome will be found right after all." To delete from the nineteenth-century Anglican Church the errors fortuitously introduced as a consequence of special circumstances in centuries past without restoring it in the image of Rome was a hopeless enterprise. After the stir over *Tract 90* and the protracted soul-searching Newman describes in his *Apologia pro Vita Sua,* he went over to the Roman Catholic Church in October, 1845. The shock was tremendous. Even Peel's reversal on the Corn Laws the next year created no greater excitement than Newman's decision. The more perceptive of those who had followed the erudite Tractarian argument had realized where its logic was leading it, but even they were unprepared for the defection of its most prominent advocate. To a country whose orientation since Tudor days had been thoroughly Protestant and in which anti-Catholic feeling was still strong, this dramatic act by so notable a churchman seemed a betrayal not only of faith but of reason.

Newman's conversion practically ended the Oxford Movement. Only he, of the original group, took the ultimate step; Keble, Pusey, and the rest remained Anglicans. Some of his followers, having picked up too much momentum to stop, followed him to Rome. Others, seeing the abyss stretching before them, pulled up at the last moment and were saved for the Church of England.

All this seems very remote from the ordinary life of the thirties and forties, most of all from the social turmoil and political crises that shook the nation in those perilous years. The issues which engaged the Tractarians' emotions as well as their intellects were, in the context of the contemporary social crisis, remote and irrelevant. Obviously their subtleties were of no interest to the man in the street. But the Oxford argumentation was far from limited to a closed circle of clerical scholars, because there was a substantial body of thoughtful middle-class laymen who were accustomed to reading sermons and following the intricacies of historical exegesis and theological debate.

To understand the principles involved in Tractarianism is to better appreciate the intellectual temper of the early Victorian period. In some respects the movement was a reassertion of the romantic spirit in a decade when Manchester materialism had tipped the scales against romantic values and attitudes. Its leaders were men of romantic sensibility. They felt toward the Church the same awed reverence which Wordsworth had felt in the presence of nature. Their deep sense of historical continuity, which amounted to a veritable mystique of the past, was romantic also. In an era impatient to move forward, they denied the prevailing assumption that whatever is new is *ipso facto* better and that the greatest obstacle to the future is the persistence of the past. The head and heart of Tractarianism dwelt, not in the age of railways and mill hands' riots, but in the remote centuries of the Church Fathers, the Middle Ages (when the undivided Church had fulfilled to perfection its priestly mission), and the reign of Charles I (when Archbishop Laud and his fellow divines had defended the English Church's prerogatives against Puritan attack). No matter that they sometimes idealized or misconstrued history; that, too, was a common romantic failing.

The Oxford Movement's affirmation of sacramentalism as a means of grace was akin to the romantic exaltation of the symbol, especially as found in nature, as the nexus between the Unseen and the Seen. Its creed rested upon the Real Presence of Christ in the Eucharist. Whereas the Evangelicals insisted that personal morality and acceptance of the Bible were the way to salvation, the Oxford Movement called upon the individual to humble himself before the corporate Church through whose sacraments Christ's truth was proclaimed. In an age of encroaching materialism it took religion into a rarer ether through the beauty of symbolic object and act.

It was only natural, then, that the Oxford Movement was (and is) popularly thought to have left England a visible bequest in the form of ritualism. This is true only in a loose sense. The confusion lies partly in the *post hoc ergo propter hoc* fallacy and partly in the ambiguity of the word "Puseyism," which in contemporary usage referred both to the Oxford Movement and to the new attention given in a portion of the Church to liturgy, ceremonial, and the physical accessories of worship. Actually, the leading Tractarians were themselves largely indifferent to ritualism, however much their veneration of ancient practices supported it in theory. But concurrently a group of "ecclesiologists" at the two universities were encouraging interest in old church architecture and appointments, and in the forties the two streams more or less merged.

From the late seventeenth century down to early Victorian times, Anglican churches had been bare, depressing buildings, their former glories vanished, mutilated, or neglected; dust, dilapidation, and debris were everywhere. To such worshipers as came, however, this was of no particular concern, for the service itself was routine and prosaic, the old splendor of the liturgy discarded in favor of an oft-repeated sedative sermon and perfunctory prayers uttered by a parson in a black gown. The lack of decoration and of dramatic ceremony symbolized the Church's rejection of Popish affectations on the one hand and of devout emotion on the other. All was cold, correct, and reasonable. The house of worship was anything but a place of aesthetic pleasure.

But by the 1830's, interest in Gothic architecture had already revived, and, with the assistance of the Oxford Movement's compelling antiquarianism, it widened by the fifties into a crusade to restore poetry and art to religious worship. Gothic architecture recalled the age of faith; it was God-centered, not man-centered in the way of Renaissance design, with its evocations of Greece and Rome. Hundreds of new churches therefore were built in neo-Gothic style, some in the grimiest parts of red-brick factory towns, and even more older ones were "restored" in the same style, to their irreparable damage. In the most ritualistic churches the clergy wore colorful vestments appropriate to the feast or season; they sang the liturgy, assisted by choirs now robed and moved from their former place of relegation in the gallery; organs replaced the choir's former limping accompaniment of violoncello, clarinet, and trombone (the orchestra mentioned in Samuel Butler's *The Way of All Flesh*); priests bowed to the altar and faced east when reciting the Creed; the congregation alternately knelt and stood; the sacred vessels were cleansed at the altar, itself adorned with elaborate cloths, candles, and arrangements of flowers; the air was laden with the odor of incense . . . All these appurtenances of worship manifested the vitality of tradition; they had behind them almost two thousand years of solemn observance, and now, once again, they led men's thoughts from the natural to the supernatural.

Far from being universal, ritualism was confined to the "High" Church, with which it has been associated ever since; outraged Low Churchmen fought it with all their considerable fund of invective. Assailed as an orgy of "Romish extravagances" and "ecclesiastical theatricals," it was so controversial that for three decades the question of whether or not to tolerate lighted altar candles, vestments, and genuflections in supposedly Protestant churches occasioned numerous lawsuits and even riots. The strife was especially bitter in London's East End, where slum priests, through either conviction or showmanlike expediency, used the bright trappings and mysterious gestures of medieval worship to fill the churches. Ritualism was one of the issues that divided the clergy in Trollope's Barsetshire, with Mr. Arabin and Mr. Oriel (the name of the college where Tractarianism began) representing the ritualists and Mr. Slope, amply assisted by the bishop's wife, expressing the prejudices of the anti-Puseyite Evangelical. In Thackeray's *The Newcomes* the Reverend Charles Honeyman, ever alert to the main chance, enhances his standing with impressionable gentlewomen when, as the impresario of Lady Whittlesea's Chapel, he goes à la mode by introducing "new scenery, dresses, and effects" into the worship.

· The association of beauty with religious devotion assisted, if it did not actually initiate, the process whereby art was liberated from the Benthamites' insistence that it have utility and the Evangelicals' that it be saturated with morality. Through its religious associations sensuous beauty eventually gained a place in the scale of Victorian values more or less comparable to that which it had had among the romantics. Not only were the churches and their services made into things of beauty: the invisible Church itself, with its mysticism and aura of transcendental sublimity, stirred the soul to responses in which, as often in the poetry of

Wordsworth and Coleridge, the religious and the aesthetic were blended. In the aftermath of the Oxford Movement, beauty was, in the most literal sense, resanctified.

More generally, the movement infused into Victorian life a much-needed element of spirituality, counteracting to a degree both the prosaic materialism of the Utilitarian temper and the indiscriminate, too readily vulgarized emotionalism of the Evangelicals. Furthermore, despite the many deep personal wounds left by the controversy it stirred, not least the family anguish caused by a beloved member's defecting to Rome, it left in its wake a dedicated clergy. Assisted by the practical reforms effected by the Ecclesiastical Commission, the slothful holders of sinecures and multiple livings gave way to men of God, austere of habit and educated of mind, who did their best to sustain the Christian faith during the decades when it was most sorely buffeted. The holiness toward which the original Oxford group aspired—driving themselves with almost neurotic compulsion—proved to be infectious.

The Tractarians also left behind them less desirable results. While the Church's corporate sense of identity was enhanced by their researches into its long history and their impassioned assertions of its inherited dignity, the resultant self-glorification intensified the culturally divisive tendencies already rife in Victorian society. Low Churchmen, despairing of a Church that tolerated Romish mumbo-jumbo, migrated to the unelaborate precincts of Dissent, and High Anglicans, uncomfortable with the intimations of Rome but still loyal to the Church of their fathers, demoted themselves into Low Churchmen. The tensions between ritualist and Evangelical over Popery, between Tractarian *and* Evangelical (combined) and Latitudinarian over doctrinal broadmindedness, between reinvigorated Anglicanism in general and doughty Dissent over other issues—all consumed energy that might better have been directed to solving more pressing problems of religion and society.

But the most tragic effect of the Oxford Movement was

that it led some of the epoch's most brilliant intellects to focus upon a remote past at a time when they should have been preparing their religion for an imminent and crucial future. In strengthening the Church's historical foundations, they neglected to protect its fabric from the coming winds of intellectual challenge. At the very moment that they were arguing the subtleties of apostolic succession, their colleagues in certain German universities such as Tübingen were developing a body of information and argument which would render largely irrelevant the Church's claim to descent from Christ through St. Peter. At that moment, too, a young Cambridge graduate named Charles Darwin was already returning from an extended voyage through the southern seas aboard a naval survey vessel, the *Beagle*. Both the German Biblical scholars and the English naturalist were also concerned, in their respective ways, with history; but it was history with a vast difference, and with a vastly different bearing on Christianity's claims to be the repository of truth about man, his origins, and his destiny.

3. The Higher Criticism and "the Testimony of the Rocks"

The German scholars' contribution to the Victorian religious crisis was in the form of the "lower" (linguistic and textual) and, deriving from it, the "higher" (historical and interpretative) criticism of the Bible. Ever since the seventeenth century, the Bible had sometimes been examined from the same standpoint from which Renaissance humanists had already been studying the Greek and Latin classics: that is, with the purpose of establishing the Bible's authorship and authenticity and, above all, of relating it to its historical background. The early nineteenth-century German linguistic and historical scholars systematized what heretofore had been no more than a tendency of Biblical scholarship into a formal discipline. Ironically, this was the kind of historical criticism which Newman and his associates had used to assert the legitimacy of the Anglican Church. Both groups were faithful to the growing nineteenth-century sense of historical development in that they recognized that documents of great age, like secular and religious traditions and institutions, had been subjected to constant change during their long course down the centuries until their origins had become obscured and their primal intentions misinterpreted.

In the treatises of the higher critics, the Old Testament was regarded not as a collection of divinely inspired and utterly authoritative books but as a mixed bag of human documents—tribal histories, genealogies, digests of laws, erotic songs, biographies, and folk myths, a kind of "Hebrew National Library" that had been quite fortuitously assembled, and endowed long after the fact with divine authority. In the process of transmission down to the nineteenth century, their secular and occasional origins had long since been forgotten, replaced by an unquestioning faith in the literal truth of every word (or, in cases where the literal truth was embarrassing—the Song of Solomon, for instance —by a convenient "allegorical" interpretation). The Gospels, similarly, comprised several versions of a biography of a historical figure named Jesus whom an early group of disciples believed to be the Son of God, the fulfillment of the Messianic prophecy, and to whom they therefore attributed miraculous powers. Thus the New Testament was a record of a particularly memorable episode of hero-worship in Hebrew-Roman times. In brief, the Bible was not what it was taken to be, the pure Word of God and from Genesis to Revelation the infallible factual basis of Christian faith.

Although most of the analysis which led to these conclusions had been conducted in Germany, Coleridge, for one, had been sufficiently in touch with it to prepare an answer before he died. In his posthumously published *Confessions of an Enquiring Spirit* (1840) he decided that the Bible retained its spiritual authority even though much of it, such as the accounts of supernatural events and Christ's miracles, could not withstand historical and scientific scrutiny. This conclusion was in harmony with that of the most influential German critic, David Friedrich Strauss, whose *Das Leben Jesu,* first published in Germany in 1835, was translated into English in 1846 by Mary Ann Evans, the future George Eliot. For although it was the negative, destructive side of the German critic's argument that claimed the most attention and caused the most distress, he himself concluded that the abiding value and authority of the Bible resided not in its "facts," which could be all too easily discredited, but in its character as a body of symbol and myth—concrete expressions, current among certain peoples at a specific place and time, of universal and timeless elements in the aspirations, fears, and experience of mankind at large. Stripped of its vulnerable historicity, Scripture retained its spiritual and ethical significance.

The principal literary reflection of this new element in the religious situation was a graphic scene in Browning's poem *Christmas-Eve* (1850), depicting the lecture room at a German university in which a heavy pedant delivered his disillusioning tidings. This scene was the third panel in a kind of poetic triptych, the first two panels of which were a Hogarthian depiction of a "Little Bethel" chapel somewhere in rainy England and a baroque evocation of Christmas Eve Mass at St. Peter's in Rome. The question was where, in fact, Truth did reside. Browning opted for Little Bethel, because it supposedly was freer of error than Roman Catholicism or the "liberal" religion based on the higher criticism.

The process of discrediting the Bible's pretensions to divine authority was continued in the sixties by such books as Ernest Renan's *La Vie de Jésus* (1860), which rewrote the Gospels as the biography of a human being, and Bishop Colenso's *The Pentateuch . . . Critically Examined* (1862). But by then it was not only the higher criticism which cast the Bible into doubt. In late November, 1859, Charles Darwin published *On the Origin of Species.*

Various elements of what is broadly called evolutionary

theory had been speculated upon by philosophers as different as Aristotle, Kant, Goethe, Hegel, and Schelling. But the Victorians' view of the history of the human race remained, on the whole, what they had learned from the Bible. Indeed, only a few months before Darwin's book appeared, a well-known clergyman, delivering the prestigious Bampton Lectures for the year, somewhat untimely re-stated the old confidence that "Moses was only separated by a few generations of oral tradition from the first man, from creation in fact. . . . Moses' mother, Jochebed, had probably met Jacob who could have known Noah's son Shem. Shem was probably acquainted with Methuselah, who had been for 243 years a contemporary of Adam—and Adam was made on the sixth day after the first day on which Time had begun." [3] Furthermore, the new science of archaeology seemed to offer powerful support for the Bible's historical authority and therefore the correctness of the Mosaic chronology. Excavations in the Near East, on the sites of nations mentioned in the Old Testament, verified their existence.

There remained, however, the evidence of geology and paleontology, which had been mounting since the middle of the eighteenth century. "The testimony of the rocks," to use the title of a popular early Victorian book, challenged the simple Biblical formulation of terrestrial history. The older geological interpretation, that of the so-called catastrophic school, was that the fossils of extinct species found embedded in rock strata were evidence of cataclysms—floods, earthquakes, devastating volcanic eruptions. Superficially, this seemed to support the Biblical account; for did not Scripture attest to one such catastrophe, the flood which Noah had ridden out? But there was a fatal difficulty, because the varying nature of the fossilized species made it necessary to assume that they had been extinguished at different stages of time separated by thousands of centuries, each such interval being many times as long as the whole putative history of the world. Unless, as some speculated, each cataclysm had been succeeded by a fresh creation, the history recounted in Genesis seemed suspect—or, at the very least, disturbingly incomplete.

A newer theory, set forth in Sir Charles Lyell's *Principles of Geology* (1830–33), was the uniformitarian. Discarding the premise of catastrophes, it maintained that the causes of geological change in the remote past were no different from those still operative in the nineteenth century —the slow, ceaseless action of wind and water, the elevation and depression of land masses. Such an assumption, of course, also required extending the chronology into veritable eons, for earth processes that are so slow as to be undetectible require such vast spans to accomplish the effects revealed by geology; and the miniature scale of history explicit in the Old Testament was accordingly rendered all the more incredible.

Lyell's book was the most influential of the several forces which sowed the seeds of religious doubt in the thirties and forties, the very years when the Oxford Movement was striving to revitalize faith. But even before the implications of the new geology and of Biblical criticism had made any headway, Christian faith was being challenged on other grounds. The prototype of the "de-conversion" experience narrated so often in Victorian personal records was that of Carlyle, whose crisis of religious alienation described in "The Everlasting No" (*Sartor Resartus,* 1833–34) had occurred some years before Lyell or Strauss wrote. In essence, Carlyle's faith had been shattered by eighteenth-century deism, which denied the presence in the universe of a personal God: "Is there no God, then; but at best an absentee God, sitting idle, ever since the first Sabbath, at the outside of his Universe, and seeing it go?" Equally destructive were the rationalistic ethical assumptions which reduced morality to a mechanical exercise in Benthamite arithmetic: "Foolish Wordmonger and Motive-grinder, who in thy Logic-mill hast an earthly mechanism for the Godlike itself, and wouldst fain grind me out Virtue from the husks of Pleasure. . . ." And so to Carlyle, "the bewildered Wanderer," "It is all a grim Desert, this once-fair world of his; wherein is heard only the howling of wild-beasts, or the shrieks of despairing, hate-filled men; and no Pillar of Cloud by day, and no Pillar of Fire by night, any longer guides the Pilgrim. . . . The whole world is . . . sold out to Unbelief; their old Temples of the Godhead, which for long have not been rainproof, crumble down; and men ask now: where is the God-head; our eyes never saw him?"

During the very years when *Sartor Resartus,* with its lament that no existing church or body of doctrine could serve man's soul, was beginning to have its effect on the religious convictions of early Victorian readers, Christian faith was proving vulnerable for other reasons. Was it consistent with an ethic grounded in compassion and justice and the conviction of human dignity to subscribe to such doctrines as those of original sin, atonement through the sacrifice of Christ, and—worst of all—eternal punishment? Here and there, a troubled man thought not, and suffered in his soul accordingly. "The loss of his religious Belief," as Carlyle said, "was the loss of everything." The unacceptability of portions, at least, of the traditional Christian dogma rendered the universe "all void of Life, of Purpose, of Volition, even of Hostility: it was one huge, dead, immeasurable Steam-engine, rolling on, in its dead indifference, to grind me limb from limb."

To admit such doubts, however, was to risk scandal and even a degree of social ostracism. Only much later, when the private letters, diaries, and conversations of men thus affected were made public, was it realized how many were troubled on religious grounds in the first decade of the reign. But a clue was available as early as 1850, when *In Memoriam* was published. Tennyson had begun writing the lyrics of which the poem is composed in 1833, as a means of finding his way out of the despair caused by the death of his closest friend in that year. He was then, as he would remain throughout life, a keen amateur scientist, and in his personal circumstances he sensed more acutely than most the terrible implications of the new geology. The immediate popularity of *In Memoriam* suggests how many people already shared his mood even though they had not confessed their doubts. They welcomed the poem because Tennyson seemed to bring reassurance that the essence of Christian faith was, after all, undamaged by the revelations of pre-Darwinian evolution.

In the forties, too, younger intellectuals like Matthew Arnold, Arthur Hugh Clough, and George Eliot were suffering the same erosion of faith. A year after *In Memoriam* appeared, John Ruskin wrote in a private letter, "If only the Geologists would let me alone, I could do very well, but those dreadful Hammers! I hear the clink of them at the end of every cadence of the Bible verses." And, as if in echo, Browning had a fictitious Roman Catholic bishop remark on the parlous state of Christian faith in 1855:

> *How you'd exult if I could put you back*
> *Six hundred years, blot out cosmogony,*
> *Geology, ethnology, what not,*
> *(Greek endings, each the little passing-bell*
> *That signifies some faith's about to die). . . .*

Lyell, a convinced Christian, attempted to quiet such fears. "In whatever direction we pursue our researches," he said, "whether in time or space, we discover everywhere the clear proofs of a Creative Intelligence, and of His foresight, wisdom, and power." But such affirmations were merely the tired echoes of Paleyan natural theology. Whatever the public statements of Lyell and other scientists, the fact, as some admitted in private, was that the Old Testament's credibility as cosmic history could not be reconciled with the account the geologists derived from the rocks. It was possible, of course, to find refuge in the supposition that while the universe was immensely older than Genesis allowed, man himself was created as Genesis said he was, by a special act of God less than six millennia ago. But this possibility was weakened, on the very eve of *The Origin of Species*, by the almost simultaneous discovery, in Devonshire and on the banks of the Somme River, of tools buried beside the remains of long-extinct mammoths—proof that human beings had co-existed with these animals eons before 4004 B.C. In 1856, also, the first remains of Neanderthal man came to light. Thus began the concept of human prehistory, which stretched the life of the race back to hundreds of times the millennia specified in the Old Testament.

4. The Darwinian Crisis

Far from introducing the idea of evolution *per se* to a totally unprepared public or initiating the religious doubts which were to trouble so many minds in the years to come, *The Origin of Species* was largely a brilliant synthesis of many scientific ideas already current, with one or two crucial additions. The concept of organic mutability was itself not new; other evidences apart, it had long been put to practical demonstration by England's botanists and breeders of race horses. But the explanation *was* new: the idea of "natural selection" accomplished by an eternal "struggle for existence"—the strong and the weak of a species pitted against the environment that determined which individuals would die and which would live to transmit their saving traits to a new generation. (In the 1872 edition of *The Origin of Species* Darwin introduced the more explicit phrase "survival of the fittest.") And, of profound significance for the future of scientific methodology, Darwin based his theory upon an unprecedented accumulation of observed and experimental data. The boldness of the argument was matched, and lent formidable persuasiveness, by the marshaling of evidence.

The shock effect the book had was due, curiously, to what Darwin did *not* say. Although he had, as he later wrote, "collected notes on the origin and descent of man," he did not include them in the *Origin*, "as I thought I should thus only add to the prejudices against my views. It seemed to me sufficient to indicate . . . that by this work 'light would be thrown on the origin of man and his history;' and this implies that man must be included with other organic beings in any general conclusion respecting his manner of appearance on this earth." But Darwin's first readers found it not only easy but inescapable to extrapolate from Galápagos reptiles to man. Indeed, the ease and inevitability of the leap had been demonstrated much earlier, when Disraeli, in his novel *Tancred* (1847), portrayed a fashionable lady's more or less lucid interpretation of a best-seller called *The Revelations of Chaos* (actually Robert Chambers' *Vestiges of the Natural History of Creation:* see below, p. 260).

"But what is most interesting is the way in which man has been developed. You know, all is development. The principle is perpetually going on. First, there was nothing, then there was something; then, I forget the next, I think there were shells, then fishes; then we came, let me see, did we come next? Never mind that, we came at last. And the next change there will be something very superior to us, something with wings. Ah! that's it; we were fishes, and I believe we shall be crows. But you must read it. . . . We are a link in the chain, as inferior animals were that preceded us; we in turn shall be inferior. All that will remain of us will be some relics in a new red sandstone. This is development. We had fins; we may have wings."

Whether Darwin said so or not (his doughty apostle Huxley made the connection explicit in his *Man's Place in Nature* [1863], and Darwin himself would do so eight years later, in *The Descent of Man*), the truth was that biological evolution made it plain, as geological evolution had not, that man was not exempt from the perpetual process of change which affected all animate nature.

Darwin's own interpretation of evolution's meaning was reassuring, even though he abstained from mentioning man. "Thus," he wrote in the last paragraph of *The Origin of Species,* "from the war of nature, from famine and death, the most exalted object which we are capable of conceiving, namely, the production of the higher animals, directly follows. There is grandeur in this view of life, with its several powers, having been originally breathed by the Creator into a few forms or into one; and that, whilst this planet has gone cycling on according to the fixed law of gravity, from so simple a beginning endless forms most beautiful and most wonderful have been, and are being evolved." This might have been interpreted as substantiating the Victorian faith in progress as a built-in attribute of the universe. But a close, candid reading of Darwin's account made it obvious that evolution did not necessarily imply progress. And even if science could somehow be interpreted as bathing the future in a rosy glow, it devastated the myth of the past upon which religious faith rested. *The Origin of Species* delivered the *coup de grâce* to whatever lingering hopes there were that the historicity of the Bible and the Judaeo-Christian view of man springing from it would somehow be substantiated by science. The long-cherished providential theory, that God had created man, in all his pristine perfection, as a special favor, and tailored the universe to his special needs, was finished. Man was merely the most highly developed (for the moment) form of animal life and subject to the same laws of development that governed the rest; he was even given a museum label, *Homo sapiens*.

And so the glorious attributes praised by poets and philosophers down through the centuries ("What a piece of work is a man!" exclaimed Hamlet) proved to be nothing more than refinements of traits already present in the lower animals. Intelligence, for instance, the "right reason" which had long been fondly thought to be the unique characteristic that differentiated man from his inferiors, a proof that God loved him above all other creatures, was not his alone. He simply possessed it in a greater degree, because of his more advanced stage of evolution, than did his four-legged, winged, and finny fellow creatures lower on the scale. In addition, intelligence had plainly been overrated. Man, it seemed, was governed not so much by intelligence as by the drives he shared with all other living things in their common grim determination to survive: sex and hunger. A little lower than the angels, indeed.

The ancient metaphor of the great chain of being therefore had to be revised. Hierarchy remained, but it was a hierarchy to which the dimension of time had been added. It gave the impression now of a vertical zoo in a state of eternal flux rather than a structure of classic design raised by the Creator and enduring unchanged to the end of time. Not a single place in it was stable or secure. If man now happened to occupy the choicest location, his supremacy was but the incident of a moment.

This blow to man's dignity as the lord of creation was shattering enough, but even more intolerable was the idea of natural selection. The present distinction of living species could no longer be explained on the traditional ground that they were all differentiated, with infinite wisdom, at the moment of creation. Instead, they were merely the present generation of victors in a ceaseless struggle for existence. Dominant today, extinct tomorrow. "Nature, red in tooth and claw," in Tennyson's famous phrase, had replaced Wordsworth's benevolent force. In the vernal wood where Wordsworth had heard only harmony, the later Victorians heard only anguished animal cries.

Science, it appeared, had liberated man only insofar as technology had enabled him to gain ascendancy—a tragically limited one—over nature. But science now revealed that in the longer view, far from being free, man was caught up in inexorable processes of nature from which there was no escape. Still, the Victorian persuasion of progress was so deep-seated that it refused to be stifled. Might not those natural processes tend toward good? Granted that man still retained all too apparent traits of the beast, might not a further refinement of the attributes which had enabled him to arrive at his present eminence enable him, as Tennyson wrote in *In Memoriam,* to "Move upward, working out the beast/And let the ape and tiger die"? It might; but in

Darwin's account of biological development there was no assurance that it would, because, *pace* Paley, the authors of the *Bridgewater Treatises,* and Darwin himself at the end of the *Origin,* the natural process contained no hint of intelligence or purpose, let alone benevolence or justice. The victory went not to the most deserving, the most virtuous, the most intelligent; it went to the most ruthless fighter—or, conceivably, the luckiest. Witness Caliban's ruminations in Browning's devastating satire of natural theology seen against the background of Darwinian evolution, "Caliban upon Setebos."

Man's particular characteristics, which happened to have brought him this far, were not necessarily those which would serve him in subsequent trials by combat in the earthly jungle. What assurance, actually, was there that he would survive? Countless other forms of life had had their little day and then ceased to be. Far from being somehow favored by whatever power lay behind the cosmos, he had to take his chance with all the rest.

"Whatever power": there, finally, was the transcendent mystery. If, as seemed reasonable to believe, there had been some sort of First Cause, analogous to the deists' divine watchmaker, there was no reason to believe in any Presence. Or if there was a grand design behind the veil, its outlines could not be discerned. Darwinism never settled upon either of the remaining two alternatives, mechanism and chance, but it really did not matter, because neither offered any but a dusty answer. If there were, indeed, laws governing all that happened, man was at their mercy; unable to detect them, let alone accommodate himself to them, he could only confess himself, like Caliban, the victim of a capricious, invisible captor. And if, instead, the only law was that of chance, before which both justice and reason were impotent, again man was helpless.

The consequence of such a world view, of course, was that the whole array of Victorian religious and moral assumptions was called into doubt. If the world was not made perfect to begin with (as geology asserted, contravening Genesis) and if there had been no such thing as a freshly created, perfect being who was benevolently set down in Paradise as the progenitor of the human race, then the whole story of Adam and Eve and the Fall of Man and, most important of all, the Redemption—the whole basis of Christian faith—collapsed. Since there was no original sin, there was no reason for God to send his son to be sacrificed in behalf of man's salvation.

These are but samples of the many issues which Darwinism brought into focus. They were the grounds of the spiritual struggle through which innumerable Victorians passed in the century's remaining decades. The popular name of the struggle was "science vs. religion," but it was much more complicated than that crude simplification would suggest, a long and crowded chapter in Victorian intellectual history which lost its urgency only toward the end of the century. The specifics need not concern us here. There is room only to recall the most famous of the fundamentalists' rebuttals of the geological evidence. Philip Gosse, father of the man of letters Edmund Gosse, was a typical mid-Victorian amateur scientist, specializing in marine biology. He was also a member of the Plymouth Brethren, one of the most fanatical of the sects. In his *Omphalos* (1857) he declared, as his son put it, "that when the catastrophic act of creation took place, the world presented, instantly, the structural appearance of a planet on which life had long existed. The theory, coarsely enough, . . . was defined by a hasty press as being this—that God hid the fossils in the rocks in order to tempt geologists into infidelity." But we must not laugh too readily: in those same years Robert Browning was explaining doubt as a divine contrivance for testing men's faith, put in the world deliberately to enable the staunch believer to qualify for heaven.

As if to compensate for its devastating effects upon religious orthodoxy as well as for the doubt it cast upon the idea of human progress, Darwinism seemed, in some minds, to substantiate another of the period's secular beliefs. The determinism of biological evolution lent authority to the determinism of political economy. Both rested on the assumption of eternal struggle and iron-bound laws, which man was powerless to breach. The history of animals, from amoeba to man, gave warrant to the assumption by analogy that cutthroat competition was an ineradicable fact of economic life and that the prizes were reserved for those best equipped to survive—the tough-bargaining employer, the hard-working employee. Thus, at the very time the Manchester School's authority was waning, natural science seemed to come to its rescue. "Social Darwinism," a concept most notably associated with the once influential but now discredited philosopher Herbert Spencer, was simply extreme laissez faire endowed with a (supposed) biological sanction. Spencer, as a matter of fact, had used the phrase Darwin was later to make famous, "survival of the fittest," as early as 1852. Needless to say, the Marxist theory of class warfare is not unrelated to this specious argument.

5. The Alternatives to Faith

To the literary imagination, the effect of Darwinism and of the new science generally was manifold and deep-reaching. It brought an awareness of mechanism to chill the warm sense of fruitful growth that permeated the romantic concept of cosmic process; it meant a drastic revision of man's view of his own nature and of his place in the universe, always a central topic of literature and now a far grimmer one—for different reasons—than had been current at any time since the Middle Ages. Above all, fulfilling the prescient fears of some romantics, science eliminated much of the poetic element from life, substituting the prosaic for the mysterious, the impersonal for the personal, the material for the impalpable. The romantic faith in the powers of the mind, broadly conceived, to command all knowledge gave way to an oppressive sense that the human intelligence, such as it was, had to content itself with a very limited comprehension of the universe in which it had its moment of ill-adapted existence. The only human certainties were that everything, in ethics, religion, history, experience, was relative, and that absolutes, if they did exist, were beyond man's grasp; and that since evolution was the basic law of life, all was flux. This was the mood in which a considerable body of mid- and late-Victorian literature was written. It formed the background of Swinburne's and Meredith's paganism, of the art for art's sake movement, of George Eliot's and Thomas Hardy's fiction.

Despite science's sponsorship of ideas which eroded Christian faith, its prestige as an intellectual frame of reference steadily increased. Regarded as it was with veneration and hope (for the pure scientists' discoveries and the technologists' practical applications proceeded apace), it finally made unbelief respectable. One's personal rejection of Christianity need no longer be kept to oneself or admitted in confidence to a few intimates. Doubt, frankly confessed, even made one a more interesting human being, as Browning's Bishop Blougram demonstrated in his own person.

Nevertheless, it was no light matter to renounce the faith in which one had been reared, and to which one's family had subscribed without question for many generations. Only after long and agonized soul-searching did many later Victorians commit themselves to various kinds of anti-religious stands—free thought, skepticism, rationalism, agnosticism, secularism, humanism. Denying the basic premises of Christianity as a supernatural and divinely inspired religion and of God as a person, they shifted the grounds of belief to man and man's experience, rejecting theism and postulating instead a vague "force" in the universe. The Church's spiritual authority steadily diminished, a process initiated, of course, in the eighteenth century but interrupted for some time, as we have seen, by the Evangelical and Tractarian movements which infused the Church with new vitality. But now these had run their course, and many minds which would earlier have found spiritual satisfaction within the doctrines and practices of organized religion were compelled to seek it outside. The result was an intellectual ferment which was in many ways the matrix of the modern religious temper.

No better symptom of that ferment, and of the earnestness with which the intellectual community participated in it, can be found than the Metaphysical Society, which brought together during the seventies, for the purposes of high-level philosophical discussion, a remarkable assortment of minds. Its members included the Roman Catholic prelate Henry Manning (cardinal from 1875), the biologist Huxley (who, finding himself without a descriptive label whereas all his fellow-members seemed classifiable by one word or another, coined for himself the word "agnostic"), Tennyson the poet laureate, several intellectual peers and Anglican bishops, Gladstone, and Ruskin. At their meetings these men, representative of the best contemporary thought, discussed the basic philosophical issues of the day. They debated in correct parliamentary fashion. A member who had missed a meeting later met one who had been present. "Well, is there a God?" he asked. "Yes," said the other, "we had a very good majority." But the counting of ayes and nays did not contribute much to the advancement of knowledge. When the society broke up in 1880 Tennyson remarked that they had spent ten years trying to define metaphysics—and failed.

John Stuart Mill was the major forerunner and inspiration of later Victorian rationalism, which attracted many of the epoch's chief intellectuals. It was upon these thinkers that science had its greatest impact, because their special kind of intellect and training made them the most receptive; it was they who most prominently and systematically adopted the scientific attitude toward matters of religion and morality.

Rationalism was essentially an escape *from* religion. A concurrent school of anti-Christian thought constituted, in a way, an escape *into* religion—of a new design. This was positivism, a form of philosophy often called Comtism after its formulator, Auguste Comte (1798–1857), a comprehensive system-maker who sought to adapt the rationalism of the French Enlightenment to the new scientific age. Comte had considerable influence on Mill, who mediated his ideas to Victorian England. For our purposes, the most memorable by-product of his far-reaching synthesis of social, scientific, and ethical thought was the so-called Religion of Humanity, an attempt to supply a rationalistic age with the emotional center, the core of faith, the object of worship that no society (according to Comte) could for long do without. This "Catholicism minus Christianity," as Huxley called it—or, alternatively, "Catholicism plus science"—prided itself on its liberation from the superstition which radical thinkers like the French *philosophes,* William Godwin, and Shelley had attributed to the traditional church. In effect, it proposed to erect a new (rationalistic) church, complete with ritual and dogma, on the site of the old one. The object of its worship was Humanity itself—a somewhat narcissistic procedure, but one for which there was precedent in revolutionary France. Like the Roman Catholic Church it dispensed with, it had its own calendar of saints, one for each day of the year, and all of them "benefactors of the human race"— philosophers, scientists, painters, poets. It possessed, too, an order of liturgy, a prayer book, a set of "social sacraments," a hierarchy of priests, and a succession of church festivals.

All this might be dismissed as a mere episode in the history of human delusions and Quixotic enterprises except that positivism's informing spirit, the conviction of the nobility of the human race metaphysically conceived, had considerable influence upon the mid-Victorian intellectual climate. Relieved of its pseudo-theological and ritualistic fripperies, it was an implicit response to Darwinism: Man Exalted instead of Man Degraded. Since no divine agency could be relied upon to ameliorate his condition, man must turn to himself to make whatever he can of his life. The only answer to his tragic destiny is found in his fully realizing and employing such powers as he possesses. In the ethics of positivism, therefore, was found a loftier statement of the familiar self-help theme. (Here, as so often in intellectual history, we find the same idea turning up on several distinct levels of thought or in several quite separate contexts.)

The conclusions that such intellectuals as George Eliot and Matthew Arnold reached after honesty required them to jettison their inherited religion suggest one crucial fact about the Victorians' situation: their need for faith was stronger than that of their forebears, simply because the grounds of faith now had become so elusive. If the quest proved fruitless, then at least the Victorians—many of them —did succeed in finding a moral *modus vivendi* which was not dependent on belief as such. If historical and dogmatic Christianity could no longer compel belief, ethical Christianity could at least serve as a guide to life. Thus the powers of mind and spirit which in other ages had gone into religious devotion were redirected to social ends, in attempts to fulfill the teaching of the Gospels. As if in recompense for the disintegration of traditional faith, the last doubt-ridden decades of the century saw a heightening of the sense of responsibility as the supreme moral imperative. The critical element in Carlyle's recovery from despair in "The Everlasting Yea"—Goethe's admonition, "Do the duty which lies nearest thee"—now served a generation which had been as yet unborn when he traversed the purgatory of religious nihilism.

Here, it seemed, was one sphere of existence in which man was free. His social conscience was more than the match of Darwinian-Spencerian determinism; no persuasion of the rule of eternal struggle in an inhospitable universe, no nightmare of a society whose first law was competition was so daunting that men did not find it possible to ameliorate their condition, and that of their fellows, by action taken in concert. As the agnostic W. K. Clifford put it, man's duty, under these circumstances, was "to do as well as possible what we can do best; to work for the improvement of the social organisation; to seek earnestly after truth and only to accept provisionally opinions one has not enquired into; to regard men as comrades in work and their freedom as a sacred thing; in fact, to recognise the enormous and fearful difference between truth and falsehood, right and wrong, and how truth and right are to be got by free enquiry and the love of our comrades for their own sake and nobody else." The later Victorians as a group were men and women of remarkable moral resolution. Living in a wasteland strewn with blasted articles of faith, they carried on, with spirit and confidence. What they lost in intellectual assurance and emotional comfort, they compensated for in sheer strength of will.

"Glory to Man in the highest! for Man is the master of things," exulted Swinburne as he concluded his "Hymn of Man," written during the first Vatican Council in 1869–70. Some Victorians thought to redeem the loss of God by erecting man in his place, to worship and serve. Their descendants' tragedy is that they have lost faith even in man.

VII

DEMOCRACY, INDUSTRY,
AND CULTURE

1. Machines and the Spirit of Man

IN VICTORIAN TIMES the quality of life among the masses of people first became a pressing social concern. The revolutionary conditions brought about by industrialization and related developments posed the question, How can society refashion and equip itself so as to provide its members with the greatest inner satisfaction and fulfillment?

It was recognized that the good society which England was hopefully building rested on something called "culture." The change the word's meaning had undergone in the first half of the century reflected the appearance of a novel concept in social thinking. As Raymond Williams has said, before the century began

it had meant, primarily, the "tending of natural growth," and then, by analogy, a process of human training [with reference specifically to the individual]. But this latter use, which had usually been a culture *of* something, was changed, in the nineteenth century, to *culture* as such, a thing in itself. It came to mean, first, "a general state or habit of the mind," having close relations with the idea of human perfection. Second, it came to mean "the general state of intellectual development, in a society as a whole." Third, it came to mean "the general body of the arts." Fourth, later in the century, it came to mean "a whole way of life, material, intellectual and spiritual." [1]

The ultimate origin of what the Victorians came to call culture was the classical-Christian and most specifically the Renaissance ideal of human perfection, of the intellect, feelings, and imagination developed in harmony. But this now became not only an individual ideal but a social one as well, an expression, as Williams puts it, of "man's need for institutions which should confirm and constitute his personal efforts. Cultivation, in fact, though an inward was never a merely individual process. What in the eighteenth century had been an ideal of personality—a personal qualification for participation in polite society—had now, in the face of radical change, to be redefined, as a condition on which society as a whole depended." [2] No longer was society to be viewed only as a means by which men could coexist for their common security and prosperity; now it came to be charged, in addition, with responsibility for enhancing its members' personal lives.

Put another way, the developing Victorian concern for culture represented the response of traditional humanism to altered social conditions. Against the narrow, pragmatic, materialistic Utilitarian spirit it posed a higher ideal. The true progress to be sought, if progress were to be the ambition of society, lay in the enriched activity of the human spirit, not in the superficial and often illusory "improvement" of the material environment and of social and political institutions. "There is no Wealth but Life," Ruskin said in *Unto This Last.*" The "happiness" derived from getting and spending was contrasted with the unmeasurable, intangible but no less real satisfactions of the mind and spirit. And the pursuit of those satisfactions provided an endeavor in which all members of society could join—a source of communal pleasure that far transcended the "cash payment nexus" which, Carlyle averred, formed the only present bond among men. Culture, diffused among the whole population, was a social necessity.

To John Stuart Mill, indeed, the very choice of political institutions was contingent on their cultural effect. Repre-

sentative democracy, he argued, was "a moral and educational question more than one of material interests . . . to
be decided mainly by the consideration, what great improvement in life and culture stands next in order for the people
concerned, as the condition of their further progress, and
what institutions are most likely to promote that. . . ." No
matter what form the machinery of democratic politics took,
social institutions—existing ones refurbished, or wholly new
ones created for the purpose—were the only means by
which this ideal of culture as a common source of happiness
could be achieved. But several powerful forces were arrayed
against it, among them the same forces which made it so
urgent a piece of national business. These were the prevailing middle-class mentality, the spread of social democracy, and the presence of the factory system which degraded
the life of men.

The first of these requires little comment beyond that
already made in Chapter IV. The middle class, dominated
as it was by the Evangelical ethic, and a large portion of it
historically separated from the humanistic tradition centering
in the universities and Anglican intellectual society, was in
need of a broader culture, but by the same token was most
resistant to it. Humorlessly self-righteous, complacent, and
impervious to criticism, it refused to embrace within its field
of approved or desired values those of the spirit (apart from
a narrowly religious one) and the imagination. In a society
battening on the material fruits of such an ethos, culture
was an irrelevancy.

The bourgeois system of values went beyond class
boundaries. It crept by osmosis into a goodly part of the
upper class, despite the condescension the nobility and gentry exhibited toward the upstart manufacturer or merchant
who presumed to aspire to a higher state. And this same
cultural poverty marked the working class as well, partly
because it was inherent in the circumstances of mass life
and partly because the middle class, through its power to
make laws and exert social pressure, imposed the code from

above—or, if "imposed" is too strong, then "set them a pattern which they willingly followed," since normally a subordinate class tends to imitate its superiors.

This fact had much to do with the way the nineteenth-century social critics viewed the progress of democracy. If the middle class proved resistant to the suggestions of a wiser and spiritually richer life beyond its present horizons, what could be said of that much larger part of the people who had always dwelt in darkness beyond the ameliorating influence of culture? If democracy was to mean any more than the right to cast a ballot and to mingle on terms of superficial equality with their betters, how could the masses be brought to participate in the nation's artistic and intellectual life? Would their presence debase or enrich it?

One great fear and one great hope were involved. The fear was that the traditional culture would be vulgarized, leveled down to the lowest common denominator of taste. In the beginning of the century, this apprehension had not been predominant among the concerns of those who opposed teaching the children of the masses to read. Their opposition was founded, rather, on the premise that even a rudimentary education would make them dissatisfied with their ordained station in life, and that literacy would make them susceptible to the inflammations of radical and atheistic propaganda. But when it turned out that the ability to read, acquired in Sunday schools and charity day schools, sent the overwhelming majority of working people to penny thrillers and sensational newspapers instead of the literature of political and religious subversion, the upper classes' concern took a new direction.

The demand for simply written books and papers suited to the semi-literate mind began, about mid-century, to prove that much money could be made in publishing for this audience. A new branch of the trade was established, shrewdly attuned to the unsophisticated tastes and limited capacities of these multitudes of readers. Dedicated to giving the people what they wanted, most entrepreneurs of cheap print cared nothing for its effects on the general level of culture. They were simply out to sell their merchandise. As the volume of their product increased year by year, the prospect grew that the mass audience, by sheer exercise of purchasing power, would eventually dominate the taste of the whole nation. A new version of Gresham's law was often cited: in the free operation of the cultural market, mediocrity and vulgarity always tend to drive out superior goods. Side by side with old-established book shops, where gentlemen of substance always dealt, sprang up innumerable neighborhood news agents' cubicles with their lurid assortment of penny and shilling thrillers. It was an ominous development. Could the culture of the drawing room and study compete with the culture of the pavement? Mill, writing in the late fifties, when the issue had not yet reached its full magnitude, presented by inference the specter of a whole society—its moral values, its intellectual life, its fine arts—succumbing to the tyranny of the majority.

The fear could, however, be translated into hope. Some of the more sanguine social observers, refusing to concede that the enfranchisement of the common mind would necessarily poison the English cultural atmosphere, argued that society's duty was to educate it up, toward the élitist level of culture. It was possible, they insisted, to enrich an ordinary man's tastes and interests so that, far from destroying that culture, he could profitably participate in it according to his capabilities, and, indeed, enhance it through the special qualities of perception he derived from experience in an inferior rank of society. A broader-based culture did not have to be a vulgarized one.

However the higher culture might benefit from an infusion of new intellectual blood, sheer humanitarianism demanded that something be done to enlighten the worker's lot in this society of factories and slums. In the forties and fifties, the fiction and poetry of protest dwelt, as, under prevailing circumstances, it should have done, on the physical misery and moral degradation of the workers rather than upon the effect the condition of their lives had on their capacity for living. A reasonably healthy and whole body and a measure of self-respect are prerequisites to enjoyment of life's less tangible rewards. But as the masses' physical wretchedness began to be abated, it was evident that their lives still admitted no light. There was no time, no money, no incentive to foster even the most elementary sense of "culture." A life on the margins of subsistence has little room for the amenities proper to human beings.

One of the worst results of existence in factory and slum was the assimilation of the individual into the mass. Hitherto, under the conditions of farm and village life, where the largest social groups were the family and the immediate community, people had retained their personal identity. Even if they were objects of charity, they were individual objects. Now, hundreds of thousands were packed into the long, dismal rows of houses near factory, mill, and mine, and their identity was largely lost. They were converted into members of the industrial proletariat; not men, women, and children, each with the precious uniqueness attributed to him in romantic social thought, but mere units in a mass.

Many factors contributed to this loss of personal identity. At their place of employment, the workers were regimented. One was a member of a shift, of a disciplined complement of toilers in a given part of the factory who came and went at the dictates of a bell. The work was monotonous in the extreme, one's allotted task being to perform, hundreds or thousands of times a day, a mere fragment, meaningless in itself, of the production routine. Wherever one worked, many others were doing the same thing at the same time; production being rigidly standardized, there was no allowance for the personal touch—a suppression of individuality which especially stirred Ruskin's indignation. After his long shift, the worker went home to a congested slum where again his sense of identity was erased by the sheer numerousness of the people around him. More subtle but no less destructive was the loss of any belief that he could command his destiny. The wage he received, indeed whether or not he worked at all, was at the mercy of so-called economic laws, often interpreted by the employer for his own convenience. When legislation gradually was passed to enable employer and worker to bargain, it turned out in practice to give the employer all the high cards.

Not least of these depersonalizing forces was the changed relation between master and worker. In the early factory system, before small handicraft operations had given way to large mechanized and steam-powered ones, the master, himself an artisan, had worked alongside his employees. Their relationship had often been warm and sympathetic, like that which had prevailed in the country between squire and tenant farmer or laborer, if conditions (the eternally unpredictable frailties and variables of human nature) were right. But in the big factories which employed hundreds or even thousands of workers, the master, as he continued to be called, typically was rich, remote, and arbitrary. The worker, or "hand," became no more than a name on a wage sheet. Under these conditions, the very word "master" lost its former connotation of an amiable relationship in which loyal acceptance of social inferiority on one side was met by human decency on the other, and acquired the connotation of petty tyranny. In the fiction of the time, apologists for the factory system, anxious to neutralize the wicked stereotype of radical propaganda, regularly portrayed mill owners as men who retained the humane virtues of their craftsman predecessors.

The individual was also the victim of statistical reductiveness. Under the sway of political economy, with its scientific, mathematical bent, the Victorians were addicted to statistics; much of the age's essential history, to say nothing of its spirit, is preserved in volumes crammed with tables and columns of figures. It was a time when, to a certain type of mind, a good round figure was worth a thousand words. The booming vitality of Victorian life could be celebrated as eloquently in charts of figures on production, exports, and mounting national wealth as in Macaulay's rhetoric. Everything in life that could be quantified, from birth to death inclusive, was quantified; so, indeed, as the Benthamite calculus showed, were some elements that could not. Thus, it was inevitable that as a member of the labor force captive in a factory town, a man was translated into an anonymous unit in economic and sociological tables and surveys. Each human being became an atom indistinguishable from all other atoms in whatever category he happened to occupy—illiterate, worker, father, victim of disease, unemployable, drunkard, thief, candidate for workhouse. Even children might be relieved of their names when they entered the Benthamite-ordered schoolroom; Sissy Jupe in *Hard Times* was "Girl Number Twenty."

Depersonalization led to dehumanization. (The jargon suits the subject.) A man or woman bound to a rackety machine was no longer a human being. One hundred persons, assigned to fixed posts, became one hundred adjuncts to the steam engines and looms which were their true masters. Machines did not tire; their operators, accordingly, were not expected to. When the people attached to them wore out, they were thrust onto the heap of human debris and promptly forgotten. Machines were more valued, because when they wore out, their still-workable parts were salvaged.

It was natural, then, that in Victorian habits of thought —not merely those of the Benthamites, which had a machinelike quality from the beginning—man and machine tended to merge. The imagery and terminology of the machine, like that of finance, constantly crept into discussions of social topics, even of religious ones. The machine's omnipresence and man's physical subjection to it had a psychic effect on people.

It was not only the machine that was everywhere. So were its products, mass-produced goods which epitomized the monotony that had become a curse of life. Their uniformity complemented the endless sameness of the streets that housed the workers, and, as time went on, the equivalent monotony of middle-class suburbia, where freshly laid out "lanes," "avenues," "ways," and "groves" were quickly lined with semi-detached houses built out of the same pattern book that served speculative builders in a hundred other suburbs. Nor was the life led by most commercial-class town dwellers less deadening to the spirit. The growing multitude of office clerks and shop assistants were slaves of dull routine throughout the long day and, in the case of the latter, into the evening, for shop hours went unregulated until the end of the century. In one respect they were worse off than factory hands, because the latter could find escape of a sort in gross amusements such as getting drunk and disorderly, whereas the clerks had to observe the forms of respectability.

In the interests of realism, however, it should be added that life in a country village or on a farm can be quite as tedious as life in town. What happened in the nineteenth century was not that ways of living which supposedly had hitherto been filled with life-refreshing variety suddenly became numbingly dull. Rather, a new source and perhaps a new quality of boredom appeared with the factory and city. And, above all, the circumstances which forced millions of people to lead lives of vacancy were for the first time recognized as a problem which demanded to be remedied by social action. The realization that enervation and monotony are not necessary conditions of life is one of the few social gains that can be credited to the factory system.

2. "The March of Mind"

It would seem, then, that nineteenth-century England afforded in large abundance all the conditions necessary to what Carlyle called "asphyxia of the soul." Whether simply neglected or over-narrowly defined, the growth of culture was inhibited on every side. But confidence persisted that democracy, industrialism, and civilization were not incompatible, and that the energies which were reconciling, however clumsily, the political and economic revolutions of the age could make room within them for a broadly based culture as well.

Education was the answer. So argued all who believed, in the spirit of the romantic social visionaries, that bourgeoisie and proletariat alike were not irredeemably doomed to labor without light. Seldom in western history had so much faith been placed in education as an agency of popular social, if not cultural, progress. One notable exception was Scotland, where, ever since the sixteenth century, Calvinism had insisted on schooling for all regardless of rank; and it was no accident that much of the impetus for English popular education came from men born and bred in Scotland.

When the Victorian age began, the most familiar catch phrase among the Benthamite improvers (it is echoed innumerable times, often with ironic intent, in the literature that comes down to us) was "the March of Mind." The idea was that, in this epoch when science and technology were transforming the physical environment and multiplying the nation's wealth, progress could be sustained only if the fund of "useful" knowledge were constantly increased and made available to as many people as could help the nation profit by it. From this practically educated class would, it was expected, spring an enlarged supply of inventors and engineers as well as of businessmen trained in the mysteries of economics and commerce. As Bentham's, and subsequently the Benthamite age's, patron saint Francis Bacon had observed centuries before, in words now blazoned across the Victorian educational landscape, "Knowledge Is Power." The schoolmaster was abroad, as still another catch phrase associated with the March of Mind had it, and, assuming he taught the right subjects, his presence was regarded in some quarters as the best possible guarantee of a prosperous and secure future.

Such were the golden hopes. The realities were something else. The history of Victorian popular education is

clouded and musty with the odor of perennial partisan controversy, but one fact emerges with saddening clarity. If
social adjustment lagged behind the new conditions of life,
even farther behind were the schools as a seed-ground of
humane culture. As the state of popular culture everywhere
in the Western world today attests, universal education has
proved not to be the panacea it once was touted as being. But
at least a working-class child has a better chance today to
share in the nation's intellectual and artistic life than did his
Victorian ancestors, whose cultural deprivation was one of the
sorest reproaches to the notion of progress and one of the age's
most intractable problems.

Out of the eighteenth-century charity schools that dispensed a smattering of education to children of the poor
developed an ill-organized, inefficient conglomeration sponsored by various religious and philanthropic bodies, the two
most important being the National Society for the Education
of the Poor in the Principles of the Established Church in
England and Wales (Anglican, needless to say) and the
British and Foreign School Society (Nonconformist). To the
continuous detriment of popular education, the two were
much less concerned with improving the quality of their instruction than with protecting their respective denominations'
interests. They operated in a permanent state of mutual
suspicion and rivalry, the bone of contention after 1833
being the distribution of governmental subsidy. Should public
money be used to indoctrinate children in the principles of
the Established Church or apportioned among the various
denominations; or should such funds be restricted to schools
committed to non-sectarian religious teaching? The weari-
some squabble stretched across the decades. "Wesleyan and
Catholic," it has been said, "Puseyite and Dissenter, Baptist
and Churchman, Evangelical and Tractarian, denouncing
one another, treated St. Paul's famous letter on charity and
the needs of the English child with equal indifference." [3]
But the contending parties did manage to agree that the
ideal products of their ministrations, such as they were,

should grow up to be pious, non-troublemaking members of "the inferior orders" who knew and accepted their station in life, rejected radical politics with horrified aversion, and put aside Paine's *The Age of Reason* in favor of their cheap Bibles.

These restrictions were in response to the influential conservative opinion that any popular education at all was undesirable and even dangerous. Farmers generally opposed it because children could be better occupied in crow scaring or hoeing for a few pennies a week. Families still engaged in cottage industry, such as hosiery knitting, lace making, and straw plaiting, needed all the little hands that were around. Textile mills, potteries, ribbon factories, brickyards —whatever industry had ill-paid drudgery to offer, offered it to children. Cheap labor, it was always maintained, was essential to Britain's competitive position, and children were the cheapest labor of all. As late as the sixties Conservative politicians were asserting that "any attempt to keep children of the labouring classes under intellectual culture after the very earliest age at which they could earn their living, would be as arbitrary and improper as it would be to keep the boys at Eton and Harrow at spade labour."

Practices in the working-class schools bore distinct tinges of Benthamism. The resemblance between the typical elementary schoolroom and a factory was not fanciful; the atmosphere of drill hall–*cum*–production line was the same in both cases. The Benthamite ideal of efficiency and economy was served—disastrously—by the widespread adoption of the monitorial system. Selected older pupils, replaced after the forties by apprentice teachers, learned from the master or mistress a certain number of prepackaged facts and painful accomplishments, such as the elements of reading, writing, and ciphering, and then were delegated to communicate these, normally in grievously imperfect form, to the pupils below them. While this sort of conveyor-belt, or sweated, education unquestionably was cheap, the products were dear at the price. But culture was not really the goal in view. From the political economists' standpoint, which was not uncongenial with that of the religious parties, the schools would serve their purpose if they guaranteed a steady flow of productive, sober, and docile recruits into the labor force. They did not aim to create a nation of readers, concertgoers, or gallery visitors.

Few working-class children had more than two or three years of desultory schooling, and those in the lower reaches of the middle class had scarcely more. They did not miss much and in fact were spared a good deal. The buildings were inadequate, the teachers even more so; until teacher-training began on a small scale in the forties, it was a commonplace that youths and men who had failed at a series of other occupations ended up behind teacher's desks. What with the physical environment—noisy, overheated, odorous from dirty clothing and a hundred unwashed and unhealthy bodies—and the atmosphere of stern discipline and unimaginative force-feeding of the rote memory, elementary schooling was an ordeal which many working-class children sought, often successfully, to avoid. Going to work was far preferable to memorizing the principal towns of France in alphabetical order, the names and dates of the prophets and the kings of Judah and Israel in chronological order, and the wanderings of the Children of Israel or the bays, creeks, and harbors of Palestine and Syria in topographical order—as well as to learning the noteworthy characteristics of Benares, Amritsar, Gujarat, Bijapur, and Pondicherry, and calculating the interest of £535 7s. 4d. at six per cent for fifteen seconds. Going to work had the additional advantage of putting coppers in ragged pockets. Although child labor gradually came to be regulated in the towns, no laws covered the employment of country children. In 1870 Forster's Education Act empowered local authorities to make school attendance compulsory up to the age of thirteen, but the requirement was not made nationwide until 1880. Until then, nothing prevented a child's dropping out at any time, to find ill-paid menial work, baby-sit at home, or loaf in the streets.

The outlook for national culture was not bright when the population included hundreds of thousands of men, women, and children like Jo, the homeless street boy in *Bleak House*:

To shuffle through the streets, unfamiliar with the shapes, and in utter darkness as to the meaning, of those mysterious symbols, so abundant over the shops, and at the corners of streets, and on the doors, and in the windows! To see people read, and to see people write, and to see the postmen deliver letters, and not to have the least idea of all that language—to be, to every scrap of it, stone blind and dumb! It must be very puzzling to see the good company going to the churches on Sundays, with their books in their hands, and to think (for perhaps Jo *does* think, at odd times) what does it all mean, and if it means anything to anybody, how comes it that it means nothing to me?

Even if a child possessed a minimal ability to read, the unpleasant circumstances under which he acquired it, as well as the general ignorance which the brevity of his schooling made inevitable, usually meant that he would seldom exercise his gift. Or, if he did, it would be over the most undemanding reading matter the press was capable of turning out.

Few people in a position of authority, either at the local level or in the London command post, showed the slightest interest in providing a more humane education. Matthew Arnold, naturally, was one who did, but even he failed to press very hard. No encouragement was given to the exercise of the mind or the feelings. On the contrary, the textbooks and classroom exercises were designed to avoid such liberating, humanizing elements, which, it was widely agreed, were inappropriate for children destined to become factory and farm hands. The essence of pedagogy was committing "useful" and "improving" facts to memory; reading for sheer pleasure was not to be thought of. And in most schools and, after 1850, in tax-built libraries, care was taken that the selection of books be limited to those which had instructive value. In many such libraries, fiction was banned. Dickens never wearied of decrying this state of affairs, in which the governors of the poor set their faces against their charges' hunger for escapist reading matter: "The English are, so far as I know, the hardest-worked people on whom the sun shines. Be content if, in their wretched intervals of pleasure, they read for amusement and do no worse. They are born at the oar, and they live and die at it. Good God, what would we have of them!"

Meanwhile, the schooling of the nobility and gentry was, in the main, what it had been since Tudor times. After home instruction or attendance at a private elementary school, the boys—their sisters, we have seen, were largely unprovided for except in finishing schools of demonstrable futility—were sent to one or another of the nine ancient public schools (English equivalents of American preparatory schools). Headed by Eton, the largest such school and traditional cradle of the aristocracy, these institutions provided the sons of the privileged few with a form of secondary education in which the emphasis was overwhelmingly classical. Translating, parsing, imitating, and memorizing the works of Greek and Latin authors was the schoolboy's principal business, year after year. The classics were studied for their presumed disciplinary value; analyzing their grammar and rhetoric was thought to be good for the mind. Their humane content was overlooked. Not surprisingly, the normal residual effect was a head crammed with Greek and Latin tags and an ineffaceable distrust of what was called polite learning.

In the course of the era, a little science, modern history, and French or German were introduced as fringe benefits. This innovation was largely due to the reform movement initiated by Dr. Thomas Arnold at Rugby and subsequently adopted by the other public schools. The cautiously liberalized curriculum was a step in the right direction, but other steps taken at the same time nullified whatever contribution it made toward broadening a boy's cultural interests. Arnold's great stress was upon character-building—understandably, because on the eve of the Victorian period the atmosphere in most of the public schools had degenerated into an evil combination of somnolence, brutality, and anarchy (troops had had to be called in more than once to put down the boys' rebellion). In time, the main vehicle of moral training was agreed to be organized games, and during the latter half of the century the public schools were more concerned with prowess on the playing field and with shaping the morality of prospective Christian gentlemen than with brainwork. But even the character-building rationale faded into mere cant, and the cult of games became an end rather than a means, another example of the fruitless machinery which Thomas Arnold's son had deplored.

Nor would John Stuart Mill have liked the conformism enforced by the public schools' new way of life. Team sports involved regimentation, discipline; and so the public schools joined the factories and the people's elementary schools in suppressing originality, devoting themselves instead to producing a standardized product at a luxury price. A favorable specimen of the system's operation would emerge from the sixth form (senior class) as an exemplar of self-control, honesty, responsibility, self-reliance, and leadership. He might well go on to distinguish himself in Empire service or in the socially exclusive upper echelons of the British Army, but little in the education that entitled him to wear the old school tie would have made him a gentleman of wide humanistic culture.

From the public schools the sons of the Anglican rich went to Oxford or Cambridge, where they spent three years learning or not learning, whichever way they were inclined. They could take a degree without having attended a single lecture; but (to be fair about it) there were some professors who, enjoying lifelong sinecures, never bothered to deliver lectures, either. Although, notwithstanding the prevalence of sloth, these two old universities remained centers of the nation's intellectual life, as they had been for centuries, the undergraduate curriculum, like that of the public schools, was heavy with anachronism. The classics (at Oxford) and mathematics (at Cambridge) ruled the roost, and "modern subjects" insinuated themselves only through the pressure of public opinion, with agonizing slowness and always against the entrenched opposition of the traditionalists. During most of the Victorian era, the universities, again like the public schools, were the monopoly of the Anglican clergy. Only in 1871 did irresistible outside pressure force them to admit Dissenters to fellowships and other academic posts.

University College ("the godless institution in Gower Street"), the first component of the University of London, was opened in 1828 to care for those excluded from Oxbridge on religious and, in effect, social grounds. Its founders were chiefly Benthamites and its curriculum, accordingly, was secular, liberal, scientific, and professional. The university soon made its presence felt, but even when allowance is made for the number of middle-class students it served, the fact remains that in Victorian England higher education, wherever provided, was reserved for a tiny minority. It was from the upper and upper-middle classes, who alone had access to it—not the obscure, rustic Judes of hopeless ambition—that the learned professions, notably the clergy and the law, were recruited.

The great majority of the middle class, therefore, were culturally disadvantaged for more reasons than the narrow Utilitarian-Evangelical estimate of life's purposes and possibilities. Their youth normally received their secondary education, if they got any at all, at local endowed grammar (classical) schools of varying quality or privately conducted academies such as Mr. Creakle's in *David Copperfield*. Most of these, like Dr. Blimber's in *Dombey and Son,* oppressed their students with the customary classical regimen, either because the terms of their endowment (in the case of the grammar schools) required them to do so or because, like the clientele they served, their chief aim was to imitate their betters. But in schools more responsive to the needs of the commercial and professional class, including the several notable institutions on the public school model founded in the mid-Victorian era, practical subjects like science, applied mathematics, and foreign languages enjoyed undisguised respectability. The classics continued to be stressed for those headed for the university, but modern subjects helped those who were going to have to make a living.

This was an undeniable gain; anything to break the stupefyingly irrelevant tyranny of disciplinary Greek and Latin and of Euclidean mathematics. If Matthew Arnold's assertion that "our middle classes are nearly the worst educated in the world" needed some qualification, at least it was unquestionable that nowhere could the son of a Victorian family, no matter how wealthy or socially favored, obtain a truly liberal education such as that proposed by Newman in *The Idea of a University* or by Mill in his great inaugural lecture at St. Andrews in 1867. Under the circumstances, it was remarkable that the genuinely cultured minority of the Victorian population was as large as it was, or had as large a middle-class representation.

3. Self-Help

There remained, however, the strong Victorian drive toward self-education. While it was generally agreed that formal education for the lower classes should be brief and confined to the harmless first elements of knowledge, the Whig-Benthamite liberals were warm advocates of education outside the classroom. It was an integral part of their program to help men adapt to the conditions of a dynamic society. "The education of the working-classes," Samuel Smiles, the future author of *Self-Help,* told a meeting of Leeds workingmen in 1845, "is to be regarded, in its highest aspect, not as a means of raising up a few clever and talented men into a higher rank of life, but of elevating and improving the whole class—of raising the entire condition of the working man. The grand object aimed at should be to make the great mass of the people virtuous, intelligent, well-informed, and well-conducted; and to open up to them new sources of pleasure and happiness. Knowledge is of itself one of the highest enjoyments."

Responding to such sentiments as these, many men in the working and artisan (lower middle) classes studied and read on their own. These self-educated readers were only a small minority, as they would be in any epoch, but contemporary evidence, including the autobiographies a number of them published, suggests that they were considerably more numerous than they are in the changed and in some respects more favorable conditions of modern life. Alton Locke, the Chartist tailor in Kingsley's novel, represents the type. His real-life model was Thomas Cooper, successively a shoemaker's apprentice, schoolmaster, and journalist by trade, who became a leading Chartist. Both the historical figure and the fictional character, overcoming formidable difficulties, managed to administer to themselves the rough equivalent of a liberalized university education, with the extra advantage that Greek and Latin were kept in their place. What their self-schooling lacked in structure it made up in substance, even though there is some reason to doubt Mrs. Gaskell's assertion, in *Mary Barton,* that Lancashire handloom weavers kept Newton's *Principia Mathematica* "open on the loom, to be snatched at in work hours, but revelled over in meal-times or at night."

Not surprisingly, most self-taught workingmen of whom we have any record were radicals of one breed or another. The Chartist leaders and their lieutenants were for the most part working-class intellectuals, men of little formal schooling who had managed to steep themselves in the writings of congenial poets like the libertarian, anti-Church Milton (a hero to most early Victorian radicals) and to read widely in general literature as well. Some memorized incredibly long swatches of poetry. More than a few composed verse of their own, much of it highly exclamatory in its assertion of working-class militancy.

Political and non-political workingmen alike were inspired to their studies by the Society for the Diffusion of Useful Knowledge, a Benthamite-oriented group founded in 1826 which promoted adult education for the sake of improving workers' efficiency and adding to the nation's pool of inventors and engineers. It had a great vogue in the First Reform Bill era, its major projects being the publication of a long series of dry treatises on applied science and political economy and the establishment of mechanics' institutes (adult night schools with libraries attached). Inevitably the S.D.-U.K. brought down upon itself the opposition and derision of conservatives, who as always feared for the nation's safety if the poor were taught to think. Carlyle complained to John Stuart Mill of the "triumphant quackle-quackling of the Diffusion Society intent only on sine and cosine" and Thomas Love Peacock satirized it, as the "Steam Intellect Society," in his novel *Crotchet Castle*.

This division of the March of Mind soon broke ranks in disorder, but it left an important heritage. It called attention to the plight of countless men who had brains but no way of learning how to put them to use, and it pioneered ways of remedying their deprivation. Like the religious organizations, it encouraged the development of cheap publishing techniques, and many of the several hundred mechanics' institutes for whose founding it was directly or indirectly responsible helped stimulate local cultural interests and activities. Both the example and the inadequacy of the institutes' libraries gave impetus to the public library movement.

Unfortunately, the Society limited itself to what might be called applied learning. True to its Utilitarian bias, it regarded education as a means to a single end, the material improvement of society and of the individual. Knowledge was power to build more productive machinery and raise one's wages so that one could enjoy a few of the comforts of life. It had nothing to do with cultivating the spirit or the imagination. Admittedly the Society's list of improving books was divided into two "libraries," one devoted to "useful" and the other to "entertaining" knowledge. But a reader would be hard put to discover any uproarious amusement in the latter, which was composed of histories and inspiring biographies. The S.D.U.K.'s world was bounded by science, technology, political economy, and whatever other disciplines (such as geography) had practical relevance.

The narrowness or misguided ambition of the "Diffusion Society's" program was most forcefully revealed by the gradual conversion of the mechanics' institutes, originally the locale of classes and lectures on science and invention designed (however overconfidently) for ambitious workingmen, into semi-frivolous institutions dominated by the middle class. Here the families of business and professional men, along with a scattering of clerks and master artisans, gathered to hear musical entertainments, platform recitals of favorite literature, and popularized lectures on belles lettres, "antiquities," travel, and other non-Utilitarian topics. The institutes' usefulness declined as their amusement value went up. At the same time, members used their libraries to read such entertaining books (especially fiction) as the board of governors allowed on the shelves; the scientific works which had been the library's nucleus gathered dust. The original spirit behind the mechanics' institute movement had gone hopelessly astray. But their continuing popularity in provincial towns, once their program had been revised, showed how hungry ordinary middle-class people were for occasional snacks of literature and art. Here culture was brought down to the level of the common understanding, and while many performances offered in its name were the very definition of vulgarization in its worst sense, they were at least a cut above both the printed pap and the strongly seasoned fare purveyed, at rock-bottom prices, to the semi-literate masses.

4. Science in the New Society

The experience of the Society for the Diffusion of Useful Knowledge and the mechanics' institutes was a significant chapter in the century-long conflict of humane learning and science. Its background lay in the late eighteenth and early nineteenth centuries, when the spirit of Utilitarianism, if not the word itself, was already abroad. In the preface to the second edition of *Lyrical Ballads* (1800) Wordsworth recognized science's anti-poetic tendencies but was hopeful of an eventual reconciliation between the Poet and the Man of Science because both dedicated their lives to the pursuit of truth. Twenty years later Peacock, in *The Four Ages of Poetry,* read the burial service over poetry: it had succumbed to the materialism of the time. Whether Peacock was serious or satiric is hard to decide, but his essay needled Shelley to reply in *The Defence of Poetry,* first published well inside the Victorian era (1840). In these prime documents of the Art vs. Utility, Imagination vs. Pragmatism battle, the word "culture" in its Victorian sense was not used, but the idea it denotes was clearly present in the debaters' minds. The opposition was between culture, which was taken to be the sum of the arts and philosophy, and "natural philosophy," or science, as it was coming to be called.

Science, as we saw in the preceding chapter, was steadily gaining in prestige as its miracle-working powers became more evident. Empiricism, as opposed to theorizing—Macaulay's Bacon vs. Plato—had been validated beyond doubt: behold the results. And this, it might confidently be assumed, was but the beginning. With every passing year the scientists, putting aside the now discredited deductive procedure and adopting in its place that which was called scientific method, would wrest more secrets from, in Browning's phrase, "nature's close reserve." Their conquests would be ever more glorious and man's control of his environment the firmer and more profitable.

The acceptance of science was all the readier because the long English tradition of scientific amateurism came into full flower in the Victorian era and a host of avocational scientists were eager to help honor their hobby and promote its intellectual authority. The famous Gilbert White, who had chronicled the natural history of the Hampshire village of Selborne for almost half a century, was among the progenitors of numerous spare-time ornithologists, botanists, geologists, and astronomers. More than a few, like the self-educated Scottish geologist Hugh Miller, a stonemason and later a bank accountant by occupation, made solid contributions to knowledge. He and men like him played a vigorous role in the controversy touched off by *Vestiges of the Natural History of Creation* (1844), a best-selling popularization of recent evolutionary thought. The author of *Vestiges,* it later became known, was himself a non-professional, Robert Chambers, who had taught himself geology in the leisure left over from his business as an Edinburgh "publisher for the people" specializing in cheap instructive books and periodicals. Tennyson kept up with scientific developments throughout his life, and Ruskin knew more about some aspects of science than do most critics of art and society. Once in a while a typical amateur scientist turns up in fiction. Mr. Farebrother, the country clergyman in *Middlemarch,* and the unschooled mill hand Job Legh, in *Mary Barton,* both were enthusiastic naturalists.

Until the middle of the century, however, except in non-Anglican or secular schools for boys of the commercial middle class, very little provision was made for scientific study in the schools and universities. Critics pointed out that such instruction as there was failed to take into account the discoveries of the past three centuries. When a student picked up an interest in "natural philosophy," as Shelley had at Eton, it was from enthusiasts, some self-taught, working outside the curriculum. Most professional scientists were men of private initiative; those who were university members seldom taught their subjects. Endowed, organized research began only in the wake of the reforms which swept Oxford and Cambridge between 1850 and 1880. Beginning in the middle of the century, it was possible to be examined for honors degrees in science, but for two decades or more few undergraduates chose, or seemingly were encouraged, to do so. It was many years before courses in scientific subjects were sufficiently common in the public schools and universities to wipe out the reproach of a commission of inquiry in 1864 that "natural science . . . is practically excluded from the education of the higher classes in England." Only in the last decades of the century, when Britain's trade lead was threatened by that of a Germany whose schools gave ample attention to science, did English education strive for parity. In the eighties the first technical schools and "polytechs" were established, with the specific purpose of turning out scientists and technicians to meet German competition.

These were, in rough outline, the circumstances behind Huxley's campaign to obtain for science what he and many fellow-professionals considered its rightful place in the concept of liberal education, co-equal with the humanities. Although Huxley was himself a reasonable man—whatever overemphasis he may have been guilty of was due to his having to compensate for the long neglect science had suffered—his speeches and articles alarmed defenders of culture as traditionally conceived. Now that science had made its belated entrance into the curriculum, both in schools and in the world outside there was the danger that the prestige of science and modes of scientific thought would obscure the claims of literature. The pendulum, the humanists feared, was swinging too far. If science had hitherto been deprived of its just share of attention, now liberal education was being sacrificed to the narrower training of professional scientists and technologists.

5. The State and the Clerisy

Whatever weight the idea of "the less government, the better" had with their laissez faire-minded contemporaries, some Victorian critics of society believed that the state must supply the leadership and support necessary to realize the ideal of national culture. In 1830—it may not have been mere coincidence that this was when the Society for the Diffusion of Useful Knowledge was pushing its own version of the March of Mind—Coleridge anticipated Arnold's mordant criticism of machinery. In his *On the Constitution of Church and State* he asked, "Has the national welfare, have the weal and happiness of the people, advanced with the increase of the circumstantial prosperity? Is the increasing number of wealthy individuals that which ought to be understood by the wealth of the nation?" He framed as questions, in other words, what Macaulay was meanwhile affirming to be cosmic truths. In so doing, he expressed value in terms independent of the cant about "civilization," "wealth," and "progress," and maintained that, with industrialism and political economy leading to the growing compartmentalization and isolation of individual lives, the true "wealth of the nation"—its culture—had to be assured by social institutions.

Such an institution Coleridge found in his proposed "National Church." The name was unfortunate insofar as it bore connotations of sectarian religion; a more accurate, though admittedly less succinct, phrase would be "the State in its cultural role." But the name was well chosen in that it recalled that the Church Universal had been the agency through which culture had been preserved, nourished, and disseminated during the Middle Ages. The scriptoria and libraries and schools, all under ecclesiastical auspices, had kept humane learning alive when their secular equivalents had been moribund, impotent, or actually non-existent. Now Coleridge would revive that function, though under secular auspices. The purpose of his National Church was to co-ordinate and direct all the nation's educational and cultural activities—in effect, to form a center of intellectual authority and to function as a propagator of a cultural norm, somewhat in the manner of the French Academy. Co-equal with those branches of the state which govern its material affairs, the National Church would have the use of a certain allotted portion of the country's wealth to support schools, universities, museums, libraries, scientific institutions, and other cultural undertakings. Coleridge's principle was recognized, in a restricted way, by the Education Act of 1870, which for the first time affirmed the state's direct responsibility to provide education for everyone. In our own day, the British Arts Council and in the United States the National Foundation of the Arts and the Humanities are practical though limited realizations of the same Coleridgean idea.

The agents of the National Church, in Coleridge's proposal, would be the "clerisy," or what would now be called the intellectual community—the sum of the nation's scholars and artists, or, as Coleridge put it, "the learned of all denominations; the sages and professors [i.e., practitioners] of . . . all the so-called liberal arts and sciences." These were to be the true educators of the nation, operating not only through schoolrooms and university lecture halls but through every means by which the nation's cultural wealth could be distributed. The elements of such a system already existed, though in most imperfect form, in the network of relatively well-educated and cultivated men stationed throughout the country as rectors and vicars, many of whom sponsored or actually taught in schools. But Coleridge's clerisy was composed of qualified laymen as well. In this concept, it must be noted, there is no hint of "cultural democracy." The clerisy were regarded as definitely superior to the large run of people, who themselves remained in an inferior cultural condition. But at least they might be visited by culture, and the attentions of the clerisy, supported by the National Church, would ensure that they might benefit by it to whatever degree their intelligence allowed.

Coleridge's clerisy reappears in Matthew Arnold's social criticism. Arnold dismissed the three conventional classes of society, one by one, as equally unfitted to be the repositories and disseminators of culture: the aristocracy ("Barbarians") because they were indifferent to it, the middle class ("Philistines") because their complacency disqualified them to recognize "the best that is known and thought in the world," and the working class ("Populace") because their only ambition was to rise to be Philistines. There remained, then, the intellectual élite, or what Arnold called the saving "remnant." These were the few men who rose above the restrictions characteristic of their respective classes and were devoted to discovering, cultivating, and propagating the truth as apprehended by the genuinely disinterested mind. Until the state assumed its full function as society's civilizing agent (Arnold followed both Coleridge and his own father in this view of the state's cultural responsibility), in the remnant resided the only immediate hope for the ideal compound of sweetness and light which would rectify the present imbalance between "Hebraism," of which the Philistines had too much, and "Hellenism," of which they could use much more.

In Arnold's own era the clerisy was in a most flourishing condition. It was the same small group of superior intelligences who had presided over English culture for at least a century: university graduates for the most part, men of wide learning who stimulated and fed one another's minds by talk and pen and who in their leisure hours read Sophocles with feet on fender; the sort of people who, in the first half of the nineteenth century, had ruled the quarterly reviews and frequented the salons of such hosts as Lord and Lady Holland. They were leading members of their various professions, including the law, the church, and the higher journalism; some were prominent in public affairs; some—far more than any analogous group would contain today—were gentlemen bent on making the best of lives subsidized by dependable inherited incomes. Although they constituted a fairly close-knit group, with headquarters in London (and, decreasingly as the age wore on, in Edinburgh) and outposts at Oxford and Cambridge, they represented a wide spectrum of opinion. In no way did they consider themselves an establishment committed to the preservation of intellectual orthodoxy. On the contrary, they were the most liberalizing force in Victorian society, coming closest to Arnold's ideal of true critics.

Their most remarkable distinction was the breadth of their interests. Despite their busy professional lives and activities in numerous learned and public organizations, they managed to be conversant with as many as half a dozen disciplines—literature, history, philology, philosophy, theology, whatever fields helped constitute the equipment of a humane polymath. Gladstone, who with Disraeli dominated national politics for a generation, delved into religious subjects and Homeric scholarship, and published books and articles which reflected his knowledge of such topics even if, as some critics suggested, his mastery left something to be desired. Possibly most representative of the mid-Victorian clerisy's intellectual versatility was George Henry Lewes, novelist, literary and dramatic critic, writer of books and articles on biology and psychology (subjects of which he had much more than an amateur's command), historian of philosophy, and author of a long-standard life of Goethe. About no realm of knowledge were some of these broad-gauged men better informed than science, a fact which had much to do with the level on which the revelations and implications of the new physics and biology were discussed. There was, as yet, no such split between "The Two Cultures" as would engage the scientist-civil servant-novelist C. P. Snow and his antagonist, the literary critic F. R. Leavis, a hundred years after Darwin.

Surrounding this intellectual aristocracy, as a distinctive feature of mid-Victorian cultural life, was a larger community composed of intelligent middlebrows typified by Mr.

Merdle's physician in *Little Dorrit,* who was "a great reader of all kinds of literature (and never at all apologetic for that weakness)." Its origins lay partially in the numerous "lit and phil" (literary and philosophical, i.e., scientific) institutions that had sprung up in provincial towns as well as London late in the eighteenth century and still prospered in the nineteenth, side by side (or sometimes merged) with the increasingly middle-class mechanics' institutes. These busy and productive cultural institutions, which combined several or all of the features of reading room, circulating library, "cabinet" (museum), scientific data exchange, paper-reading assembly, and social meeting-place, enrolled the town's most active minds—physicians, lawyers, clergymen, book-reading businessmen, even possibly a sprinkling of skilled artisans, who in the aggregate constituted a kind of minor local clerisy.

Beginning in some such fashion, the democratization of culture gained momentum in the thirties and forties. Many workingmen's groups, radical or non-political, went in for mutual improvement classes and other "lit and phil" activities suited to their purposes and walk of life. Stimulated by the prevailing self-help enthusiasm and by their awareness of how unsatisfactory their formal education had been, many small employers, superior-grade shopkeepers, ordinary professional men, and the like spent their leisure reading and talking among themselves on topics of intellectual substance. They were men who, but for the grace of their lively minds, might have been exemplary Philistines. They were not specialists or professionals, and least of all pedants; their interest in the affairs of man and his universe was simply the result of an insatiable curiosity, a true avocation. The existence of so many provincial "athenaeums" and other grandly titled societies, and, later, the popularity of university extension courses suggest how widely diffused was this eagerness for culture. But the best evidence comes from the history of the press. The success of serious and semi-popular magazines covering a broad range of subjects in a style that seldom condescended is witness of the size of the audience they were meant to educate, and their quality testifies to the quality of that audience's mind. The men who read them read, among much else of less distinction, what we most value in Victorian literature.

True, neither the élite nor the middlebrow clerisy functioned as Coleridge and Arnold hoped they would, as culture-bearers to the multitude. They received and treasured knowledge, but they did not spread it except among themselves. But in a period when social democracy seemed to be threatening to sink the cultural level of the nation lower and lower, this relatively small group, liberal, inquisitive, never wearying of the play of ideas, maintained the humanistic ideal. Consciously or not, they tried to keep a balance between what was most worth preserving in the inherited literary culture and what was most promising in the new literary-scientific one.

The class of thinking laymen probably reached the peak of its size, vigor, and influence between the fifties and the eighties. As leisure shrank and the pool of knowledge inexorably widened, fewer and fewer men, of whatever gifts, could pretend to a comfortable command of even one field, let alone several. It has been remarked more than once that the dissolution of the Metaphysical Society in 1880 foreshadowed the end of such interdisciplinary communities; the subject-matter of their various interests was becoming too complex and even its language too recondite for men to talk about them with their former easy familiarity. As in education, the generalist (as he was not then called) had to give way to the specialist. By the last years of the century the clerisy was fragmented, along with so much else in English life. Replacing it was the cellular structure of the expert society, whose members communicated, for the most part, only among themselves. Many of the nation's most brilliant men, who under happier circumstances would have belonged to the Coleridgean clerisy, left the mainstream of contemporary intellectual life to master their specialties. The wholeness which had been an ideal of Western culture from the Greeks down through the English romantics to Matthew Arnold was now seen to have a steadily diminishing prospect of realization, either for the individual human being or for society at large.

If the sum of intellectual laymen was small in proportion to the total population then, it is infinitesimal now. A generation ago G. M. Young sounded a lament for the vanished Victorian clerisy:

And where shall we look for the successors of the Mills and Ruskins and Tennysons? Or of the public for which they wrote? The common residual intelligence is becoming impoverished for the benefit of the specialist, the technician, and the aesthete: we leave behind us the world of historical ironmasters and banker historians, geological divines and scholar tobacconists, with its genial watchword: to know something of everything and everything of something: and through the gateway of the Competitive Examination [for the civil service, which helped turn the universities into institutions for specialized professional training] we go out into the Waste Land of Experts, each knowing so much about so little that he can neither be contradicted nor is worth contradicting.

VIII

THE NATURE OF ART AND

ITS PLACE IN SOCIETY

1. Art and the Middle-Class Mind

WORDSWORTH'S AND SHELLEY'S defenses of poetry (a term
they sometimes expanded to mean "imaginative vision")
responded to an ominous trend already apparent in the
century's first decades. To the distrust of broad humane
culture on moral and social grounds was added Utilitarian
opposition to art on philosophical grounds. "All poetry,"
Bentham announced, "is misrepresentation." It dealt with
matters that are often patently untrue, hence it corrupted the
strict rationalism which ought always to govern men's minds.
To the Utilitarian way of thinking, Keats's kind of truth
which could be tested on one's pulse was unadulterated
nonsense.

The ventriloquistic Peacock, anticipating Macaulay's
dictum that "as civilization advances, poetry almost necessarily declines," put the case in behalf of most Benthamites
(John Stuart Mill, of course, later entering a vigorous dissent):

A poet in our times is a semi-barbarian in a civilized community.
He lives in the days that are past. His ideas, thoughts, feelings,
associations, are all with barbarous manners, obsolete customs,
and exploded superstitions. The march of his intellect is like that

of a crab, backward. The brighter the light diffused around him by the progress of reason, the thicker is the darkness of antiquated barbarism, in which he buries himself like a mole, to throw up the barren hillocks of his Cimmerian labours. The philosophic mental tranquillity which looks round with an equal eye on all external things, collects a store of ideas, discriminates their relative value, assigns to all their proper place, and from the materials of useful knowledge thus collected, appreciated, and arranged, forms new combinations that impress the stamp of their power and utility on the real business of life, is diametrically the reverse of that frame of mind which poetry inspires, or from which poetry can emanate.

Is poetry useful? Can it be proved to contribute to the sum of human happiness? Obviously not, although once in a while verse might serve a practical purpose as a mnemonic device. Thus Bentham himself invented a triad of couplets to set forth his "whole fabric of morals and legislation":

> Intense, long, certain, speedy, fruitful, pure—
> *Such marks in* pleasures *and in* pains *endure.*
> *Such pleasures seek, if* private *be thy end:*
> *If it be* public, *wide let them* extend.
> *Such* pains *avoid, whichever be thy view:*
> *If* pains *must come, let them* extend *to few.*

But it was a general Utilitarian principle that imaginative literature, far from advancing men's affairs, distracted attention from their proper business. As a writer in the Benthamite *Westminster Review* commented in 1825, "Ledgers do not keep well in rhyme, nor are three-deckers * built by songs, as towns were of yore. . . . Literature is a seducer; we had almost said a harlot. She may do to trifle with; but woe be to the state whose statesmen write verses, and whose lawyers read more in Tom Moore than in Bracton." This was the true spirit of the Victorian businessman, ancestor of the twentieth-century Babbitt.

It was not only men of affairs, however, who doubted

---

* *Three-deckers:* warships. Later in the same quotation, *Tom Moore:* fashionable poet and songwriter; *Bracton:* medieval codifier of English law.

whether the arts had much place in a busy society like theirs. Their devaluation was concurred in by many intellectuals, not necessarily Benthamite in sympathies, who yet had a similar commitment to rational and scientific thought. The romantics had unintentionally encouraged a belief that the reason and the imagination were two discrete and antithetical faculties. This was, as we now realize, a perversion of the true romantic ideal, which held that all of men's faculties should be perfectly harmonized, even though, as Coleridge said, the harmony involved the reconciliation of opposites, or, as Keats maintained, the imaginative faculty was superior to the reason. But, misinterpreting this doctrine, the Victorians tended to relegate sensory and imaginative experience—the aesthetic side of life—to a separate compartment, indulged at certain appropriate times but not absorbed as a co-equal element of man's life.

Sometimes the intellect, often in the form of "the scientific spirit," simply overruled the aesthetic sense. There is no more touching passage in Victorian annals than Darwin's lament in late middle age, "I have tried lately to read Shakespeare, and found it so intolerably dull that it nauseated me. I have also almost lost my taste for pictures or music. I am glad you were at the 'Messiah,' but I dare say I should find my soul too dried up to appreciate it; and then I should feel very flat, for it is a horrid bore to feel as I constantly do, that I am a withered leaf for every subject except Science. The loss of these tastes is a loss of happiness." * But it had to be sustained. Science possessed the superior claim, if a choice had to be made.

The Evangelicals rejected art as decisively as the Utilitarians did, and for some of the same reasons. To them, also, or at least the more strict among them, it was an either-or proposition: art, if one looked at the statements of its most dedicated romantic apologists in a certain light,

* This statement was synthesized from separate sources—a letter of 1868 and Darwin's *Autobiography* (1876)—by Donald Fleming in an article in *Victorian Studies,* March, 1961.

seemed to claim as complete an autonomy as religion, and one could not have both. The choice was clear, or, more precisely, there was no choice. The claims of the other world reduced those of this world to nullity. Poetry therefore shared in the Evangelical disapprobation of secular distractions.

Just as the Benthamites decried art because it drained off attention and energies from more profitable activities, so did the Evangelicals, the profitable activities in their case being those which were entered in the celestial time sheet. Every available moment on earth should be devoted to preening one's soul for heaven, and the indulgence of the un-religious imagination and of aesthetic propensities, however bland and innocent, distracted one from that supreme endeavor, because then the seductive senses were given priority over the soul. This fear of sensuousness extended to all the arts—not poetry alone, but music, painting, and drama. The only exception was made for religious poetry and hymnody, where cautious indulgence in appropriate imagery and rhythm served a spiritual end.

Of course this battery of objections did not stem artistic production in Victorian times; and the many who failed to share these austere views constituted an eager and appreciative audience. But the influence of Utilitarian and Evangelical biases was so pervasive that those who felt free to indulge their sense of beauty nevertheless hedged it with restrictions. The age's criteria of acceptable art are usually summed up in the term "moral aesthetic." The idea that art should teach and inspire as well as give pleasure was not new; it was, indeed, older than Horace's *dulce et utile*. But seldom had it been so firmly established as it was in this period, when society's need for self-understanding, criticism, and direction was so urgent. While the Evangelicals rejected the secular arts because they seemed to usurp the supremacy of religion, other, more sophisticated Victorians cultivated them because they seemed to offer what, to many, religion could no longer provide, a guide to life. Poetry and painting supplemented the pulpit if they did not actually replace it.

The early and mid-Victorian emphasis thus was upon theme rather than expression, upon intention and substance rather than technique. The more pleasing a style was, the better; but style should never be so conspicuous as to distract attention from content. This was one of the main charges which critics of the day made against romantic poetry, notably Byron's—that it was deficient in thought, over-abundant in emotion. "A feeling came more easily to them than a reflection," wrote the critic Sir Henry Taylor, "and an image was always at hand when a thought was not forthcoming." And so ornateness of language and luxuriance of imagery gave way, in critical preference though by no means always in practice (Tennyson's "Enoch Arden" and, in a different way, Swinburne's most characteristic poetry are examples here), to restraint, always with the aim of a socially desirable idea lucidly expressed. The classic manifestations of this Victorian emphasis upon moral content as the supreme criterion of great art—taking "moral" in its widest sense—are found in Arnold's literary criticism and Ruskin's art criticism.

The romantics' unrestrained expression of the self obviously found little favor with most Victorian critics, although popular taste remained responsive to it. One reason was that with the romantics, critics felt, subjectivism had been carried to an "unhealthy" extreme (once again Byron was the leading instance) and a reaction was bound to set in. Another reason was the growing influence of the scientific-rationalistic spirit, which devalued the importance of individual perceptions. And so, in a rough sense, the Victorians revived a major principle of eighteenth-century literary theory: the inward-looking self must be effaced in favor of the outward view.

Like most such doctrines, however, this one was heavily qualified in practice. Notwithstanding his later strictures against the lyric, Matthew Arnold bared his *Angst* in some of the most moving lyrics any Victorian produced. It was ironic as well as symbolic that one of the most intensely confessional of Victorian poems, *In Memoriam,* appeared in the same year in which the greatest romantic autobiographical poem, Wordsworth's *Prelude,* was first published. When one realizes how many memorable Victorian poems are outpourings of the poet's soul—Rossetti's *House of Life* is another prime example—it is plain that the decline of subjective poetry in the period can easily be exaggerated.

Whatever else was required of Victorian art, it had to be faithful to familiar human experience. In Ruskin's aesthetic this was a basic principle, never used to better purpose than in his opportune defense of the Pre-Raphaelites, whom we shall meet formally in a little while. To convey its intended meaning to people—people in general, not connoisseurs—art must renounce tired stereotypes and conventions and speak the language of fresh, everyday observation and experience, which is the indispensable bond of communication between artist and audience. This is the presiding idea in Browning's poems on the nature of art, especially "Fra Lippo Lippi" and "Pictor Ignotus." Art, like Antaeus, draws its vitality and relevance from the earth of everyday life.

The positivist, pragmatic spirit of the time, combined with the emphasis upon art's appealing immediately to the ordinary beholder through subject-matter conformable to his everyday observation, led to realism (though the term itself did not enter the critical vocabulary until the middle of the Victorian period). Part of Tennyson's fortune as a popular poet lay in his nearsightedness, which, by forcing him to examine natural objects such as flowers and leaves more closely than did most persons, enabled him to describe them in exceptionally fresh and faithful terms and thus to win his readers' admiration for his "truth to nature." Browning's particular forte was a realism of both external description and psychology. He had an extraordinarily acute sense of concreteness as applied to specific objects and physical locale as well as a pre-Jamesian desire to portray the interior landscape of men's motives and thoughts. The former added credibility to the latter. A similar painstaking representationalism is also characteristic of much Victorian fiction. Dickens and George Eliot in particular wrought extended, detailed descriptions of scene and person. When reviewers took up one of Dickens' earlier novels, comparison with Hogarth was almost *de rigueur,* just as, later on, George Eliot's characteristic method was constantly likened to that of the Dutch genre painters.

With the Victorians, therefore, "painting from life" was no mere convenient figure of speech. When the first Pre-Raphaelites set out to paint a picture, they went to great lengths to insure fidelity. John Millais, portraying the watery death of Ophelia, had his model, Rossetti's future wife Elizabeth Siddal, lie in a bathtub half-filled with water and heated by lamps underneath. The lamps went out; Elizabeth, growing numb, said nothing for several hours, in order not to disturb the artist; she caught a bad cold, and her father threatened to sue for £50.

These were the days when the artist William P. Frith grew famous and rich from the crowd-appeal (in two senses) of *The Railway Station (Paddington), Ramsgate Sands,* and *Derby Day,* large canvases populated with scores of carefully drawn figures from many walks of life, each caught in some typical and credible posture or act. (Of the last-named picture, Oscar Wilde bemusedly inquired whether it was all really painted by hand.) At this time also, photography emerged from inventors' workshops and was practiced in studios and then in the open air, outdoing the human eye and hand at capturing the *vraisemblance* of face and scene, with the ultimate effect of directing palette-and-canvas art away from literal representation toward impressionism.

There was, then, a general insistence that art should conform to the scientific spirit of the age in its accurate representation of fact. Whenever it seemed to deviate from common human experience, novelists were at pains to appease the reader's disbelief with the show, at least, of documentation. Dickens, taxed with the unlikelihood of Krook's death from spontaneous combustion in *Bleak House,* replied that there were "about thirty cases on record" of such greasy demises, including "the recorded opinions and experience of distinguished medical professors." In the prefaces to *The Moonstone* and *The Woman in White,* Wilkie Collins assured his readers that the "physiological experiment" and the crucial legal points respectively involved had been checked out with the experts. Even when credibility was not in question, some novelists did extensive research for the sake of authentic background details. Before she wrote *Felix Holt, the Radical* and *Middlemarch,* for instance, George Eliot immersed herself in the atmosphere of the First Reform Bill period by taking copious notes from contemporary sources.

Novels like Thackeray's *Henry Esmond* and its sequel, *The Virginians,* beginning in Queen Anne's time and ending with the American Revolution, and Dickens' *Barnaby Rudge* and *A Tale of Two Cities,* both set in the last two decades of the century, exemplified the enduring "passion for the past," to borrow Tennyson's phrase in "The Ancient Sage," which guided the Victorian artist's choice of theme and background just as it had his romantic predecessors'. Every major poet and every Victorian painter and sculptor of consequence repeatedly drew his subjects from faraway times and places, most notably but by no means exclusively the age of classical antiquity and the Middle Ages. But, to a greater extent than the romantics, the Victorian artists tended to choose their historical and exotic themes with an eye to their present-day relevance.

It is noteworthy, however, that when Browning, in his earlier, as yet unhonored, phase, set his poems in Renaissance Italy and France, the critics roundly reproached him for ignoring the Victorian present. For side by side with the continuing enthusiasm for historically oriented art, and sometimes pushing it into the shadow, existed the strong Victorian persuasion that the prime subject matter of art was things near at hand, such as domestic incidents and scenes of everyday contemporary existence (barring only the repulsively sordid). To a considerable body of Victorian critical and popular taste, art, like charity, began at home. This preference for the here and now was in part the reflection of the general insularity of English culture. People such as those who deplored Browning's neglect of the contemporary scene took the view that the artist's obligation to the society which supported him was to pay it the compliment of drawing his subject matter from it. Thus another main source of Tennyson's popularity lay in his poetizing of scenes and stories from familiar life in the poems he categorized as "English Idyls"—"Audley Court," "The Gardener's Daughter," "Lady Clara Vere de Vere." *In Memoriam,* which made him a best-selling poet, owed much of its wide appeal to the domestic setting in which the poet's spiritual crisis was portrayed as taking place—the country rectory in Lincolnshire, with its homely Christmas and New Year's observances and the tea urn bubbling on the lawn as the family gathered in the long summer twilight.

Tennyson's genre studies and domestic narratives typified the close bond between Victorian popular art and literature. Indifferent or blind to aesthetic effects, the ordinary man and woman "read" pictures, as Lamb said people read Hogarth's. Sometimes, as in Frith's panoramic scenes, a whole assortment of little episodes could be fitted into one such picture. Other painters, emulating Hogarth, told a connected narrative in a series of scenes, as did George Cruikshank in his famous pictorial temperance lecture, *The Bottle.* The important thing was that each episode or story should have immediate and unmistakable impact on the prepared reactions and elementary sensibilities of the beholder. It was no accident that when Victorian painting took a holiday from historical and contemporary subjects it drew heavily upon such literary sources as Scott, Byron, Shakespeare, and the eighteenth-century novel, with whose characters and episodes the viewer was already comfortably familiar. No explication or interpretation was needed: the meaning was instantly clear. And when artists chose, instead, the allegorical mode, they took pains that the lesson be spelled out as plainly as it was in *Pilgrim's Progress.*

Subtlety and indirection were not highly valued in Victorian art, because they delayed and confused rather than assisted the beholder's response. Though the Victorians, sauntering through an art gallery or sitting with a book, appreciated deft handling of small literal details—when *Derby Day* was first exhibited, it had to be railed off to discourage those who wanted to linger in order to "read" it close-up, square foot by square foot—their artistic sensitivity was not otherwise attuned to the unobtrusive. They wanted to be addressed directly, on a single unambiguous level of communication. Seeking edification rather than aesthetic pleasure, they expected, and got, an art that aimed for unmistakable over-all effect. Although modern criticism has detected a wealth of subtleties in the work of some major Victorian novelists and poets, notably Dickens, George Eliot, Emily Brontë, Hardy, Tennyson, Browning, and Arnold, there is little evidence that contemporary critics or ordinary readers noticed them.

2. *The Victorian Artist*

The Victorians' attitude toward the artist, as artist, was ambivalent. They inherited and added substance to the romantic view of the poet (the archetypal artist) as hero and prophet. It is significant that Shelley's celebration of the poet's supremacy among men was published the same year (1840) that Carlyle delivered his lectures on the Hero as Poet and as Man of Letters. Although each had his own ideal of the heroic and prophetic qualities involved, both Shelley and Carlyle exalted poets as constituting a modern priesthood, secular oracles who interpreted the purposes of the universe to ordinary men. The readiness with which ordinary men subscribed to this view is suggested by the quantity and content of the fan mail received by literary celebrities like Tennyson and Dickens. Tennyson was applied to for spiritual counsel, consolation, and information on how the poetic faculty works; Dickens for rather more down-to-earth assistance, such as advice on how to become a successful author, and outright gifts of money. (The difference may reflect the relative prestige of poetry and fiction at the time. Other things being equal, a poet outranked a novelist.) Tennyson's and Dickens' names, at least, were familiar to countless households which would have had trouble naming the current chancellor of the exchequer.

The reverse side of the coin was less agreeable. The no-nonsense climate of middle-class commercial society, like that of the Puritan society which stirred Sidney to his *Defence of Poesy,* had little time or tolerance for the "mere" artist. To those of Evangelical persuasion, he was a wastrel, and very probably immoral. The cautionary literature circulating among the Nonconformist sects in particular included a fair number of stories of artists coming to bad ends, and the name of Shelley, where it was known, sufficed to remind the young of the dangers of verse-making linked with atheism, ultra-radical political views, wife-desertion, and adultery. To those holding Benthamite values, the artist was a parasite, a non-producer except of luxury items; in no way did he contribute to the national wealth or physical well-being.

But this dour view of the value of art in a bourgeois society came to be modified as evidence accumulated that, with an immensely expanded reading public, there was money to be made in literature. The professional man of letters, as distinct from the writer whose chief income came from other sources, became a prominent figure in society for the first time. Journalism, which at the beginning of the period was commonly thought of as the trade of alcoholic penny-a-line hacks, gradually acquired prestige as more and more educated men, such as Thackeray, entered the occupation and periodicals paid well for their work. Writing for periodicals like the *Cornhill,* the *Saturday Review,* and the *Contemporary Review* was a sure way of achieving respect among people who counted.

How, then, did the artist view himself, his world, and his art? On the whole, down through the middle of the era the typical Victorian poet or prose writer felt himself at home in his time. He may have denounced the age for its manifold errors—Carlyle was hard at work doing so in the thirties, Dickens by the end of the next decade was sharpening his weapons of social criticism, Thackeray at the same time was portraying the vanities and pretensions of fashionable life, and Tennyson was indicting certain aspects of the age in poems like "Locksley Hall" and (a little later) *Maud*. Nevertheless, the Victorian writer did not look upon himself as a misfit or an outcast. Regardless of the extent to which he felt intellectually at odds with some facets of contemporary society, he still belonged to it and proposed to correct its errors from within. Only Matthew Arnold, writing his melancholy lyrics in the late forties and early fifties, conveys a sense of personal isolation comparable to Byron's. The conventionality of most Victorian authors' private lives testifies at least as much to their acceptance of the status quo as to the strength of conformist pressures. It is true that Dickens and Rossetti had mistresses, and that George Eliot lived openly with a man who could not divorce the adulterous wife who bore two children to the son of Leigh Hunt. But these merely are famous exceptions to a broad rule.

It is more certain that the greatest Victorian poets were torn between two impulses, their natural bent and the public's insistence that they devote themselves to society's interests as sources of spiritual counsel, moral guidance, admonition, and reassurance. Tennyson's bent plainly was toward intensely personal expression, in the manner of the true romantics who were at their zenith in his childhood. But, as such poems as "The Palace of Art," "The Lotos Eaters," and "Ulysses" attest, early in his career he felt very keenly the claims of society; and in 1850, at the age of forty-one, he became the official poet of that society. Browning, three years his junior, experienced the same conflict and the same resolution in somewhat different terms. His unique gift, as we see it, was for dramatic portrayal and psychological analysis—yet the age pressured him to speak with vatic voice, which he was only too willing to do once he discovered, after long years in the wilderness, that he had the ear of his contemporaries. So too with Arnold, who under the same impulse turned from the poetry of melancholy sensibility to literary and social criticism. In none of these poets was the conversion thorough and complete; the tension between the two forces was never wholly resolved, nor was it in the age at large.

3. Society Redeemed by Art

Important though the didactic function of art was, in the view of Ruskin, William Morris, and their followers there was a still greater one: in art lay the only means by which modern society could be redeemed and the world made a decent place for man to work and live. Since this idea was so specifically identified with Ruskin and Morris, tireless activists and propagandizing taste-makers who were constantly in the public eye, it is convenient to depart from the usual practice in these pages and focus upon its advocates, who were as much cultural phenomena of their epoch as they were men.

Ruskin maintained that culture (as he conceived it) was a function, in the first instance, of the eyes. Whereas to Arnold it centered in the inspiration offered by literature and to Huxley in the habits of the scientific mind, to Ruskin it lay in aesthetic experience. The quality of man's inner life was determined by the presence or absence of beauty in his everyday surroundings. Nor was it a matter only of culture in the Arnoldian sense: the optic nerve led, so to speak, directly to the soul. Man's visual sensibility enabled him to be receptive to the religious intimations available both through nature (Ruskin was a devout Wordsworthian) and through art. To Ruskin as to Browning—their aesthetic creeds had much in common—religion and art were inseparable. Art in its highest and purest form is a manifestation of the Divine expressing itself through the artist's genius. It is therefore vital to man's private existence, the one element in experience which can permeate and unify his spirit. The presence of man-made beauty in whatever form, whether it be apocalyptic windows in a cathedral or a dish in a humble workman's cottage, is requisite to human well-being.

As with the individual, so with society. In one of the most influential passages Victorian literature contains, the chapter "On the Nature of Gothic" in *The Stones of Venice,* Ruskin lamented the disappearance of the wholeness which in happier days, specifically the Middle Ages, had made life worth living. "We have much studied and much perfected, of late, the great civilised invention of the division of labour; only we give it a false name. It is not, truly speaking, the labour that is divided; but the men:—Divided into mere segments of men—broken into small fragments and crumbs of life. . . ." The experience of art was the sole way by which the fragmentizing, dispersive forces of modern industrial society could be countered. Carlyle had prescribed renewed spiritual faith as a cure for the social malaise; Ruskin, whose role as prophet and scourge of contemporary society owed much to Carlyle's example, agreed with the diagnosis but prescribed a different cure. Reintegration would come only when men could universally share the beauties of nature and art.

Public beauty, as embodied in buildings, gardens, and landscaping, the totality of any man-made scene, was a function of social health. A noble building was an outward manifestation of the contentedness, freedom, spontaneous joy, and religious faith of the workers who joined in making it, just as a painting or sculpture reflected those same qualities in the soul of the individual artist. In the case of Victorian England, the gaunt iron bridges, the incongruously styled and hideously overornamented public and commercial buildings, the grim red-brick factories lining streams choked with refuse, and in the home the mass-produced interior appointments, including furniture carved by machine—all these were the outward sign and partial cause of society's illness. Ruskin and after him Morris, who had been converted to Ruskin's doctrines by reading "On the Nature of Gothic," saw it as their mission to awaken their contemporaries to the aesthetic and therefore moral ugliness around them and to point out how beauty might come to the rescue of society. To them, art was supremely "useful," but in a sense the political economists, their main whipping boys, never dreamed of.

Until the sixties, Ruskin believed that this renewal could occur within the existing framework of economic society. But his faith succumbed to reluctant awareness that art was impotent against the forces which then prevailed. From the outset he had looked upon art as a product of labor. To Carlyle's insistence upon work, regardless of its product, as a kind of grim Calvinistic self-flagellation, Ruskin opposed the conception of work as joyous fulfillment. In *The Seven Lamps of Architecture* he had asserted: "I believe the right question to ask respecting all ornament [for example, carvings in a cathedral], is simply this: was it done with enjoyment—was the carver happy while he was about it?" To him, the crowning injustice in the factory system was that it made impossible the spontaneous joy of creativity which the hand worker derived from his everyday occupation. Work was an ever-available means of expression, a daily satisfaction of the imaginative urge which resides in even the humblest of men. Under modern conditions, that joy was lost for two reasons: the division of labor, which, in the interests of efficient output, meant that the product was not that of one man but of many; and the standardization of design, required by machine production, which left no room for individual expression. And so man had been degraded into a tool.

(Thus, at any rate, went Ruskin's argument. But if their dust could speak, the handicraftsmen whose occupational joy he took for granted might have entered a strong demurrer. It is conceivable that their work, pursued day after day throughout their lives, gave them as little satisfaction as did that of a Lancashire machine tender. They could, and did, turn out shoddy goods, badly designed and indifferently executed. The pride in their work, the spirit-contenting skill and devotion which Ruskin ascribed to them, is very likely another of those sentimental myths upon which the Victorians were prone to build towering ideologies. But the important thing is that Ruskin believed it—and persuaded others to believe it.)

The necessity of providing scope for the workman's (supposed) creativity and encouraging his enjoyment of the creativity of others formed the basis of Ruskin's social criticism and his nebulous ideal of a paternalistic, collectivist society. In such a society the highest goal would be to guarantee to each person, not political equality (for Ruskin had no democratic leanings) but what was far more precious: equal access to beauty and equal opportunity to create it on his own. The details of Ruskin's program do not concern us here. His importance for our purposes is that he brought to the materialistic culture of the second half of the nineteenth century an awareness of how indispensable were beauty and the making of beauty to any society worth living in. In his writings art acquired supreme social dignity, partly through his insistence on its sacramental nature and partly through his proposing it as a sovereign remedy for the new society's dehumanizing infection.

William Morris made the same vital connection between art, the individual man's labor, and the quality of his life. In his social criticism he laid stress on an art that springs from the people, that is, crafts of all kinds, and on the creation of a comely environment in which all people, regardless of occupation, might live. Morris insisted that every bit of interior decoration and every household article, however utilitarian, should possess a beauty of its own. Outside the home, the eye should be gladdened and the soul nourished by well-designed structures of every sort, from cottages to office buildings, their architecture suiting their function and complementing the natural features of the landscape. Like Ruskin, he was convinced that beauty within the soul could be achieved only by the constant experience of beauty without.

Despairing of any improvement in the condition of industrial society so long as capitalism prevailed, Morris turned to revolutionary socialism. His collectivist, machineless Utopia is not a very exciting one. Like the beauty that suffuses their surroundings, the pleasure his workers find in such toil as is necessary is rather pallid. Probably no one regrets that his dream never was in danger of coming true. Nor did his political creed bear fruit except as it affected the emergent Fabian movement. But Morris is unique among writers in that he left his easily seen mark upon the late Victorian domestic environment. One of the most versatile of men, in addition to being a poet and writer of prose romances and political tracts, he was a skilled textile and furniture designer, weaver, tapestry maker, inventor of new dyestuffs, and maker of fine hand-printed and hand-bound books, the most famous of which was the sumptuous Kelmscott Chaucer. The products of his interior decorating firm, widely imitated, set the visual tone of many a well-to-do home where his socialist pamphlets never penetrated, and within a short time Morris-inspired wallpaper, chintz, carpets, furniture, and stained glass had become a national fashion, an epoch in the history of British (and American) household appointments.

This was something new, a long-overdue rectification of the aesthetic felonies committed in display after display in the Crystal Palace and enshrined thereafter in countless British parlors. Whatever one may think of the *art nouveau* in whose English version he had a hand, it is largely thanks to Morris and those who followed him that the twentieth century has placed as much stress as it has upon taste in interior decoration and the design of furniture and household accessories, and upon the architecture of public buildings and the layout of housing developments. To the extent that considerations of beauty do play some role in the arrangement of our physical environment, we, like the late Victorians, are deeply in Morris'—and ultimately Ruskin's—debt. They popularized the idea of art as an accompaniment to everyday life. And they did so for a characteristically Victorian purpose—to point the way to a happier society. Only in that age, one is tempted to say, could the veneration of beauty have provided the rationale of a program looking to the comprehensive transformation of economics and society.

But there was another aspect to Morris' view of art. His ambivalence was that of his era at large: on the one hand, devotion to the Ruskinian conception of art as inseparable from the concerns of society; on the other, an assertion of the autonomy of beauty. Long before his conviction that a happy society must be sustained by pervasive contact with beauty led, first, to his awareness that the conditions for such fulfilment could not be realized under the capitalistic system and then to his becoming a militant socialist, Morris was writing poetry, notably *The Earthly Paradise,* in which art was conceived of as a thing apart and the poet an "idle singer of an empty day." An activist and optimist in one mood, in the other Morris typified the later Victorian's quite opposite response to the darkening atmosphere.

By now, the factories, foundries, collieries, and smoky cities which had spread across England's once green and pleasant land had become an offense to every moderately perceptive observer. But the artist was worst off, and not only for reasons having to do with environmental ugliness. The mid- and late Victorian world was largely alien to his temperament and assumptions. The encroachment of the ignorant, insensitive multitude upon contemporary culture, the gospel of Social Darwinism, the new science that had revealed a universe from which the human values that hitherto had fed the artistic vision were summarily expunged —all these combined to form a world singularly inhospitable to the artist's aspirations. He shared with his fellow-Victorians the need for a haven against which the waves of disintegrating change washed unavailingly. Some of them found it in the religion of humanity. The artist found it in a substitute universe created through the exercise of art. His religion was dedicated to the sanctification of beauty, with himself and his kind seeking to protect it from the debasement of a hostile world.

This elevation of beauty as the cardinal value of life and of art as its avatar, and the removal of both from the hostile world, stemmed both from Ruskin's over-success and from his failure. In his effective rebuke of the Utilitarians' dismissal of beauty and art from their crass universe, he had stressed art's indispensability as the cohesive element of the total human experience; others, extending this doctrine to a length he would have regarded as untenable, now asserted that beauty was the criterion by which all other values, religious, social, moral, should be judged. In this respect, Ruskin had succeeded all too well. But, in more practical terms, he had also sought to install beauty in existing society—to wave the wand of art and transform a civilization encrusted with soot, deafened by steam engines, and riven by social conflict and intellectual discord into a community as peaceful and harmonious as any to which the vital craftsmen's art of the medieval cathedrals supposedly bore witness. He had failed, not only in this grand venture but also in the more modest attempt somehow to bring even a small touch of art into everyday life. England had listened politely and then responded by speeding up the production of ugly household goods and defacing additional ancient churches in behalf of neo-Gothic modernity. The most apparent effect of his preaching the social message of medieval art was

merely to load contemporary architecture with Gothic ornament ("gingerbread" was too polite a word for it) as a means
of disguising or, in the event, accentuating the building's
inherent affront to the eye. The functionalism which lay at
the heart of his aesthetic argument went disregarded. And
so it was Victorian England's refusal to act upon Ruskin's
prescription for its salvation that impelled the artist to
withdraw himself from it. Beauty must be sought in the pri-
vacy of one's own imagination.

4. The Pre-Raphaelites

This process reached across the whole second half of
the century. In cultural history, it is conventionally though
arbitrarily divided into three successive phases: the Pre-
Raphaelitism of the 1850's, the Aesthetic Movement which
succeeded it after an interval and lasted through the eighties,
and the Decadence of the nineties.

The first stage of artists' reaction against the materialistic tide coincided, aptly enough, with the Crystal Palace
exhibition of 1851, which marked the high point of the nation's satisfaction with that tide. It was fitting, also, that the
Pre-Raphaelite Brotherhood was actually founded three
years earlier, the year of the continental revolutions. For
this coterie of enthusiastic young artists dedicated themselves at the beginning to a revolt against what they regarded
as the artificiality and stultifying influence of the school of
painting which had succeeded Raphael (1483–1520). They
revered Raphael himself and the primitive religious painters
before him; their indignation centered upon his less talented
successors, who in their estimation had merely imitated the
master and hardened his techniques into conventions. The
Pre-Raphaelites sought therefore to restore to painting the
naturalness and simplicity they insisted it had lost after
Raphael by demonstrating in their own art the superiority of
realism—freshly observed nature transferred to canvas—

to timid emulation. In this respect the movement bore a striking resemblance to the romantic revolt, half a century earlier, against eighteenth-century artificiality in poetry.

The Pre-Raphaelites were also anti-establishment. Their particular *bêtes noires* were the academic painters, members of Britain's prestigious Royal Academy, who perpetuated the dead weight of the conservative tradition epitomized by "Sir Sloshua" Reynolds. After a few years, in the manner of such spontaneous and high-minded campaigns, the founders and the associates they had attracted went their separate ways as painters, and such small unity of principle and aim as they had initially had disappeared. Despite its vacillations and inconsistencies, however, Pre-Raphaelitism clearly marked a turning point in the history of Victorian society's involvement with and attitude toward art.

For one thing, the Pre-Raphaelites put to fresh use the persistent romantic-Victorian attachment to the Middle Ages. Whereas Carlyle, Ruskin, and others used their idealized vision of medieval society as a stick with which to belabor modern civilization, the Pre-Raphaelites seized upon medieval characters, settings, and incidents in the first place for frankly escapist purposes, to provide life-giving relief from the oppressiveness of a materialistic society. Their archaism was simply an emotional—it might even be said a sentimental—one. Moreover, although there was no direct cause-effect relationship between them, it is notable that the Pre-Raphaelite movement originated in the very years when the ritualistic movement, the sequel to Tractarianism, was beginning to flourish. In the prominence the two gave to early Christian symbolism they bore a more than casual resemblance to each other. They also shared, incidentally, in the obloquy all things presumably "Romish" in tendency or allusion suffered at the moment, when the Pope's setting up English bishoprics in 1850 (the so-called Papal Aggression) exacerbated the normal ultra-Protestant loathing of Catholicism. The suspicion of Romishness was hardly allayed by the presence of the monogram "P.R.B." instead of the irreproachable "R.A." after the artists' names. To some uneasy visitors to the first exhibitions in which Pre-Raphaelite work was shown, the cryptic letters were the sign of a subversive conspiracy, probably Jesuitical in origin.

The Pre-Raphaelites were famed, in some quarters notorious, for their mixture of mysticism and "fleshliness" (i.e., sensuousness), especially in connection with female subjects. The typical Pre-Raphaelite woman was no robust Rubensesque sexpot—instead, she was long-necked, reddish-haired, slender, and tending toward consumption—but to the Victorians, if not to us, there was something unsettlingly fascinating about her. They were better accustomed to the rosy-cheeked country maidens who figured in the genre paintings that captivated popular taste and won medals at the Academy's shows. At the same time, in both painting and poetry Dante Gabriel Rossetti, a second-generation Anglo-Italian who constituted the Pre-Raphaelites' principal link with literature, portrayed a Dantesque quest for Ideal Love, a sort of counterpart of Shelley's Ideal Beauty and a far cry from the placid, sexless, emphatically un-mystical domesticity that dominated British art. To the conventionally minded, this exoticism was disturbing, even vaguely immoral. But Victorian art needed such innovations to redeem it from stagnation.

Finally, Pre-Raphaelitism revived in art the literary romanticism of half a century earlier. The movement was much indebted to Keats, whose fame the Pre-Raphaelites did much to promote and several of whose poetic subjects they borrowed for their canvases. Keats was pre-eminently the painter's poet among the romantics; of them, he had the most pronounced aesthetic, as opposed to philosophical, bent. In adopting him as one of their heroes and inspirers, the Pre-Raphaelites seemed to imply, whether or not they meant to do so, that like him they valued art for sheer beauty rather than content.

There was a contradiction here, as elsewhere in this abnormally inconsistent movement, because the Pre-Raphaelites' paintings often were loaded with messages both literal and symbolic. Furthermore, despite the initial preference for romantic (not exclusively medieval) subjects, several of the Brotherhood later took up the domestic, anecdotal themes so beloved of the middle-class Victorian public and won much honest fame and not a little fortune thereby. In thus obliging popular taste, including that of Manchester cotton million-aires who commissioned their work, they were not really betraying their earlier principles, because they had never proclaimed the autonomy of art or in any formal way sought to withdraw themselves, as artists, from the common world. Rossetti's personal indifference to the social, political, and religious questions which troubled the era was not a matter of principle. It was merely dictated by a temperament which could not be excited by anything except painting, poetry, collecting blue china, and installing a private menagerie in a London garden. But in the long run the effect of Pre-Raph-aelitism was to re-direct attention to art as art, not as a vehicle for social or moral commentary, and thus to diminish the authority of Ruskin's moral aesthetic. Just as the Oxford Movement had invested the Anglican Church with new gran-deur, so the Pre-Raphaelites ennobled the concept of art.

5. The Primacy of Art

The Aesthetic vogue of the later seventies and the eighties was an outgrowth of Pre-Raphaelitism, with a dif-ferent cast of characters. The connecting link was Rossetti, whose poetry and painting inspired the Aesthetes. The most publicity-conscious of the group, Oscar Wilde, borrowed one of his famous stage properties from either Rossetti's poem "The Blessed Damozel" or his picture *Ecce Ancilla Domini* as (in the words of W. S. Gilbert) he walked down Piccadilly with a lily in his medieval hand. Rightly or wrongly—Rossetti himself protested the assumption—the Aesthetes interpreted his artistic aim as the pursuit of beauty, divorced from social meaning. More justifiably, they recognized in him their own strong inclination to look into their souls as they wrote or painted. In Rossetti's poetry the Victorian bias in favor of objectivity was reversed, and the romantic mode of introspection and confession resumed. In Rossetti the Aesthetes read also, though the phrase was Arnold's, the "infinite yearning, infinite pain" that was their chosen interpretation of human experience.

Considerably more uncomfortable than Rossetti in his role of lawgiver to the Aesthetes was Walter Pater, a Victorian moralist with a difference. Beginning with his *Studies in the History of the Renaissance* (1873), Pater was the exponent of a *carpe diem* philosophy suited to an age when the old certainties were crumbling. Wring from experience, it urged, as much refined sensuous pleasure as you can, because it is all that life affords. Live "intensely" (a favorite word with the Aesthetes: it conveyed intimations of Keats's similar desire), abandon your delicately responsive sensibility to the constant play of sensations and impressions—sight, sound, odor, touch, taste.

This is, intentionally, a gross over-simplification, though not necessarily a falsification, of Pater's "new Cyrenaicism," or hedonism. It has the advantage of suggesting the way he was read and explaining the kind of influence he had. In his over-exquisite essays there is no hint of flight to the fleshpots. On the contrary, Pater was almost Puritanical as he stressed the necessity of unremitting discrimination in one's choice of pleasures. But Pater soon became aware how readily his recommendation at the end of *The Renaissance,* that "not the fruit of experience, but experience itself, is the end" of life, could, in his own words, "mislead some of those young men into whose hands it might fall," and he therefore suppressed the concluding chapter in the second edition.

Irrespective of what Pater really meant by his aesthetic philosophy, it resulted in the apotheosis of beauty as the supreme experience of life, and of art as a superior reality, atoning for the deficiencies of nature and totally unlike any other kind of human activity, with laws and values unique to it. Aestheticism thus offered the mode of experience farthest removed from anything else available in an industrial world. On the part of the artist, it meant projecting and preserving his personal apprehension of beauty in whatever form he deemed most fitting. Art's purpose was solely to afford him pleasure, and he was the sole judge of its quality; he was superior both to criticism and to whatever claims the public might make upon him. The beholder's experience was likewise an intensely personal event, unique and sacrosanct, occurring without reference to any fellow human being except the artist. The vehicle of communication between the two participants in this closed transaction was the form of the art object, not its content.

It followed that life itself was viewed as an art. The Aesthetes replaced the brassy hedonism of the pleasure-pain calculus with the ethereal hedonism of pure beauty, however captured and savored. In so doing, they disavowed the twin philosophical assumptions of their period, that the only reality was the material and that time, to the Darwinians at least, was nothing more than the scene of universal senseless brutality. To Pater's disciples, the only reality worth seeking was not material goods but an intangible—the individual human experience. The detached "spots of time" (to use Wordsworth's phrase), whether immediate moments or vividly remembered ones, were the *summum bonum* of life. One who cultivated the spirit of beauty within himself discovered that time, whatever Darwinian connotation it possessed, was also the site of ecstasy. "Life," said Wilde in *A Woman of No Importance,* "is a *mauvais quart d'heure* made up of exquisite moments." And art captured those moments in glowing amber. "A sonnet," wrote Rossetti, "is a moment's monument."

And so Aestheticism involved a complete revulsion against received standards of value. It vehemently disowned the "vulgarity" of middle-class taste, or what passed for taste; in this respect, it was one of the most fervent elements in the anti-democratic reaction which was intensifying in the years between the reform bills of 1867 and 1884. Instead of contributing, like good Victorian Englishmen, to the wealth of the nation, the Aesthetes devoted themselves to exploring the mystery of human consciousness and emotion as they beheld it on the screen of their own vivid sensibilities. For the prudential life-view of the political economists, law-bound, material, and social in emphasis, they substituted the most subjective ethic conceivable, independent of all outward laws and customs, governed only by the inclinations and desires of the inner spirit. To replace Carlylean activism, with its insistence upon productive work, they cultivated a philosophy that exalted being over doing, and instead of the Ruskinian moral aesthetic, one that was completely amoral and divorced from social implications. And, reverting to Wordsworth's and Shelley's position, the Aesthetes asserted the superior claims of "poetic" over "scientific" truth. Thus the movement carried romantic individualism and epistemology as far as they could go. The only wisdom attainable was that achieved by devotion to the exquisitely refined inner sensibility. For participation was substituted solitude: for society, the ego.

Thus artists came to regard themselves as belonging to a separate class, not only detached from the common run of men but superior to them. From the social viewpoint, Aestheticism was élitism carried to its ultimate, defiant extreme. This process of isolation coincided with a larger trend already noted—the growing specialization of later Victorian times and the withdrawal of the expert from the broad cultural scene in favor of the civil servant's office, the laboratory, or the academic study. The artist, for his part, regarded himself as a man whose interests and skills were so concentrated and rare that he could expect little understanding from those about him, people of coarser grain, little sensibility, and less experience. The later romantics, of course, had exhibited the same tendency when, in their despair over a world that gave no promise of remaking itself to their specifications, they sought refuge in that other world of private sensation. But the drift to artistic autonomy had been stemmed by the moral rigors of a new generation, when "the Soul" in Tennyson's poem, sorely tempted by the glamor of the Palace of Art, resolutely turned her back on it and opted for a cottage in the vale. Now, after another generation had passed, the artist, renouncing the role of citizen and public man, vacated the marketplace and the forum in favor of the ivory tower, where he could consult and indulge his most private wishes. It was at this point, roughly a century ago, that the modern schism between the world of artists and the world of men had its origin. Now the artist was truly alienated.

The Aesthetic movement ended the cultural parochialism which had been one of the most deadening aspects of English life under Philistine middle-class rule. Although it was essentially a native strain of theory and practice somewhat tenuously derived from Pre-Raphaelitism, it would not have assumed the form it did without the inspiration it received from France. English and French avant-gardism had been running in parallel channels. Gautier's doctrine of art for art's sake, a phrase which served then, as it does now, as a convenient shorthand description of Aestheticism, had flourished in France as part of the artists' revolt against the illiberalism of the Second Empire. Thanks to Swinburne's enthusiasm, the poetic principles and techniques of the Parnassiens, especially Gautier and Baudelaire, were taken up by the Aesthetes. By the eighties, as the Aesthetes fell under the influence of the Symbolistes—Verlaine, Rimbaud, and Mallarmé—the English Channel ceased to be regarded as a defensive moat providentially located to protect native art, including literature, from French corruption. Paris became the spiritual home of the new wave of English poets and painters. Nor did the quest for beauty in the form of pure art end in France. Under Pater's auspices it led to ancient Greece and Rome, to the Middle Ages, to a Renaissance freshly liberated from Ruskin's moral disapproval, to Japan

—for whatever moments of ecstasy could be derived from evoking those remote sites of supposed aesthetic fulfillment.

Nothing better symbolized this spirit of revolt against the contemporary bourgeois spirit than the flamboyant costumes the publicity-conscious Wilde set adopted as an outward sign of their defiance. It was most fitting that an age which had been ushered in by the Regency dandy should be ushered out by his grandchildren in velvet knee breeches. Dandyism framed the Victorian period. But these men and their willowy, Rossetti-inspired women postured, as their forebears decidedly had not done, in the cause of Beauty. For better or worse, they made Beauty a humorous byword among all who laughed at their long hair, haggard faces, and affectations of costume, manner, and speech as satirized by George Du Maurier's cartoons in *Punch* and by Gilbert and Sullivan in *Patience*. When the craze wore off and the freakishness took a new, rather more private and indeed sinister turn among a fresh set of Aesthetes, it may be that a gain had been recorded. The participants in the movement had been relatively few; the publicity they reaped was grossly incommensurate with their actual number. Nor did they leave behind them many enduring works of art, in whatever medium. But their influence on their epoch was far from negligible. Relieved of its weight of Ruskinian moralism, the idea of aesthetic experience as an end in itself and of art as an exalted activity independent of social obligation became part of the advanced late Victorian creed.

Although the term "Aestheticism" sometimes is stretched to cover the last phase of the reaction against Victorian orthodoxy in art and morals, the Decadence of the "Yellow Nineties" is better regarded as a separate, though derivative, phenomenon. Also known as *fin de siècle,* the Decadence was authoritatively described early in its hectic course by Arthur Symons, a participant-observer who was also its historian: ". . . it has all the qualities that mark the end of great periods, the qualities that we find in the Greek, the Latin, decadence; an intense self-consciousness, a restless curiosity in research, an over-subtilising refinement upon refinement, a spiritual and moral perversity." With the Decadents—men like Ernest Dowson, Aubrey Beardsley, Lionel Johnson, and such wildly eccentric fringe-figures as Frederick Rolfe ("Baron Corvo")—the inward-turningness of Aestheticism was carried to the final bizarre extreme.

As a token of their contempt for respectability, the Decadents extended the Aesthetes' cultivation of the senses to the realm of the abnormal and perverse (according to the prevailing moral standards): sexual aberrations, drug-taking, absinthe-drinking—an array of vices sufficient to rend the whole massive monolith of Victorian morality. The "fascination of corruption," in Pater's phrase, lured a small band of rebellious youth, desperately searching for new sensations, into a preoccupation with morbid and exotic experience. Or so they were at pains to imply in their poetry and art; a sober examination of the record suggests that their practices did not quite live up to their pretensions. But the importance of their brief occupation of the limelight resides in the impression they meant to give and succeeded in giving. They were the victims of a society dominated by the blusterings of a patriotism running to jingoistic seed—following its zenith at the time of the Queen's Jubilee (1887), the imperial spirit was itself now showing premonitory signs of degeneration—and of the philosophical near-nihilism bred by science's freshest advances. They sought forgetfulness in vice, and when the sweets of nameless forbidden fruit were sucked to the dregs (the metaphor is slightly askew, but its components are faithful to the context) the result was total, irremediable ennui. The fulfillment of wild desire led to an arid satiety from which, in more than one case, the only escape was death. These prematurely aged young men were remarkably tragedy-prone; nine of them died, by their own hand or by miserable accident or disease, at an average age of slightly under forty.

The Aestheticism which culminated in Decadence represented a revival and an exaggeration—almost a *reductio ad absurdum,* if we do not take the tragic fin-de-sièclists too seriously—of certain tendencies apparent in the second romantic generation. Keats's reputed experiments with claret and cayenne pepper on the tongue had their less innocent sequels in the Decadents' desperate search for new excitements—or numb oblivion—in alcohol, sex, and drugs. Both, from somewhat different motives, were seeking to widen the boundaries of experience, even to the audacious extent of somehow reconciling their private world and the world of men. The history of this latter-day pseudo-romanticism, it has been observed, is one of "an immense number of explorations, many false starts and blind alleys, and not a few personal tragedies, all directed to finding some sort of accommodation between art and a bourgeois industrial society." [1] But nobody found such an accommodation and so the problem is still with us, in more acute form, seventy years later.

All the Aesthetic energies were not wasted, however. Since the artist was no longer obligated to deliver a socially intelligible and useful message, he could devote himself solely to form—pure design in graphic art, complete concentration on the ordering of language, images, and sound in poetry (and mannered prose as well). And while the direct results of this preoccupation with technique strike us as being the finger exercises of self-conscious experimenters rather than the sonatas of matured genius, the by-product was momentous. "The 'aesthetic' regard for craftsmanship remained the controlling force behind many a serious and powerful work of art, from the subtle moral geometries of James to the enormous intellectual labyrinths of Joyce." [2] The seed of Aestheticism was well sowed, albeit the fruit confounded the sowers' intentions. By the time the fruit ripened the Victorian age was itself ripe for review.

IX

PROGRESS OF A

REPUTATION

1. The Anti-Victorian Reaction

"WHATEVER we may think or affect to think of the present age," wrote John Stuart Mill in 1831, in the same essay quoted at the beginning of Chapter III, "we cannot get out of it; we must suffer with its sufferings, and enjoy with its enjoyments; we must share in its lot, and, to be either useful or at ease, we must even partake its character." But participation, as Carlyle and Dickens, for example, would demonstrate in the next twenty years, did not bar criticism. One of the notable characteristics of Victorian literature, indeed, is its capacity for simultaneous involvement and detachment. And the longer Victoria's reign lasted, the more abundant were the omens of what would happen to its reputation when it had passed into history. The critics of its present self were joined by critics of its earlier phases, so that the age sponsored numerous reactions against itself while it was still running its course.

If "Victorianism" means simply subscription to current orthodoxy, Carlyle, Dickens, Arnold, Ruskin, and Morris were as anti-Victorian as any disciple of Lytton Strachey in the next century. Less strenuously, but sometimes with no less bite, *Punch* conducted a continuous once-a-week critique of the day's social and cultural fashions and follies for sixty Victorian years, and the subversive humor of Gilbert and Sullivan's operas, their geniality diverting attention from their sting, was merely the most popular theatrical element in a long tradition of satire and parody which reminds us that in a certain mood many Victorians delighted in laughing at themselves. Self-criticism, after all, is not necessarily defanged when cast in comic form. And it is worth remembering, too, that Samuel Butler's iconoclastic *Erewhon* was published in the same year as the Imperial Library edition of Tennyson's poems, in which *Idylls of the King* were for the first time collected.

From the seventies onward, as we have seen, a strong tide set in against the confident orthodoxies of the mid-Victorian period. Economic and social individualism was retreating before a mild, tentative, but, in comparison with what had gone before, revolutionary expansion of the powers of the state; the moral aesthetic was turned inside out by art for art's sake; the evasiveness of conventional fiction was challenged by realists like Hardy, Moore, and Gissing; Tennyson, though still the age's most popular poet, suffered a marked decline in critical esteem. Oscar Wilde discovered that the easiest way to celebrity was to posture and speak *pour épater le bourgeoisie:* in his epigrams and in plays like *The Importance of Being Earnest* he deflated the platitudes and moral pomposities that still constituted the middle-class credo. In the years just preceding his eclipse a fellow Irishman, equally irreverent, had been unwittingly grooming himself to take Wilde's place. Shaw and Wilde (though both would have been appalled by the idea of their collaboration) together wrote the comic afterpiece to the high Victorian drama.

Thus the panoply of dogma and dicta which had nourished the conventional Victorian mind had come under attack long before the Queen died. The very epithet "Victorian" had acquired a derogatory penumbra among the advanced. And the whole atmosphere of the short-lived Edwardian era was electric with an exultant and slightly self-conscious sense of liberation—liberation, that is, from the stuffiness, the obscurantism, the false verities, the repressions and taboos now attributed, fairly or not, to the Victorian mind. The Edwardian reaction took numerous forms: the "new woman" demanding social if not sexual emancipation as well as political equality; the "new drama" dedicated to the treatment of risky moral and social themes; the "new poetry" that rebelled against Tennysonian domesticity and mellifluousness; the "new art" impatient with the pallid didacticism of later Pre-Raphaelite painting. The spirit that informed them was captured in the determined religious and moral unorthodoxy of the Bloomsbury group, some of whose parents and grandparents had ornamented the highest Victorian social and intellectual circles, and in the caricatures of Max Beerbohm, the self-appointed (and deadly effective) illustrator of anti-Victorianism. His drawing of a hulking middle-aged Prince of Wales, sent by a stern mother in widow's weeds to do silent penance for some unspecified misdeed in a corner of a room at Windsor, might have been interpreted as an allegory of the era. The Edwardians felt that at long last they had broken the silver cord against whose restraints their fathers, some of them, had grown increasingly restive, even as their King, reaching the throne at the age of fifty-nine, subconsciously reacted against the prolonged domination of his mother.

Outdated as the Victorians seemed to many Edwardians, they were still in control in high places. At the time of the First World War, most of the nation's scientific, political, ecclesiastical, industrial, and military leaders were Victorians by birth and upbringing. Swinburne and Meredith had died only in 1909, and Hardy would live on until 1928. As a group, the many distinguished survivors of the Queen's reign were regarded with respect. After all, they were the Older Generation, and Victorian morality had not overlooked the fifth commandment. But in the course of four years (1914–18) the former attitude of tolerant affection

tempered by awe changed to bitterness mingled with super-
cilious scorn. It was the late Victorians' bungling of the art
of geopolitics and their monumental stupidity, complacency,
and shortsightedness which had condemned Britain to an
exhausting conflict, as grossly mismanaged on the home front
as in the theaters of war. Whether or not the Victorians de-
served to be the scapegoats, the familiar fallacy which gov-
erns the human mind in such circumstances made it virtually
inevitable. The onus of guilt had to be borne by the preceding
generation.

In the last months of the war, Lytton Strachey's *Eminent
Victorians,* epitomizing this intensified feeling of betrayal,
ushered in the most virulent phase of anti-Victorianism. The
book's ironic iconoclasm was exquisitely attuned to the
nation's mood. Its very title was part of its fortune: "Eminent," with a wry curl of the lip which bore witness to all
that four years of war had exposed of eminent men's capacity for stupidity and selfishness; "Victorians"—a single
word which stood for all (it was now thought) that had been
wrong with British society for the past fifty years. *Eminent
Victorians,* making game of the personal absurdities, pretensions, artificial pieties—the moral littleness—of four selected specimens of Victorianism (Dr. Thomas Arnold,
Cardinal Manning, General Gordon, and Florence Nightingale), summed up the cynical spirit of the surviving young
and middle-aged as they looked back upon catastrophe and
forward into a land of meager promise.

In this twilight of the Victorian gods, both the spirit
and the technical brilliance of Strachey's performance
aroused almost hysterical enthusiasm among the emancipated. Even before he followed up his first success with a
slightly more sympathetic biographical portrait of the Queen
herself, his posture and his methods (including a wanton
disregard of historical truth wherever necessary for rhe-
torical or dramatic effect) were adopted by a host of imitators in England and the United States. The Stracheyan
mode of debunking biography became all the rage, and

every time its subject was a Victorian eminence such as Tennyson, Matthew Arnold, or Disraeli the period's reputation sank still lower. It now became a favorite parlor trick at sophisticated parties to declaim a few choice lines of bathos from Tennyson, to which the Pavlovian response on the part of all auditors was a concerted "My God!" The word "Victorian" was always good for a cheap laugh.[1]

In the elongated shadow of Lytton Strachey, the Victorians' overvaluation of themselves was transformed into their grandchildren's equally exaggerated underestimation. Although the indictment was more comprehensive than that to which the age had been subjected by its own indigenous critics, it was often wide of the mark, and it concentrated upon superficialities, because superficialities are most vulnerable to facile ridicule. To compound the injury, this was the time when amateur Freudianism was all the rage among biographers, and sometimes it seemed as if psychoanalysis had been invented for the express purpose of revealing what horrid Ids festered beneath the Victorians' pretentious Egos.

2. Recovery

Not all accounts of the Victorians written between the two world wars were total losses. A few historians were offering better-informed studies. Even before the outbreak of the First World War, the Fabian social historians J. L. and Barbara Hammond had begun a series of books on conditions of pre- and early Victorian labor and life which culminated in *The Age of the Chartists* (1930). The most authoritative history of the period, regrettably less than half-finished at its author's death, was the French scholar Élie Halévy's *Histoire du peuple anglais au XIXᵉ siècle*. An encouraging sign that Victorian history was not monopolized by the pseudo-Stracheyites in the mid-thirties was the publication of *Early Victorian England 1830–1865*, a two-volume collection of authoritative chapters on subjects ranging from sport, music, and drama to economics and domestic life.

Writers like the Hammonds, Halévy, and some of the contributors to *Early Victorian England,* not content to rely as most biographers and popular historians did upon easily available secondary sources, drew upon hitherto unused primary materials—newspaper and magazine files, contemporary memoirs, ephemeral controversial literature, blue books, private and official archives. Gradually it became evident that it was not prejudice alone which stood in the way of a just understanding of the Victorians and what they were about. Prejudice could be nullified in time, especially prejudice as violent as this anti-Victorianism was; its excesses guaranteed that in time it would prove self-defeating. But it could be replaced with something more positive only if all the pertinent facts were known, and the sheer volume of data preserved from the Victorian age was staggering. One modern expert has said, without exaggeration, that it comprises "a larger mass than exists for any country in any previous century." [2] By the forties, however, unconvinced and undeterred by Strachey's pronouncement at the beginning of his famous *Eminent Victorians* manifesto— "The history of the Victorian Age will never be written: we know too much about it"—students were bent on knowing more. For the sake of a better-informed view of what had become an intolerably maligned period and cast of characters, they burrowed ever deeper into the vast accumulation of Victoriana—handwritten, printed, painted, and photographed.

The leaders of the trend toward greater comprehension were literary biographers and those critics who, against the new-critical fashion of the time, used biographical data for interpretive purposes. Nothing did more to rehabilitate the Victorians as a society worthy not only of study but of deep respect than, for instance, the discovery that Dickens, far from being the mere popular entertainer he had been tagged by previous criticism, was a great artist; or that George

Eliot was a genius of almost equal stature, an intellectual and moralist as well as a novelist of the first rank; or that Ruskin's thought was worth at least as much attention as his tragic psyche. One by one, the straw figures who populated the "official" biographies of Victorian writers were replaced with men and women whom one was enabled to know, thanks to energetic research, with almost unmatched intimacy—and confidence in their historical reality. The accompanying critical revaluation (upward, in nearly all cases) had the effect of suggesting that an age which could produce and in most instances recognize such literary giants as Carlyle, Dickens, Tennyson, Ruskin, George Eliot, Browning, and Arnold could not easily be dismissed as a laughable or deplorable interlude in English history.

In 1948 the British Broadcasting Corporation made a notable contribution to the "historic revaluation of the Victorian age," as the subtitle of the resulting printed volume described it, by producing a series of sixty talks by authorities on various aspects of Victorianism. This ambitious project undoubtedly stirred much fresh and respectful interest in Victorian society and culture on the part of the high- and middle-brow audience to whom the BBC's "Third Programme" was directed.

And so, from the Second World War onward, the historians of Victorian politics, social life, and ideas produced studies which added immeasurably to our understanding of the time and its leading and representative personalities. They have been, for the most part, dispassionate, in the best tradition of modern academic scholarship; but they have also been sympathetic, in conspicuous contrast to their journalistic predecessors. Old notions have sometimes been discredited, such as the assumption that the middle class achieved political and social supremacy with the passage of the First Reform Bill, or the one that insisted that laissez faire was a virtual principle of life which governed all significant economic and political action—or inaction—in the first four Victorian decades. Some aspects of the Hammonds' ground-breaking studies of working-class history have had to be re-examined, particularly because the Hammonds, with their Fabian zeal—an early species of anti-Victorianism —selected or misinterpreted their evidence to fit their bias.

Some basic questions still are debated. Historians have not, so far, agreed on whether the post-Napoleonic era in which Cobbett lived was truly worse off, as far as the life of the common people was concerned, than the England of the 1760's which served as his ideal measure of prosperity and social contentment. Might it not have been a new awareness rather than an actual increase of poverty that darkened the early Victorian era? Were the masses worse or better off as a result of the factory system? And—an especially intractable problem—what caused the great population increase in the late eighteenth century and the first half of the nineteenth which set off the Malthusian alarm? The demographers continue to speculate over the riddle.

The legend of the Victorians' prudery lasted longer than most of the other vulgar errors associated with them. In an "emancipated" period like that between the two world wars, when talk of sex was thought to be deliciously daring, it was titillating as well as merely amusing to think of a people who were so nervous about the human body and its suggestibilities that they put frilly pantaloons on piano legs. (The fact is that this was sometimes done—but more in America than in England, and with the dismayingly practical intent of protecting the finish.) The rehabilitation of the Victorians in the popular mind was virtually completed when Steven Marcus' *The Other Victorians* (1966) revealed to a gratified general public what no student of the period who was acquainted with birth statistics and contemporary accounts of the prevalence of prostitution had presumed to doubt, namely, that the Victorians were well aware of sex and even practiced it both inside and outside marriage. The reprinting of *My Secret Life,* the excruciatingly tedious diary of an anonymous sex-obsessed gentleman, supplemented Marcus' account by giving the Victorians the final credentials they required for modern respect: they also contributed to the classic library of pornography.

In recent years, too, the Victorian revival has been advanced by the supporting agencies that now normally accompany intensified interest in a particular period or culture. Two learned journals, the multi-disciplinary *Victorian Studies* and *Victorian Poetry,* are devoted to the period. There is a Victorian Studies Center at the University of Leicester, England; an American society is working to make accessible and encouraging the study of the many hundreds of periodicals the age produced; again in England, a Victorian Society opposes the threatened destruction of select Victorian buildings and conducts walking tours for enthusiasts. The architecture of the period, so long the occasion of shudders or laughter, has lately been taken more seriously than it perhaps deserves, thanks especially to the beguiling partisanship of Sir John Betjeman and the scholarship of Sir Nikolaus Pevsner. Victorian art and furniture also have been rescued from the lumber room to which they were consigned many years ago and have become both fashionable and the subject of earnest professional study. In 1971 the famous London firm of Sotheby's took over a fine Regency building for the sole purpose of selling nineteenth-century antiques and works of art. No year passes without at least one gallery or museum in Britain or America mounting an elaborate exhibit devoted to some phase of Victorian art or society.

The consequence of all this attention, far from finally clarifying our conception of the Victorians, has been an enlarged appreciation of just how complex their age was. It is possible to "prove" almost anything one wants to believe about it. The late W. L. Burn described "the game of selective Victorianism": "The material is abundant. The society which provides it is lavishly documented and was of a fecundity which can give every investigator of 'patterns' and 'trends' enough 'clues' to follow to last him a lifetime. The rules are simple. Indeed, there is only one important rule:

to determine beforehand the 'pattern' you wish to discover or the 'trend' you wish to follow and then go on to find the evidence for its existence."[3] The game, when played by enough people, produces an understanding perplexity in anyone who tries to see the Victorians steadily and see them whole. More than twenty years ago, Jerome Buckley admirably summarized the imposing lack of consensus on almost any point connected with the Victorians:

The Victorians, we are told, were "a poor, blind, complacent people"; yet they were torn by doubt, spiritually bewildered, lost in a troubled universe. They were crass materialists, wholly absorbed in the present, quite unconcerned "with abstract verities and eternal values"; but they were also excessively religious, lamentably idealistic, nostalgic for the past, and ready to forego present delights for the vision of a world beyond. Despite their slavish "conformity," their purblind respect for convention, they were, we learn, "rugged individualists," given to "doing as one likes," heedless of culture, careless of a great tradition; they were iconoclasts who worshiped the idols of authority. They were, besides, at once sentimental humanitarians and hard-boiled proponents of free enterprise. Politically, they were governed by narrow insular prejudice, but swayed by dark imperialistic designs. Intellectually and emotionally, they believed in progress, denied original sin, and affirmed the death of the Devil; yet by temperament they were patently Manichaeans to whom living was a desperate struggle between the force of good and the power of darkness. While they professed "manliness," they yielded to feminine standards; if they emancipated woman from age-old bondage, they also robbed her of a vital place in society. Though they were sexually inhibited and even failed to consider the existence of physical love, they begat incredibly large families and flaunted in their verses a morbidly overdeveloped erotic sensibility. Their art constitutes a shameless record of both hypocrisy and ingenuousness. And their literature remains too purposeful, propagandistic, didactic, with too palpable a design upon the reader; yet it is clearly so romantic, aesthetic, "escapist," that it carries to posterity but a tale of little meaning.[4]

Every assertion is met with a counter-assertion. Some have more weight than others, but every one, charge and tribute alike, has ample warrant in the literary and non-literary annals of the time. It is all a matter of where one chooses to look, and from what angle of view.

The balance sheet is constantly changing, and of course there never will be a definitive judgment on the Victorian age; its reputation will continue to endure vicissitudes as the values of successive generations change. The desire— and lately, thanks to the work of many specialists, the ability —to see the age close-up, in its habit as it lived, has led to some sacrifice of perspective. In recent years a stock which once was priced absurdly low has climbed to what are quite possibly unrealistic heights. Sooner or later, no doubt, there will be a compensating adjustment.

Meanwhile, as the process of revaluating the Victorians continues, it is worthwhile to bear this in mind: If the Victorians had been the fools the Stracheyan generation thought they were, grossly incompetent in their conduct of life both personal and public, their society would have collapsed in utter chaos, leaving little room for subsequent laughter. If, on the other hand, their leading figures were the colossi of wisdom some of their contemporaries took them to be, they would not have left the twentieth century quite so daunting a heritage of unsolved problems. But if they failed, it was not for want of trying, for, faced as they were by an experience with which nothing in the history of the race had prepared them to deal, they did their human best, in their various ways and according to their various lights, to bequeath us a stabler, happier world. Notwithstanding the inroads of Darwinian and later science, with its bleak account of man's nature and destiny, they steadfastly maintained what Carlyle called, in "Signs of the Times," "a faith in the imperishable dignity of man; in the high vocation to which, throughout this his earthly history, he has been appointed." That, perhaps, is the chief thing the Victorians' literature tells us about them.

CHRONOLOGY

Social, cultural, and political events are set in lightface, **literary events in boldface.** (Books first published in numbers or serialized in periodicals are dated accordingly. In the case of novels, the latter year is normally the date of first publication in volume form.)

The Pre-Victorian Era

1802   Peace of Amiens (–03). Paley: *Natural Theology.* **Edinburgh Review founded.**

1803   Malthus: *Essay on the Principle of Population* (2nd ed).

1805   **Scott: *The Lay of the Last Minstrel.***

1807   Gas lights introduced in London. Slave trade abolished. **Wordsworth: *Poems in Two Volumes.* Byron: *Hours of Idleness.***

1808   **Scott: *Marmion.***

1809   ***Quarterly Review* founded. Byron: *English Bards and Scotch Reviewers.***

1810   **Scott: *The Lady of the Lake.* Shelley: *Original Poetry by Victor and Cazire; Zastrozzi.***

1811   Regency begins (Prince of Wales acting for the insane George III). Luddite riots (–12). National Society for the Education of the Poor founded.

1812   **Byron: *Childe Harold's Pilgrimage* I–II (III 1816; IV 1818).**

1813   **Shelley: *Queen Mab.* Austen: *Pride and Prejudice.***

1814   First use of steam in printing. British and Foreign School Society founded. **Wordsworth: *The Excursion.* Scott: *Waverley.* Austen: *Mansfield Park.***

1815   Battle of Waterloo; end of Napoleonic War. Resumption of agitation for parliamentary reform. Corn Law passed. Wordsworth: *The White Doe of Rylstone.*

1816   Coleridge: *Christabel and Kubla Khan.* Shelley: *Alastor and Other Poems.* Austen: *Emma.* Scott: *The Antiquary.*

1817   Ricardo: *On the Principles of Political Economy and Taxation.* Coleridge: *Biographia Literaria.* Keats: *Poems.* Hazlitt: *The Characters of Shakespeare's Plays. Blackwood's Edinburgh Magazine* founded.

1818   Bowdler's *Family Shakspeare.* Keats: *Endymion.* Austen: *Northanger Abbey; Persuasion.* Lamb: *Works.* Hazlitt: *Lectures on the English Poets.* Scott: *The Heart of Midlothian.*

1819   Peterloo Massacre. "Six Acts" abridging freedom of speech, print, and assembly; radical agitation subsides (–30). Byron: *Don Juan* I–II (III–XVI 1821–24). Wordsworth: *Peter Bell; The Waggoner.* Hazlitt: *Lectures on the English Comic Writers.* Shelley: *The Cenci.*
QUEEN VICTORIA born.

1820   George III dies; succeeded by Prince Regent as George IV. Keats: *Lamia, Isabella, The Eve of St. Agnes, and Other Poems.* Shelley: *Prometheus Unbound.* Lamb: *Essays of Elia* (in *London Magazine* –22). Peacock: *The Four Ages of Poetry.* Scott: *Ivanhoe.*

1821   Beginning of decade in which spread of factory system is reflected by immense growth of industrial towns. Shelley: *Epipsychidion, Adonais.* De Quincey: *Confessions of an English Opium Eater.* Scott: *Kenilworth.* Hazlitt: *Table Talk* (–22).

1823   London Mechanics' Institute founded: beginning of nationwide movement. Shelley: *Poetical Pieces.*

1824   *Westminster Review* founded. Coleridge: *Aids to Reflection.*

1825   Repeal of Combination Laws results in short-lived spate of union activity. Hazlitt: *The Spirit of the Age.* Macaulay's first essay in *Edinburgh Review* ("Milton"). "Silver fork" school of fiction begins (–45).

1826   Society for the Diffusion of Useful Knowledge founded.

1827   Thomas Arnold becomes headmaster of Rugby (–42). Tennyson: *Poems by Two Brothers.*

1828   Test and Corporation Acts repealed. University College, first component of University of London, opened.

1829   Catholic Emancipation Act. Carlyle: **"Signs of the Times"** in *Edinburgh Review.*

The Victorian Era

1830   George III dies; succeeded by his brother, William IV. July
        Revolution in France. Manchester and Liverpool Railway
        opened. Lyell: *Principles of Geology* I (II–III 1833). **Cole-
        ridge: *On the Constitution of Church and State.* Cobbett:
        Rural Rides. Tennyson's first independent volume, *Poems,
        Chiefly Lyrical. Fraser's Magazine* founded.**

1831   Reform Bill introduced and rejected by House of Lords;
        riots at Bristol and elsewhere. "Captain Swing" farm labor-
        ers' riots. Prosecutions of unstamped radical papers (–36).
        Cholera epidemic. **J. S. Mill: "The Spirit of the Age" (*Ex-
        aminer*).**

1832   First Reform bill passed. Jeremy Bentham dies. *Penny Maga-
        zine* and *Chambers's Edinburgh Journal* founded: first
        cheap mass-circulation weeklies. **Tennyson: *Poems.***

1833   Keble's "National Apostasy" sermon: Oxford Movement be-
        gins. *Tracts for the Times* (–41). First effective Factory
        Act. Abolition of slavery in colonies. *Bridgewater Treatises*
        (–36). **Carlyle: *Sartor Resartus* serialized in *Fraser's*
        (–34) (First English publication in book form, 1838).
        Browning: *Pauline.***

1834   Poor Law Amendment Act. Grand National Consolidated
        Trades Union (abortive labor movement).

1835   Ecclesiastical Commission appointed. Municipal Corpora-
        tions Act.

1836   Pugin: *Contrasts.* London Working Men's Association
        founded: beginning of Chartist movement. **Dickens: *Pick-
        wick Papers* (–37).**

1837   William IV dies; succeeded by niece, Princess Victoria.
        **Carlyle: *History of the French Revolution.* Dickens: *Oliver
        Twist* (–39). Thackeray: *Yellowplush Papers* (–38).**

1838   People's Charter published. Anti-Corn Law League founded.
        First regular Atlantic steamship service begins. Railroad
        opened to London (Birmingham line). **Dickens: *Nicholas
        Nickleby* (–39).**

1839   Chartist riots after Parliament rejects petition. Fox Talbot
        publishes account of photographic process. Child Custody
        Act. Eglinton Tournament. Ecclesiological movement: be-
        ginning of ritualism. **Carlyle: *Chartism.***

1840   Queen marries her first cousin, Albert, Prince of Saxe-
        Coburg-Gotha, who becomes Prince Consort. Penny post
        established. **Dickens: *The Old Curiosity Shop; Barnaby
        Rudge* (–41). Browning: *Sordello.***

1841 Newman: *Tract 90* (end of *Tracts for the Times*). *Punch* founded. Browning: *Bells and Pomegranates* (—46). Carlyle: *Heroes and Hero Worship.*

1842 Ashley's Act (women and children in mines). Chadwick Report on Sanitary Condition of the Labouring Population. Chartist riots at peak. Young England movement (—45). Tennyson: *Poems* (2 vols.). Dickens: *American Notes.* Mudie's Circulating Library founded.

1843 Wordsworth succeeds Southey as poet laureate. Carlyle: *Past and Present.* Hood: "Song of the Shirt." Dickens: *Martin Chuzzlewit* (—44). Ruskin: *Modern Painters* I (II–V 1846–60). Macaulay: *Critical and Historical Essays.*

1844 Factory Act (women and children). Beginning of cooperative movement at Rochdale. [Chambers]: *Vestiges of the Natural History of Creation.* "Railway mania" (speculation) (—47). Disraeli: *Coningsby.* Elizabeth Barrett: "Cry of the Children"; *Poems* (2 vols.).

1845 Newman joins Roman Catholic Church. Irish famine (—47). Engels: *Condition of the Working Class in England* (published at Leipzig). Disraeli: *Sybil.*

1846 Repeal of Corn Laws; free trade triumphs. Mary Ann Evans (George Eliot): translation of Strauss's *Das Leben Jesu.* Commercial telegraph service begins. Dickens: *Dombey and Son* (—48). Thackeray: *Book of Snobs* (—47). Lear: *A Book of Nonsense.*

1847 First operation using chloroform. Ten Hours Act. C. Brontë: *Jane Eyre.* E. Brontë: *Wuthering Heights.* Thackeray: *Vanity Fair* (—48). Tennyson: *The Princess.*

1848 Revolutions throughout western Europe. Chartist crisis (April 10). Public Health Act. Pre-Raphaelite Brotherhood founded. Christian Socialist movement begins. Queen's College founded. Gaskell: *Mary Barton.* Kingsley: *Yeast* (serialized in *Fraser's;* book 1851). Thackeray: *Pendennis* (—50).

1849 Bedford College for Women founded. Dickens: *David Copperfield* (—50). C. Brontë: *Shirley.* Arnold: *The Strayed Reveller and Other Poems.* Ruskin: *The Seven Lamps of Architecture.* Macaulay: *History of England* I–II (III–IV 1855).

1850 Restoration of Roman Catholic hierarchy in England ("Papal Aggression"). Oxford institutes degrees in science (Cambridge 1851). Public Libraries Act permits taxation for library buildings. Tennyson (new poet laureate): *In Memoriam.* Carlyle: *Latter-Day Pamphlets.* Kingsley: *Alton Locke.* Browning: *Christmas-Eve and Easter-Day. Household Words* founded (Dickens' first mass-circulation weekly).

1851 Crystal Palace exhibition. Spencer: *Social Statics.* Census reveals half of population lives in towns. **Ruskin:** *The Stones of Venice* **I (II–III 1853). Meredith:** *Poems.*

1852 Death of Duke of Wellington. **Newman:** *The Idea of a University.* **Arnold:** *Empedocles on Etna and Other Poems.* **Dickens:** *Bleak House* **(–53). Thackeray:** *Henry Esmond.*

1853 Cheltenham Women's College founded. **Arnold:** *Poems.* **Thackeray:** *The Newcomes* **(–55).**

1854 London Workingmen's College founded. Crimean War (–56). Dissenters admitted to Oxford degrees (Cambridge 1856). **Dickens:** *Hard Times.*

1855 Abolition of newspaper tax; *Daily Telegraph,* first mass-circulation daily, founded. **Trollope:** *The Warden.* **Tennyson:** *Maud and Other Poems.* **Browning:** *Men and Women.* **Dickens:** *Little Dorrit* **(–57). Gaskell:** *North and South.*

1856 *Oxford and Cambridge Magazine* **prints important poems by Rossetti and Morris.**

1857 Matrimonial Causes Act establishes divorce courts. **Trollope:** *Barchester Towers.* **Hughes:** *Tom Brown's School Days.* **Thackeray:** *The Virginians* **(–59).**

1858 **Trollope:** *Dr. Thorne.* **Morris:** *The Defence of Guinevere and Other Poems.*

1859 Darwin: *The Origin of Species.* Smiles: *Self-Help.* Mill: *On Liberty.* **Eliot:** *Adam Bede.* **Meredith:** *The Ordeal of Richard Feverel.* **FitzGerald's translation of** *Rubáiyát of Omar Khayyám.* **Dickens:** *A Tale of Two Cities.* **Collins:** *The Woman in White* **(–60). Tennyson:** *Idylls of the King* **(first four; others 1869–85). Dickens:** *All the Year Round* **succeeds** *Household Words.*

1860 *Essays and Reviews* stirs religious controversy. Food and Drugs Act. **Eliot:** *The Mill on the Floss.* **Dickens:** *Great Expectations* **(–61).** *Cornhill Magazine* **founded: first successful shilling magazine. Ruskin:** *"Unto This Last"* **in** *Cornhill* **(book 1862).**

1861 William Morris opens interior decorating and crafts business. Prince Consort dies; Queen retires into mourning. Mill: *Utilitarianism* serialized in *Fraser's* (book 1863). **Eliot:** *Silas Marner.* **Meredith:** *Evan Harrington.*

1862 Colenso's *The Pentateuch . . . Critically Examined* stirs new controversy. **Meredith:** *Modern Love.* **Clough:** *Poems.* **C. Rossetti:** *Goblin Market and Other Poems.* **Ruskin:** *Munera Pulveris* **in** *Fraser's* **(–63; book 1872).**

1863 Huxley: *Man's Place in Nature.*

1864 **Newman:** *Apologia pro Vita Sua.* **Dickens:** *Our Mutual*

Friend (–65). Tennyson: *Enoch Arden and Other Poems.*
Browning: *Dramatis Personae.*

1865   Antiseptic surgery (Lister). *Fortnightly Review* founded:
chief organ of rationalism and secularism. Transatlantic
cable opened. Swinburne: *Atalanta in Calydon.* Arnold:
Essays in Criticism (2nd series 1888). Ruskin: *Sesame and
Lilies.* Carroll: *Alice in Wonderland.*

1866   Hyde Park riots: agitation for extended franchise. Eliot:
Felix Holt. Swinburne: *Poems and Ballads* (2nd–3rd series
1878, 1889). Trollope: *Last Chronicle of Barset* serialized
(book 1867).

1867   Revival of Irish Nationalist (Fenian) movement; frequent
violence. Second Reform Bill passed. Arnold: *New Poems;
Culture and Anarchy* in *Cornhill* (–68; book 1869). Carlyle: "Shooting Niagara: and After?" in *Macmillan's.*

1868   Abolition of compulsory church rates. Both Disraeli and
Gladstone become prime minister for first time. Collins:
The Moonstone. Morris: *The Earthly Paradise* (–70).
Browning: *The Ring and the Book* (–69).

1869   First women's college at Cambridge (Girton). Mill: *On
the Subjection of Women.* Metaphysical Society founded
(–80). Tennyson: *The Holy Grail and Other Poems.*

1870   Franco-Prussian War: Germany, the winner, begins to rival
Britain as leading industrial power. Competitive examina-
tions for home civil service instituted. First Married Wom-
en's Property Act. (Forster's) Education Act. Huxley: *Lay
Sermons.* Dickens: *The Mystery of Edwin Drood.* Rossetti:
Poems.

1871   Religious tests for university teachers and officials abolished.
Trade unions legalized. Darwin: *The Descent of Man.*
Arnold: *Friendship's Garland.* Ruskin: *Fors Clavigera*
(–84). Swinburne: *Songs Before Sunrise.* Carroll: *Through
the Looking Glass.* Buchanan: "The Fleshly School of
Poetry" (attack on Swinburne and Rossetti). Trollope: *The
Eustace Diamonds* (–73). Eliot: *Middlemarch* (–72).

1872   National Agricultural Labourers Union founded. Secret ballot adopted in national elections. Butler: *Erewhon.*

1873   Agricultural depression begins. Pater: *Studies in the History of the Renaissance.* Mill: *Autobiography.* Arnold: *Literature and Dogma.*

1874   Hardy: *Far from the Madding Crowd.* Thomson: *The City
of Dreadful Night* in *National Reformer* (book 1880). Trollope: *The Way We Live Now* (–75).

1875   Artisans' Dwelling Act (first public housing legislation).

Gilbert and Sullivan begin collaboration with *Trial by Jury.*

1876   Victoria proclaimed Empress of India. **Meredith: *Beauchamp's Career.* Morris: *Sigurd the Volsung.***

1877   Society for the Protection of Ancient Buildings founded.

1878   Aesthetic movement under way. Lawsuit for libel: Whistler vs. Ruskin. **Gilbert and Sullivan: *H.M.S. Pinafore.* Hardy: *The Return of the Native.***

1879   First women's colleges at Oxford (Somerville and Lady Margaret Hall). **Meredith: *The Egoist.***

1880   Women admitted to degrees at University of London. Elementary education made compulsory. **Gissing: *Workers in the Dawn.***

1881   Henry George: *Progress and Poverty.* Irish question becomes major political issue. **Gilbert and Sullivan: *Patience.* Rossetti: *Ballads and Sonnets.* Wilde: *Poems.***

1882   Married Women's Property Act (the chief one). **Stevenson: *Treasure Island; New Arabian Nights.***

1883   **Trollope: *Autobiography.* Moore: *A Modern Lover.***

1884   Fabian Society founded. National Socialist League founded. Third Reform Bill passed. **Shaw: *An Unsocial Socialist* in *Today*** (book 1887). **Meredith: *Diana of the Crossways*** (—85).

1885   **Gilbert and Sullivan: *The Mikado.* Ruskin: *Praeterita*** (—89). **Pater: *Marius the Epicurean.***

1886   Political crisis over Gladstone's Irish Home Rule Bill (defeated). **Gissing: *Demos.* Hardy: *The Mayor of Casterbridge.* Kipling: *Departmental Ditties.***

1887   "Bloody Sunday" (Socialist demonstration at Trafalgar Square). Queen's golden jubilee: outpouring of imperialistic sentiment. **Hardy: *The Woodlanders.* Pater: *Imaginary Portraits.***

1888   **Kipling: *Plain Tales from the Hills.***

1889   London dock strike. **Pater: *Appreciations.* Browning: *Asolando*** (his last volume).

1890   **Morris: *News from Nowhere* in *Commonweal*** (book 1891).

1891   **Gissing: *New Grub Street.* Hardy: *Tess of the d'Urbervilles.* Wilde: *The Picture of Dorian Gray; Intentions.***

1892   **Kipling: *Barrack-Room Ballads.* Wilde: *Lady Windermere's Fan.***

1893   Art nouveau in fashion. **Hopkins: selection of poems published in Miles's *Poets and Poetry of the Century.* Yeats: *The Celtic Twilight.* Pinero: *The Second Mrs. Tanqueray.***

1894   *The Yellow Book* (—97). **Kipling: *The Jungle Book.***

Yeats: *The Land of Heart's Desire.* Shaw: *Arms and the Man.* Moore: *Esther Waters.* Wilde: *Salome.*

1895 Conrad: *Almayer's Folly.* Wells: *The Time Machine.* Hardy: *Jude the Obscure.* Yeats: *Poems.* Wilde: *The Importance of Being Earnest.* Shaw: *Candida.*

1896 Kelmscott Chaucer printed by William Morris. *Daily Mail* founded: first halfpenny daily. Beerbohm: *Works of Max Beerbohm.* Housman: *A Shropshire Lad.*

1897 Queen's diamond jubilee. Havelock Ellis: *Studies in the Psychology of Sex* (–1910). Conrad: *The Nigger of the "Narcissus."*

1898 Hardy: *Wessex Poems.* Shaw: *Plays Pleasant and Unpleasant.* Wells: *The War of the Worlds.*

1899 Boer War (–1902).

1900 Conrad: *Lord Jim.*

1901 Queen Victoria dies; succeeded by Prince of Wales as Edward VII. Shaw: *Three Plays for Puritans.* Hardy: *Poems of the Past and the Present.*

SOURCES OF QUOTATIONS
FROM MODERN BOOKS

Chapter II
1. R. H. S. Crossman, "The Testament of Change," *Ideas and Beliefs of the Victorians* (London, 1949), p. 431.

Chapter III
1. Esmé Wingfield-Stratford, *Those Earnest Victorians* (1930), p. 318.
2. Bertrand Russell in *Ideas and Beliefs of the Victorians,* p. 20.

Chapter IV
1. G. S. R. Kitson Clark, *An Expanding Society* (1967), pp. 34–35.
2. Gamaliel Milner, *The Threshold of the Victorian Age* (1934), p. 121.
3. Charles Coulston Gillispie, *Genesis and Geology* (1951), p. 216.
4. George Macaulay Trevelyan, *Illustrated English Social History* (1952), IV, 83.

Chapter V
1. Élie Halévy, *England in 1815* (1924), p. 509.
2. G. D. H. Cole, "Personal Responsibility," *Ideas and Beliefs of the Victorians,* p. 372.
3. G. M. Young, *Victorian England: Portrait of an Age* (1936), p. 5.

Chapter VI
1. Kitson Clark, *The Making of Victorian England* (1962), p. 20.

2. Horton Davies, *Worship and Theology in England: From Watts and Wesley to Maurice, 1690–1850* (1961), pp. 254–55.

3. Paraphrased from George Rawlinson's lecture by F. Sherwood Taylor, "Geology Changes the Outlook," *Ideas and Beliefs of the Victorians,* p. 189.

Chapter VII

1. Raymond Williams, *Culture and Society, 1780–1950* (1958), p. xvi.

2. Williams, p. 62.

3. J. L. and Barbara Hammond, *The Age of the Chartists* (1930), p. 215.

4. Young, *Victorian England,* p. 160.

Chapter VIII

1. Graham Hough, *The Last Romantics* (1949), p. xix.

2. Jerome H. Buckley, *The Victorian Temper* (1951), p. 224.

Chapter IX

1. Most of this paragraph and the preceding one is loosely and selectively quoted from Richard D. Altick, *Lives and Letters: A History of Literary Biography in England and America* (1965), pp. 282–85.

2. Kitson Clark, *The Making of Victorian England,* p. 2.

3. W. L. Burn, *The Age of Equipoise* (1964), p. 36.

4. Buckley, *The Victorian Temper,* pp. 2–3.

OTHER BOOKS TO READ

Two STANDARD HISTORIES of nineteenth-century England, both in the Oxford History of England series, are Sir Llewellyn Woodward, *The Age of Reform 1815–70* (2nd ed., 1962) and R. C. K. Ensor, *England, 1870–1914* (1936). A long-respected volume, *British History in the Nineteenth Century* (1922; enlarged edition, 1937) by Macaulay's grand-nephew, George Macaulay Trevelyan, is now somewhat dated. R. K. Webb's *Modern England from the Eighteenth Century to the Present* (1968) is ample on the Victorian era and has the benefit of recent scholarship. Derek Beales, *From Castlereagh to Gladstone* (1969) is equally well-informed and more compact. On too large a scale for the ordinary reader but still unsurpassed for penetration and authority is Élie Halévy's *Histoire du peuple anglais au XIX e siècle* (1913–46; translated as *A History of the English People in the Nineteenth Century*, 6 vols., 1924–48). The first volume, *England in 1815*, is a masterly panorama of English society and culture on the eve of the Victorian era; unfortunately the series reaches only to 1852, although one of the "Epilogue" volumes covers the last Victorian years. Asa Briggs's *The Age of Improvement 1783–1867* (1959; American paperback title, *The Making of Modern England*) is an excellent account of the pre-Victorian age as well as of the first half of the period itself. Another of Briggs's books, *Victorian People: A Reassessment of Persons and Themes 1851–67* (1965), studies the mid-Victorian era through some of its representative figures, from Smiles and Bright to Disraeli and Trollope. W. L. Burn's *The Age of Equipoise: A Study of the Mid-Victorian Generation* (1964) deals with the same epoch. It is probably too specialized for the novice, but it is indispensable for an understanding of the cross-currents and anomalies of mid-Victorian society. Somewhat broader in scope is G. Kitson Clark's *The Making of Victorian England* (1962), gracelessly written but valuable for its presentation of "revisionist" views on various topics.

Most of the works already mentioned give generous space to social history, among other concerns. The following volumes are more specifically interested in "the way people lived." G. M. Trevelyan, *Illustrated English Social History,* Vol. IV: *The Nineteenth Century* (1952; text first published as the last portion of his *English Social History,* 1942) paints the scene with broad though not always accurate strokes, and is enhanced by a wealth of well-chosen and unhackneyed pictures. On a more modest scale there is W. J. Reader's *Life in Victorian England* (1964), half pictures, half text. The two portly volumes of *Early Victorian England 1830–1865* (1934), edited by G. M. Young, are noteworthy for their copious contemporary illustrations, their sixteen chapters by various specialists on many aspects of early Victorian life, and the magisterial concluding chapter by the editor, subsequently expanded to cover the whole of the Victorian period and published separately as *Victorian England: Portrait of an Age* (1936). Even readers who are not fully prepared to understand Young's constant allusiveness delight in his dry wit, which makes Lytton Strachey's comic effects seem shoddy (as they were), just as his intimate and curious knowledge of the period makes Strachey's scholarship seem a mere pretense (as it was).

J. L. and Barbara Hammond's *The Age of the Chartists, 1832–1854* (1930; shortened as *The Bleak Age,* 1934), while its Fabian Socialist bias is now more apparent and disturbing than it was a generation ago, remains among the classic works of English social history. A livelier and broader narrative of a single Victorian decade is John W. Dodds's *The Age of Paradox: A Biography of England 1841–1851* (1952), another lavishly illustrated volume which ably portrays the chiaroscuro of the period between the worst Chartist disturbances and the sunlight of the Crystal Palace year. Esmé Wingfield-Stratford's *Those Earnest Victorians* (1930; English title, *The Victorian Tragedy*) and *The Victorian Sunset* (1932), collected, along with *The Victorian Aftermath* (1934) as *The Victorian Cycle* (1935), are Stracheyan in vivacity but not wholly in intent; though arch and sardonic, they are, on balance, sympathetic to the Victorians. Two recent volumes on the History of British Society series, J. F. C. Harrison, *The Early Victorians 1832–1851* (1971) and Geoffrey Best, *Mid-Victorian Britain 1851–1875* (1971), treat their subjects from the fresh viewpoint of recent scholarship.

On the intellectual history of the period, perhaps the best summary is the long "introductory survey" prefixed to Charles Frederick Harrold and William D. Templeman's anthology, *English Prose of the Victorian Era* (1938). This fine essay regrettably is not available in separate form. D. C. Sommervell's *English Thought in the Nineteenth Century* (1929) is equally succinct but to some degree misleadingly oversimplified and superficial. *Ideas and Beliefs of the Victorians: An Historic Revaluation of the Victorian Age,* with an introduction by Harman Grisewood (1949), containing the sixty talks given on the BBC, is of uneven quality, as might be expected from the number of participants, but many of the essays are both stimulating and informative. Basil Willey's *Nineteenth Century Studies* (1949) is an indispensable collection of chapters on selected but salient aspects of the thought of Coleridge, Thomas and Matthew Arnold, Newman, Carlyle, Mill, and George Eliot. The sequel, Willey's *More Nineteenth Century Studies* (1956), continuing the theme begun in the later chapters of its predecessor, is concerned with "A Group of Honest Doubters" which includes Tennyson. Jerome H. Buckley, *The Triumph of Time* (1966) is a model study of one aspect of the Victorian consciousness and sensibility to which Chapter III of the present book is much indebted. J. B. Schneewind, *Backgrounds of English Victorian Literature* (1970) covers some of the materials on Victorian politics, religion, and morality discussed in this book, but from the viewpoint of the professional historian and, despite the title, with no attempt to indicate their literary bearings.

Two important books deal explicitly and comprehensively with the Victorian spirit as manifested in literature: J. H. Buckley's *The Victorian Temper: A Study in Literary Culture* (1951), especially valuable for its relating of aesthetic theories and trends to literature, and Walter E. Houghton's *The Victorian Frame of Mind 1830–1870* (1957), which impressively documents the extent to which that mind was "a bundle of various and often paradoxical ideas and attitudes." Raymond Williams, *Culture and Society 1780–1950* (1958) shows how "responses in thought and feeling to the changes in English society since the late eighteenth century" are reflected in the writings of a number of representative (or atypical) Victorians.

The Victorian reading public is studied from the informal records of their tastes and experience left by individual men and women and from evidence found in the literature itself in Amy Cruse, *The Victorians and Their Reading* (1935; English title, *The Victorians and Their Books*). Richard D. Altick, *The English Common Reader: A Social History of the Mass Reading Public 1800–1900* (1957) examines the manifold social and cultural factors which contributed to—or in some cases inhibited —the expansion of the audience for print.

Excerpts from contemporary documents which illustrate many aspects of Victorian social life are gathered in three volumes by E. Royston Pike: *"Hard Times": Human Documents of the Industrial Revolution* (1966); *"Golden Times": Human Documents of the Victorian Age* (1967); and *"Busy Times": Human Documents of the Age of the Forsytes* (1969). (The titles of the original English editions omit the quoted phrases.) *Backgrounds to Victorian Literature,* edited by Richard A. Levine (1967), is a useful anthology of excerpts from modern scholarly works on various subjects discussed in this book. Another anthology, *The Emergence of Victorian Consciousness,* edited by George Levine (1967), offers a generous assortment of contemporary statements, including many by non-literary figures, on the chief aspects of "the spirit of the age."

In addition to the several books already mentioned which are noteworthy for their illustrations, there have been a number of fairly recent volumes devoted chiefly to the graphic evocation of the Victorian milieu. Of these, perhaps the one with the widest compass is Nicolas Bentley's *The Victorian Scene* (1968). Both James Laver's *Victorian Vista* (1955) and Joan Evans' *The Victorians* (1966) combine illustrations with letterpress composed of quotations from a large variety of contemporary sources. The effect in each case is *sui generis.* Between them, Raymond Lister, *Victorian Narrative Paintings* (1966) and Graham Reynolds, *Painters of the Victorian Scene* (1953) provide a good idea of the way artists used genre and episodic materials from their own day. Two books by John Gloag, *Victorian Comfort: A Social History of Design from 1830 to 1900* (1961) and *Victorian Taste: Some Social Aspects of Architecture and Industrial Design from 1820 to 1900* (1962), along with John Steegman's *Consort of Taste, 1830–1870* (1950), are adequate introductions to the Victorian "look" of everything from Valentines and newel posts to rural railroad stations and remodeled cathedrals. On the history of the medieval impulse in nineteenth-century architecture, the standard work is Kenneth Clark, *The Gothic Revival: An Essay in the History of Taste* (1928)—written, it is worth noting, when the author, now Lord Clark, was but twenty-two.

INDEX

Boldface type indicates pages on which terms are explained.